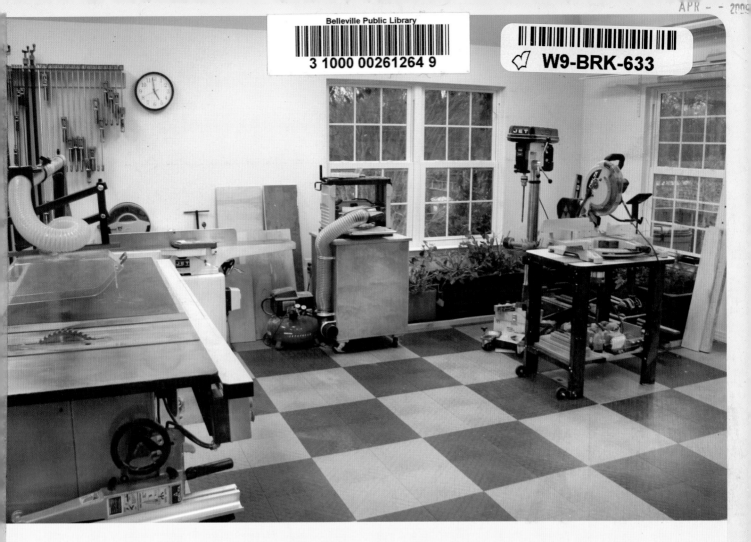

Creating Your Own
WOODSHOP

CHARLIE **SELF**

POPULAR WOODWORKING BOOKS
CINCINNATI, OHIO
www.popularwoodworking.com

READ THIS IMPORTANT SAFETY NOTICE

To prevent accidents, keep safety in mind while you work. Use the safety guards installed on power equipment; they are for your protection. When working on power equipment, keep fingers away from saw blades, wear safety goggles to prevent injuries from flying wood chips and sawdust, wear hearing protection and consider installing a dust vacuum to reduce the amount of airborne sawdust in your woodshop. Don't wear loose clothing, such as neckties or shirts with loose sleeves, or jewelry, such as rings, necklaces or bracelets, when working on power equipment. Tie back long hair to prevent it from getting caught in your equipment. People who are sensitive to certain chemicals should check the chemical content of any product before using it. The authors and editors who compiled this book have tried to make the contents as accurate and correct as possible. Plans, illustrations, photographs and text have been carefully checked. All instructions, plans and projects should be carefully read, studied and understood before beginning construction. Due to the variability of local conditions, construction materials, skill levels, etc., neither the author nor Popular Woodworking Books assumes any responsibility for any accidents, injuries, damages or other losses incurred resulting from the material presented in this book. Prices listed for supplies and equipment were current at the time of publication and are subject to change.

METRIC CONVERSION CHART

to convert	to	multiply by
Inches	Centimeters	2.54
Centimeters	Inches	0.4
Feet	Centimeters	30.5
Centimeters	Feet	0.03
Yards	Meters	0.9
Meters	Yards	1.1

CREATING YOUR OWN WOODSHOP. Copyright © 2009 by Charlie Self. Printed and bound in China. All rights reserved. No part of this book may be reproduced in any form or by any electronic or mechanical means including information storage and retrieval systems without permission in writing from the publisher, except by a reviewer, who may quote brief passages in a review. Published by Popular Woodworking Books, an imprint of F+W Publications, Inc., 4700 East Galbraith Road, Cincinnati, Ohio, 45236. Second edition.

Distributed in Canada by Fraser Direct
100 Armstrong Avenue
Georgetown, Ontario L7G 5S4
Canada

Distributed in the U.K. and Europe by David & Charles
Brunel House
Newton Abbot
Devon TQ12 4PU
England
Tel: (+44) 1626 323200
Fax: (+44) 1626 323319
E-mail: postmaster@davidandcharles.co.uk

Distributed in Australia by Capricorn Link
P.O. Box 704
Windsor, NSW 2756
Australia

 Visit our Web site at www.popularwoodworking.com or our consumer Web site at www.fwbookstore.com for information on more resources for woodworkers and other arts and crafts projects.

Other fine Popular Woodworking Books are available from your local bookstore or direct from the publisher.

13   12   11   10   09   5   4   3   2   1

Library of Congress Cataloging-in-Publication Data

Self, Charles R.
  Creating your own woodshop / by Charlie Self.-- revised ed
    p. cm.
  ISBN 978-1-55870-841-9 (pbk. : alk. paper)
  1. Woodshops. I. Title.

TT185.5.S45 2008
684'.08--dc22
                                    2008039181

Acquisitions Editor: David Thiel
Senior Editor: Jim Stack
Designer: Brian Roeth
Production Coordinator: Mark Griffin

ABOUT THE AUTHOR

Charlie Self is a writer and photographer who first worked in the Katonah Altar Factory before he was 17, a whole lot of years ago. For the past 40 years, he's worked as a freelance writer, with more than 20 of those years devoted to writing about woodworking. Charlie is currently starting his second term as President of the National Association of Home & Workshop Writers. He is also a multiple winner of the Golden Hammer awards presented by NAHWW for excellence in writing or photography in his field.

ACKNOWLEDGEMENTS

I dedicate this book to my wife Frances, for all the obvious reasons and some not so obvious.

My particular thanks go out to all of those who contributed time and photographs of their own shops to the book. Thanks also to all who allowed me to photograph their lairs. It was a lot of fun for me. You're all named within the book, so I'll let that stand for a mention.

Companies and individuals always contribute largely to any book of this type. I think my best way is to say thanks alphabetically: American Plywood Association (APA); American Workbench; Asphalt Roofing Manufacturers' Assoc.; Bosch Tools; Colonial Williamsburg; Craftsman; DAP; DeWalt; Delta Industrial Machinery; Felder; Festool; Georgia-Pacific; Grizzly; Jet Tools; Lee Valley & Veritas Tools; Palmgren Tools; Ridgid Tools; Ryobi Tools; Simonton Windows; Square D; Stanley; Velux; Woodworker's Supply.

Of course, it was individuals within these companies (or contracting to them) who made the work possible, but naming them all is impossible. Know that you have my thanks; you know who you are.

My special thanks to David Thiel for the care and work he has put into this book.

Contents

My shop at the beginning, with batter boards still in place and post holes dug.

Introduction

A FRESHER LOOK AT WOODWORKING SHOPS FOR THE 21ST CENTURY

Every woodworker has a different story, at least in detail, as to how he, or she, became acquainted with woodworking. I should have been ready from the cradle, because my maternal granddad owned a sawmill, but it didn't work that way. My first interest was cars, then motorcycles. Because Dad was an auto mechanic, my first introduction to tools was handing him wrenches as he worked under a vehicle. Later, I worked in an altar factory in Katonah, NY to pay my way through the gas station pumps, but that was only until I found a job working with grease in a gas station. It wasn't a vocation and some of the machinery scared the daylights out of me (some still do).

In the woodworking shop, I served as the primary dust collection system (in conjunction with a push broom, a grain shovel and a huge stack of burlap sacks), while being terrified of the noise made by the 18" radial arm saw when I had to operate that. All of this led, naturally, to the U.S. Marines and work as a helicopter avionics tech. Getting out eventually led to college, and more motorcycles (I covered off-road competitions), but also a need to put into practice some of the real woodworking skills I'd learned nearly a decade earlier — building bookcases. Unlike younger students I wasn't in love with blocks and boards as furniture. And I didn't have the limits of a dorm, as I was older and only lasted through one semester of barracks — whoops, dorm life.

Seven or eight years later, things got serious and a decent table saw made its way into the space available. Before that, almost everything was done by hand — apartment life creates some measure of consideration for others. As woodworkers in general know, the addiction grows, and you start to move through a series of shops, adding tools as you go. A double decade ago, my tools were in the dining room of a rental house. After that, the saws and drills and bits and lathe moved into a second parlor in an old farmhouse, with a back porch about 50' long and 10' deep that served as more shop space and storage — great place for a radial arm saw on that long wall.

From that, I've moved my tools through a sandwich shop basement (19' × 63') to my current freestanding 25' × 48' shop.

More than a decade ago, I started building my own woodworking shop (at left), using pole construction, wood siding and flooring, tin roof, reasonable insulation and, at that time, a used electric furnace. I'm now in the process of reconsidering the heating, with a dead furnace on hand.

It all came together, but it took my wife and myself about three years from the time a neighbor dug the postholes, to hiring a crew to put the roofing on: We did the rest. What I have now is still incomplete, and always will be, but it is a workshop like none I had before. With 200 amp Square D service, and a host of 240 and 120 outlets (and plenty in reserve, if needed), I'm reasonably happy with it, but I can see changes I would make if I were starting over; that's where this book can help you. I'll look at changes I'd like, and I'll look at changes a couple of friends made in their shops to better suit skilled hobby woodworking. I'd start with a taller ceiling. I started this shop based

on a 9' ceiling, a mistake based on the 7' ceiling in the basement shop I had immediately before. 10' is close to essential for comfortable larger scale woodworking; swing a board and having it come up short against a ceiling joist, or the ceiling, makes your teeth rattle.

The day we finished nailing the flooring (I used ¾" sanded, tongue-and-groove plywood), Frances looked towards the back of our lot and noted the space in the shop (the walls weren't on yet): "You'll never fill all this space." Shortly after the roof was on, I had eleven table saws in there for testing. I hope that you don't ever have a similar assembly need, regardless of the space you have.

My shop is 1,200 square feet (25' × 48') and is often crowded and cramped, though less so now that I don't do much tool testing. If I start building cabinets, at my normal snail's pace, it gets crowded and stays that way.

If your workshop is like some of mine have been, what you have is probably best described as a disorganized and near total mess. You may spend almost as much time cussing the difficulty you have setting up as you do planning and working on projects, and the odds are superb the place is seldom as safe as it needs to be. Stumbling over obstacles is too often the major form of locomotion in amateur woodworking shops. Other shops seem to take on a high sheen of cleanliness that can mean one of two things: Either it's seldom used, or the owner spends most of his or her time cleaning up, instead of working on projects.

Workshops don't have to be that way, but many are. Small pro shops tend to be almost as badly organized as amateur shops. Information from several large woodworking (furniture) companies was part of the aim of this book, but I received a slew of turndowns based on a desire to

My shop had a lonely first winter.

Colonial Williamsburg's 18th-century woodshop uses the traditional tools that are making a comeback in today's woodshops.
COURTESY OF COLONIAL WILLIAMSBURG

keep proprietary methods and machinery as secret as possible. Regardless, even though a large, or even moderate sized, woodworking operation isn't going to work with the same machinery you or I do, handling of materials in an efficient manner, from intake through finish and removal (shipping), plus dust removal and prevention, and safety will all have corollaries between larger and smaller shops. Spend some of your planning time visiting local woodworkers, and, if at all possible, visiting local furniture makers. More than anything else, check their work flow. What we're interested in is the process of getting raw wood in one end, and a finished project out the other end, as safely as possible, while having an enjoyable time.

We'll dig out details on how to make the most of whatever space you now have, whether it's a corner of a basement, or an entire building. For apartment dwellers, woodworking is a difficult hobby to pursue without at least a minimum of space (that minimum is probably about 8' × 8', unavailable in many apartments), and neighbors at a far enough distance that the high pitched whine of power tools won't drive them straight up the walls (on the fifth or sixth day of your new hobby, they go for your throat). Hand tool woodworking makes much less noise, with the accom-

The interior of a garden shed can serve many woodworking needs. Though small, tools and the woodworker's habits will adapt to the space. COURTESY OF MIKE GIROUARD

panying sounds usually limited to thumps, bumps and cussing. Hand-tool woodworking is far quieter than shrieks from power tools.

If you plan to stay with small projects readily done with hand tools, or are a carver or turner (especially pen turn-

Modern woodshops are often a comfortable blend of power tools and hand tools. There are benefits to both.

COURTESY OF JOE ZEH

used fluorescent light fixtures (I got my original 8' units at a local school sale spending less than $30 for eight, of which at least six were fully usable — and I traded those for some other materials — and then traded some of that for 4' units under the mistaken impression that the bulbs are easier to change than 8' bulbs) to rough cut wood for framing and sheathing, and, in some instances, siding. There are many steps in-between, some related to scavenging as practiced in an earlier century, and some to the resurrection of scavenging enjoyed in the 1970s. It all adds up to more workshop for less money, with greater safety, efficiency and enjoyment.

We live in a era when hobby and small production woodworking shops can be equipped with more tools than at any earlier time in history. Often these tools are easier to use, and give more accurate results than ever before. It's up to us to use the space, and the tools occupying that space, to come up with projects that are enjoyable to make, and that others enjoy using, or looking at — or both. In some senses, this is the golden age of woodworking tools, at least for the average person.

The true golden age, like most golden ages, probably never did exist, and most likely never will. The concept of hand-made, for example, is superb, but the great wood furniture producers of the past had a slew of apprentices to do the grunt work. Today, we use machines. We can do the work in the same manner as our fathers and grandfathers and great-grandfathers did, and there's no reason not to do so if we enjoy that kind of work. At the same time, it's a simple matter to turn out work that appears the same when finished, but that is made with far less effort — though it may take just as much thought. Today, an amateur woodworker can equip a shop that helps make up for the skills he or she doesn't have.

This book will show you how to get the most use from your space, and how to increase that space when it becomes necessary. We'll look at the best sites in the shop for various saws, lathes, planers, jointers, and other equipment, while considering the amount of working space each major tool needs for safe, efficient operation. Your specific combination of tools, needs, and space determines your particular shop layout and size. Those tool needs vary according to your interests: lathe work requires specific spaces, and, if turning is the only task, lowers any need for other tools; full-blown cabinetry or furniture building makes some major needs apparent right away. Others may wish to work only with miniatures, decorative inlays, scrolling, band saw work, or total hand construction of large and small projects. Each demands different tools, different layouts, different expenditures and different planning. For many of us the new lines of benchtop tools available from most major makers serve admirably. For others, those tools give neither the size cuts, nor the accuracy of cut, needed.

You'll read, and see, how to project needs from current uses, how to plan the workshop (often as much fun as

ing), an apartment shop works. Generally, noise and space needs make house ownership or rental necessary. Some of the rough plans we set up here require more space than that, including a bit of extra land on which to build. Others present the methods of converting current space to shop uses, always with the proviso that you keep in mind the problems having a woodworking shop inside any home can cause. At one point, I lived in an old farmhouse and used the second living room, or parlor, as a woodworking shop. Life became interesting when it was time to dust and vacuum the rest of the house, and certainly limited the nighttime pursuit of my hobby until I lived alone for a bit.

Woodworking shops serve a wide variety of purposes and suit a wide variety of work. Many people who work with lathes do little other woodworking. Beyond preparing the wood to be turned, the tools and shop layout needed are very different from those of us who build furniture or cabinets. Toy builders need smaller amounts of space than do cabinetmakers and furniture makers. Those of us who want to do it all, and who wish to take the work from green, rough wood, through finished projects need the most space.

Creating one's own workshop generally requires using the least costly materials possible. These may range from

Living the nostalgic life of an 18th-century woodworker can be quaint, until sunset when you end up working by candlelight.
COURTESY OF COLONIAL WILLIAMSBURG

using it after completion), and how to set up one of several types of spaces for your own woodworking style, project desires and safety.

The latter point, safety, is one that is not made often enough. Power woodworking tools are far more dangerous than hand tools, and hand tools can be extremely hazardous. One of my worst injuries happened while woodworking a few years ago. I got impatient in completing a project, rushed, slipped and jammed a chisel into my left hand. The bone-deep cut took weeks to heal. The fault was totally mine, because the chisel was razor sharp, of good quality, and all I needed to do was to slow down and think. I didn't, thus got a slice I'll remember for many years (and enforcement of an old, old lesson: attitude plays a major part in woodworking — or any other — safety efforts: think safe and you are well on the path to being safe).

I can't change your attitude, but I can recommend the basic shop layouts that my experience, and that of other experts, show to be the safest. If you approach any of these plans with the right attitude, you can certainly make your shop as safe as it possibly can be. At the same time, you are ultimately responsible for your own safety and the safety of visitors and others in your shop. If something I

recommend, or present as recommended by others, doesn't seem safe to you, regardless of your level of experience, do NOT follow that recommendation. Work out a different way of doing things, one that makes you feel safe.

FIRST AID

For those times when all the safety concerns in the world don't seem to work, I cannot recommend strongly enough that you take a first aid course: usually, local Red Cross units present such courses several times a year. Then stock up on first aid supplies for the shop. I've looked around friends' shops and seen nary a band-aid, while in others, there are a few, a pair of tweezers and some alcohol. A bit more than that is wise.

There's also the problem that the workshop is often outside the house and you don't want to be dripping blood and sawdust across the carpets and up to the bathroom in an emergency, not to mention those times when it is enough

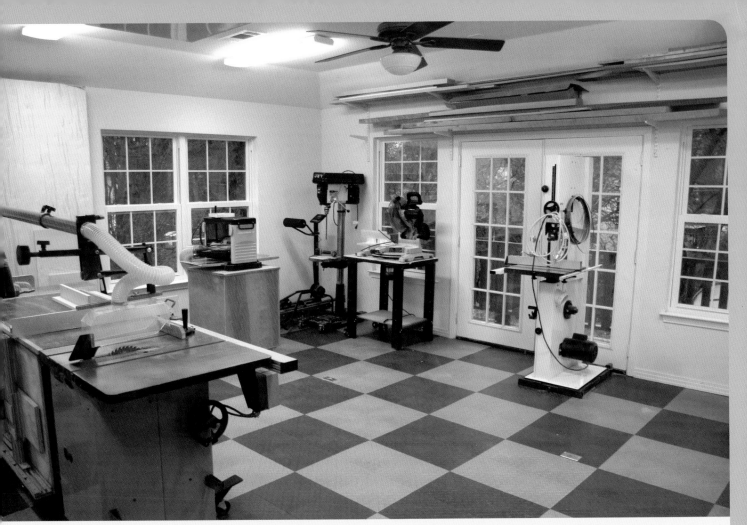

Bright walls and plenty of windows and overhead lighting are high on the list of most woodworkers when planning and constructing their woodshop. COURTESY OF DOUG JOHNSON

of an emergency to require immediate treatment. A workshop first-aid kit that is actually in the shop is necessary. My shop is 48' long, and I have one near each end, though one is a lot more complete than the other.

What do you need in yours? Needs vary, but you make a good start with tweezers, scissors, scalpel blades and disposable needles, plus a small 3X or 4X magnifying glass or lens. The lens helps eyes, aging or otherwise, locate those small wood or metal splinters and get to them with the tweezers. One quick thought, do not buy low cost tweezers. They are hard-to-impossible to use because the faces don't mate properly. Like most woodworkers, my biggest first aid need in the shop is pulling splinters out of my own hands. Sometimes I really need to dig, so a good pair of tweezers that grips firmly is going to create less pain. A sharp needle is often handy to pry splinters out to the point where tweezers can get a grip.

Other important first aid items for your shop include:

• Yellow or red sharps box. Labeled as such. Also works for workshop sharps like snap-off knife blades.

• Tea tree oil or other effective antiseptic (iodine, etc.). Tea tree oil is a quick treatment for small cuts and scrapes. It is antiseptic and appears to help the healing process.

• Band-Aids. Get several sizes, but don't depend on them staying in place without a finger stall over them.

• Gauze pads. Keep a 1" gauze roll on hand, plus 2", 3" 4" gauze squares, all in their sterile wrappings. You may also want to place two or three pressure dressings in the first aid kit. When possible, pressure on a wound is safer than a tourniquet for stopping bleeding. Probably the simplest good instruction I've seen for using tourniquets and pressure bandages is in a little tome entitled "United States Marine Guidebook of Essential Subjects." It is unlike my original such guide book in many ways, including the fact that it is pocket-sized, and done in almost comic book style, where the 1957 manual used photos and was in no way pocket-sized. You can check eBay for such manuals: that's where I got mine.

• Tourniquet. Make sure the instructions are with it, in at least 18 point type. A tourniquet is great for stopping really bad bleeding, but can cause loss of a limb if used improperly.

• Eyewash: there are sealed sterile one-shot bottles for washing big things out. There is also a standard non-sterile (after the first use) everyday bottle.

• Medical alcohol.

11

- Burn ointment.
- Petroleum jelly for scrapes, rashes or chapped lips.
- Aspirin.
- Tylenol®
- Benadryl®
- Other medications you or other shop users might need to hold on until a doctor gets there.

Look for a big box to put it in, easy to open and easy to close, with easy-to-use clips and large enough so there's no need to sit on it to get the lid shut. There are numerous plastic toolboxes with metal clasps now on the market. One of those is fine, and actually provides a tray to keep the most commonly used items on top.

Because I have no medical training or experience, I make no claims as to the correctness or completeness of the above list. It is short, and doesn't include anything to help in the case of a catastrophic injury. In fact, if you're alone in a hobby woodshop, and you chop off a limb, I'm not sure any first aid kit is going to save you. I would strongly suggest you check with your local Red Cross chapter to determine what is best in your first aid box, matched to your own personal needs. Also, make sure any workshop phone, cellular or other, is programmed for one-touch 911, and that the phone is within easy reach if

you're knocked down, fall down or otherwise can't get up to wall phone height. A corded phone at desk height, with the cord hanging within a couple of feet of the floor can work. Cellular is probably better, but I've yet to find a cell phone that works in my shop — down in a hollow (holler around here), with a tin roof, and in a dead spot.

This is not a project book as such, nor is it a tips book, nor, really, is it a book that shows you multitudes of shops and says "Pick one, and it's yours." What I've done is gather my experience and lots of advice from others, and checked out construction methods, plus layout styles for several different types of construction and space. If you want absolute details on laying out a shop, it's here if you apply some thought about your own situation. If you want a recommendation as to exactly what tools your shop should have, you're going to miss the point. Such recommendations are impossible. I don't work as you do, and you don't work as I do. And that's as it should be. Pick and choose and set up your own shop as it suits your needs.

Most of the information is on power tool woodworking. Woodworkers I meet today are interested in getting the most and best use from their power tools. Hand work is a sideline, one that is a great deal of fun, and interesting, but isn't often used for all facets of woodworking today.

While hand tools are making a comeback, it's still rare to find a woodshop specifically designed for wheelwrights.

You will see a number of "ordinary" shops, if any shop that pleases its owner can be called ordinary. Some of the work that comes out of such shops is stunning.

Enjoy the planning of your fresh woodworking shop. Fresh is always fun. When you've carefully planned for efficiency, fun and safety, using established planning boundaries the resulting use is going to fit those criteria, and be easier to use.

And remember, things don't change all that much.

A NOVELIST'S DESCRIPTION OF A 1715 ERA WOODSHOP

"The chamber, into which he stole, like all carpenters' workshops, was crowded with the implements and materials of that ancient and honourable art. Saws, hammers, planes, axes, augers, adzes, chisels, gimlets, and an endless variety of tools were ranged, like a stand of martial weapons at an armory, in racks against the walls. Over these hung levels, bevels, squares, and other instruments of measurement. Amid a litter of nails without heads, screws without worms, and locks without wards, lay a glue-pot and an oilstone, two articles which their owner was wont to term "his right hand and his left." On a shelf was placed a row of paint-jars; the contents of which had been daubed in rainbow streaks upon the adjacent closet and window sill. Divers plans and figures were chalked upon the walls; and the spaces between them were filled up with an almanac for the year; a godly ballad, adorned Page 77 with a rude wood-cut, purporting to be "The History of Chaste Susannah;" an old print of the Seven Golden Candlesticks; an abstract of the various Acts of Parliament against drinking, swearing, and all manner of profaneness; and a view of the interior of Doctor Daniel Burgess's Presbyterian meeting-house in Russell Court, with portraits of the reverend gentleman and the principal members of his flock. The floor was thickly strewn with sawdust and shavings; and across the room ran a long and wide bench, furnished at one end with a powerful vise; next to which three nails driven into the boards served, it would appear from the lump of unconsumed tallow left in their custody, as a substitute for a candlestick."

From *Jack Sheppard*, by William Harrison Ainsworth circa 1840. Examples of Colonial style workshops are easily found these days, most particularly at Colonial Williamsburg, where the below shop is located.

Bobby Weaver's new shop rises almost literally on the ashes of the old. He is using the same foundation and floor, which needed only minor clean-up and restoration, though the entire building was otherwise destroyed.

CHAPTER ONE

Figuring Out Your Best Shop

To start, look at your workshop aims. What do you want your shop to be? This is an essential step to meeting anyone's requirement for shop layout and the tools needed. The ideal here is the perfect shop for any individual, within limits of available space, and cash, to meet particular craft needs and desires. While one person may be totally satisfied with a simple layout where the primary tool is either a table or radial arm saw, differences are wide, as are combinations of use. Some woodworkers move from band saw, to lathe, to finish. Others move from planer, to jointer, to table saw, to assembly, to finish, varying with project and personal needs and desires. The concept of handling wood doesn't change, regardless of the machine size. The variables of interest are size and efficiency in methods and speed of handling at any one point in the production process, whether amateur or not. What others do to increase efficiency and safety of handling materials in various types and sizes, can often be adapted to our own current, and future or immediate uses. The easiest way for most of us to deal with all of this is to get a suitable sheet of graph paper, maybe twice the standard $8^1/_2$" × 11" size, then make a drawing of shop outlines, either as desired or existing. Place windows and doors and electrical outlets, as existing or desired. Then, as we go along, make close-to-scale cut-outs of top views of the tools you want. Slide those around to see how each tool positions, how the flow looks, and where you want to go with it.

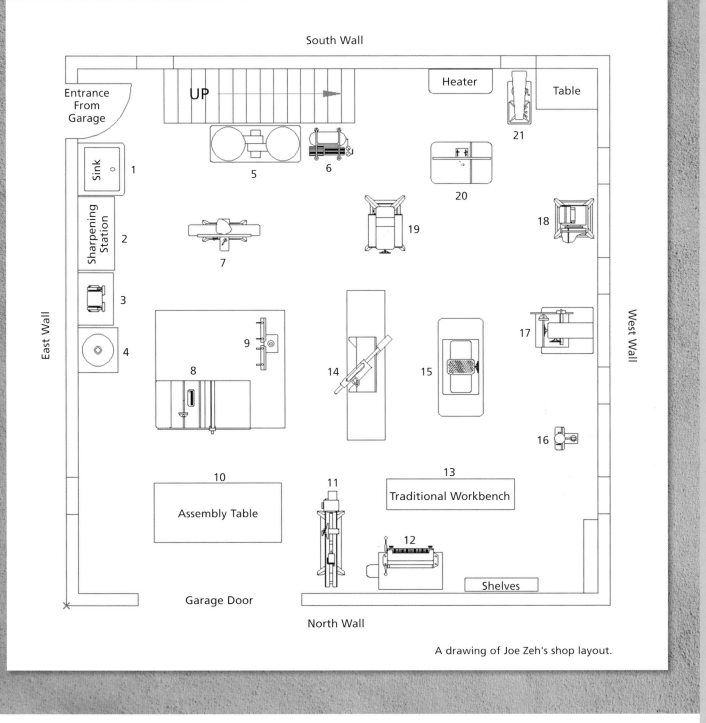

South Wall

Entrance From Garage

Sink 1

Sharpening Station 2

3

4

UP

5

6

7

Heater

Table

21

20

19

18

East Wall

9

8

14

15

17

West Wall

16

10

Assembly Table

11

13

Traditional Workbench

12

Shelves

Garage Door

North Wall

A drawing of Joe Zeh's shop layout.

The primary purpose of any woodworking shop is to have raw material, wood, come in one end, and a finished product move out the other end. Those ends may be only a couple of feet apart, but the process works better if there is a distinct setting for the varied operations, from wood storage to working up rough wood, to cutting wood to size, to assembly, to sanding and to finishing. Most of us have to combine the space for different processes, at least in part. An ideal shop might begin with a planer, backed by a door, or even a double door, for easy materials feeding. The table saw might be next in line. Next to the table saw is

the jointer, and just past those two is a workbench for test assembly and general hand woodworking. The band saw may be near this bench, as might the drill press. I suggest keeping them on one side of the bench and placing a lathe, if you want one, on the other side. Always leave room for benchtop work, though. Any tools placed near a bench are best sited at least three feet away from that bench. Other major power tools, such as scroll saws, sanders and radial arm saws, are placed where work flow to-and-from them is both most efficient and safest. In a single person shop work flow safety should never be a problem. But if you

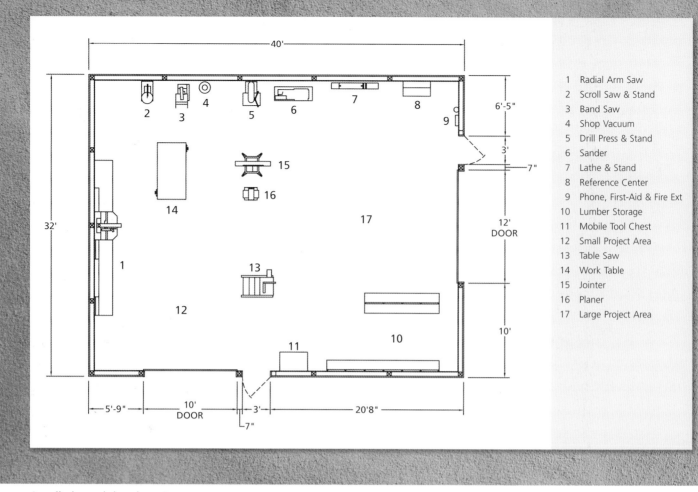

1	Radial Arm Saw
2	Scroll Saw & Stand
3	Band Saw
4	Shop Vacuum
5	Drill Press & Stand
6	Sander
7	Lathe & Stand
8	Reference Center
9	Phone, First-Aid & Fire Ext
10	Lumber Storage
11	Mobile Tool Chest
12	Small Project Area
13	Table Saw
14	Work Table
15	Jointer
16	Planer
17	Large Project Area

A well-planned shop layout. COURTESY OF THE UNIVERISTY OF TENNESSEE

have friends who occasionally work with you in the shop, it may become one. Keep that in mind as you plan.

Finishing areas present the most problems for both safety and quality of work in the small shop, whether amateur or professional. It is difficult to afford both the space and a method of closing off the dust from the rest of the shop. As amateurs, we've got an advantage. We can shut down all other operations while we're finishing. Too many of us let things ride as far as clean-up goes, so there's enough old and new dust in the air to mess up the finish on projects. One of the giveaways of an amateur job is a rough, bubbled finish, something that isn't acceptable any more. It's more a sign of haste than of anything else. Shut down long enough for the dust to settle, and make sure the project surface is clean and free of grease as well as dust. Use a tack rag, after letting the shop air settle for at least four hours, and you'll get much better looking finishes.

Arrange ventilation to clear fumes quickly — a spark-free fan works best — or use non-volatile finishes. Use a good mask or respirator, too.

This book isn't concerned with projects to make an existing shop more efficient, but ideas that make small shops easier to use. We aren't going to spend a lot of time telling you to save old coffee cans (and icing containers, and for-

mula cans, and nut containers, and almost any non-glass container, including detergent bottles — which serve admirably to hold small, squirtable amounts of mineral spirits, among other substances). The idea is to take the space you have available and either buy, or arrange already bought machines and benches, to give the best woodworking efficiency for your particular form of woodworking, without spending any more money than you have to.

You'll find information on building, as well as on converting spaces and buildings, that will be useful for some of you. We look at the amount of space needed to work with a tool, and to work with one tool in conjunction with another tool. The fact is, it's always more efficient to have specific machines close to the entry areas of a shop — planers and table saws — and others stuffed off in corners — lathes and drill presses. But you may want to change the order of stuffing those items in corners, and change from planer to table saw at the closest entry point, though in almost every instance, I'd put the table saw first (you may need it to rip boards to width for feeding through the planer, for one thing). Next in line is the jointer. And on to a wide array of others, plus benches.

A small shop is not always inefficient, while a large one isn't automatically efficient. Desires and needs must be

Dale Tom's shop upstairs main door. Dale's place has a full basement, with two other overhead doors and another swinging door.

taken into consideration during planning, but, too, remember that the larger a shop gets, the further you may have to walk to get a tool that's not at hand. I've placed full sets of screwdrivers, plus a selection of hammers at both ends, and at both centers (or nearly so) of my shop, which is 48' long. I originally wanted to go to 28' × 64' (or, really in my dreams, 32' × 64') until I checked costs. The walk then would have been even worse. I once had a workshop 63' deep. It sometimes felt like a long hike in the desert when I was loaded with wood or a heavy tool that had to go at the back end. At that time, I first started keeping extra tools at different spots in the shop, something I still do. Full sets of screwdrivers and hammers adorn the walls at the ends and in the middle of both sides, along with other selected tools. I really don't want to duplicate every tool in my shop, but most smaller hand tools can be set up this way, whether center punches and awls or ball peen and claw hammers.

Each of us has different wants in a workshop, different working methods, and thus, different needs. Where commonality falls, it is within the use of individual tools, no matter the user. A table saw does specific jobs well and needs space of a particular shape, plus a particular type of lighting, to suit those jobs. In what order you do the jobs and how you combine them with other jobs done by other

tools at other times is what gives your work its individuality. But the table saw still needs space in front and behind, for rip cuts of the lengths you are most likely to require, and for grooving and moulding operations. The table saw also must have space at one or both ends for cutting off long panels, or boards, the length of that space depending on the size and type of materials you work with.

If you lay out space for a shop and leave the same size and shape of space for each tool, you'll either reduce the efficiency (and safety) of the tools, or waste a lot of floor area. A drill press doesn't require anything like the amount of working space that you need for a table saw, radial arm saw, shaper, router table, jointer or planer. Neither does a band saw, except in certain instances when working with very long stock.

One of the first hard parts in shop design is to come to some decision as to tools you feel you must, or will, have. These tools may already be on hand, or tools you plan to buy in the future, or tools you only wish to own. Decide on the areas of woodworking that interest you most, and aim for a shop that suits those needs. If more space or a different design is needed for later, you can start with your current layout as a basis, and move on some years down the road. Attempting at this moment to design and build a shop to suit everything you think you will ever want can be exceptionally expensive, even without buying the tools to complete filling the space. Designing and building to suit actual current (and close future) needs is cheaper, usually easier, and tends to get you up and working in your shop a lot sooner. A large problem with designing a shop is the amount of time that can be wasted doing plans that will never get used in any way, shape or form. I once had a disc load of those, designs that are too extensive to be affordable — at least for me. Those dreamy designs are not a complete waste of time and energy, though. During planning, you may strike the spark that allows you to produce that perfect shop for you. What your shop should be is affordable, efficient, effective for all of your current projects and expandable for more ambitious later projects.

You may also reduce building costs considerably by using a few fairly simple tips and methods. It's impossible to eliminate the need for certain materials and processes, though. Two-hundred and forty volt tools, for example, require 240 volt circuits. Not all home electrical systems are designed to add several of these with any real ease. Thus, costs rise. Look for the 120-volt versions wherever you can. This limits the size of the tool, because it limits power, but it can reduce wiring costs tremendously if you're setting up in a basement or garage (and if you've priced wire today, reducing extra use seems like a great idea).

Designing for shops is far simpler if you know what kind of work you wish to do — simple woodworking gets very complex when all varieties are considered. Many shops work well for a variety of wood-shaping activities. Plan for and design for your own personal variety of machinery and tools arranged to do the jobs you like most and find important, in the order you find most important.

A very simple power woodworking shop may have only a single stationary tool, either a band saw, radial arm saw or table saw. It is far more likely, and effective, that one of those basic saws is combined with a jointer, and, if a table saw isn't the basic saw, maybe a scroll or band saw. With this kind of basic set-up, it's possible to do most kinds of woodworking, from making simple boxes to making extremely complex projects of varied shapes. You are limited to buying planed seasoned wood, though, and that can be tough on a budget.

Along the way, we'll look at the shops, the tools, and the jobs they do, around the world. Well, not exactly around the world, but one small shop in England and many in the U.S. This may assist you in determining exactly what to plan for. We'll examine those shops in Chapter 10.

By the time you get to the point of wanting a designed shop that works for you, you should have a good idea of what kind of woodworking you prefer. If not, decide what kind of woodworking you wish to emphasize, and how its space needs fit in with your space possibilities. If you have room to construct a freestanding shop, your freedom of choice in various woodworking areas is obviously a lot greater

than it is if you have to use part of a basement. Better than a basement shop is a garage, either attached or freestanding.

Over the years, I've had a shop that consisted of a platform of plywood laid on two 2×4s over two sawhorses (with problems finding space for storing tools and platform). That "shop" was set in the yard with a 10-gauge extension cord. Much later, I had an $18^1/2' \times 63'$ basement shop that was exceptionally handy, but hard to keep clean, and hard to move tools and materials into, or projects out of. The exterior doors were set at a 90° angle to the interior doors, with the door height being under 6', though the doors were almost 8' wide. That one was probably dangerous as all get out, too, as it had the door in one end, a window halfway down one wall, and no other exits.

I've used a parlor in a very old country home, and a portion of an over-sized office room in another large, old rented house. I've used a WorkMate in the yard, the dining room, and a hall. I've used a Shopsmith Mark V attached to one of their large drum dust collectors in an unused dining room area.

I now have a freestanding shop, one that will serve, I hope, the rest of my working life, and on into retirement. It is 25' wide, 48' long, with its own 200-amp electrical supply, shown at right. (Yes, I know the grass needed cutting that day.)

We built nothing fancy. Fluorescent lighting dominates, because the 4' fixtures were cheap, but I have a centerline of incandescent bulbs for winter before the shop is warm. Pole construction (4×4s and 4×6s and a couple of 6×6s). The poles are on 8' centers, with nailers on 2' centers. Two posts and built up beams are all that break up the shop, but I found the 6x6 posts provided excellent locations for two, quadruple 120-volt receptacles per post. That's more handy than you might suppose.

The inside shop walls with nailers (run vertically) effectively give a good, thick wall, without losing enough space to matter. They do save some money in framing (nailers are 2" rough-cut Southern pine, installed green).

The poles are pressure treated SYP (southern yellow pine), available just about everywhere but especially low in cost in Virginia. My center row of posts rests on cement block piers. Actually, the posts rest on the center beam for the floor, which is supported by the piers. I'd have loved to use some of the newer, fancy floor-joist systems for this project, but pressure treated 2×10s cost next to nothing in comparison.

One of my neighbors built a pole shop some years ago, with old telephone poles. His biggest problem was getting anything on the inside square and plumb. Mike's shop isn't in here because he's primarily a metal worker, with electrical and automobile additional interests. He does carpentry instead of woodworking, with any woodworking incidental to building structures.

I planned for and installed no plumbing. Remember, I live in a rural area. A shop with no plumbing may be less practical in suburban and urban settings.

My shop's exterior, completed. It's not fancy, but it does work, and is reasonable in cost. Construction used rough-saw poplar for boards and battens.

A full 200-ampere Square Deal 40-circuit service entrance panel lets me run all the tool circuits, on ground fault circuit interrupters, anyone could need in a small shop. One-twenty circuits require only single breakers, with one breaker space. Two-forty volt requires a double breaker with two spaces each.

I put in three lighting circuits. This isn't code required for the square footage of the building, it's a personal preference. It means a tripped breaker doesn't leave you completely in the dark. One bank of lights always works, assuming the neighborhood doesn't lose power. That still leaves plenty of circuits for the rest of the building.

Some detail on electrical wiring and lighting is supplied in Chapter 9, covering absolute and theoretical needs for freestanding and other shops. There's also some information on doing the wiring yourself, though that's not a process I generally recommend for someone without experience, and it may well be illegal in your particular locale. Always check local codes. As far as I know, all local codes conform to the National Electrical Code (NEC), but some, especially in larger cities, are a great deal stricter.

At the outset, shop walls were open studs or nailers. As time passed, I put up $^7/_{16}$" waferboard, pegboard and similar materials to provide an enclosed space. I also insulated behind the interior walls, using as much inexpensive fiberglass insulation as the wall thickness would accept, but at least $3^1/_2$" of fiberglass.

Exterior walls are 1" rough yellow poplar, 6" wide, placed as board-and-batten (vertical 6" boards, $2^1/_2$" battens

— not all the battens are poplar, as I also had some oak, pine and walnut lying around at the time).

The shop floor is wood. I do not care for concrete shop floors for a couple of reasons. First, they're rough on the feet, ankles and lower legs after a few hours. They are particularly rough on my knees, especially after three knee surgeries. Second, they're rough on any edged tool that gets dropped. Drop a new plane on a concrete floor and the odds are excellent it will be ruined. Drop the same plane on a wood floor, and it's usually fine or fixable. Still, concrete fits well with pole construction, and costs less than low level floor framing where joists and beams would have to be of surfaced, pressure treated wood. This shop, though, is on uneven ground, where fill and general work-up for a concrete floor would add considerably to costs, so an actual framed wood floor is about the same cost (especially after my wife, Frances, presented me with the tongue-and-groove plywood for the finish floor as a Christmas present, some years ago). For those who have to go with concrete, in coming years you may want to put in sleepers and come back over that with $^3/_4$" tongue-and-groove plywood. I saved some cost by making the subfloor, atop treated floor joists, of rough cut poplar, installed diagonally.

Windows are few, and start about 50" from the floor: I can place any tool anywhere, without restriction from glass. Too, it has been my experience that natural light in a shop is much over-rated. It always seems to be either too dim for sensible use, or too glaring to be any good. In

This outlet is on one of the centerline posts in my shop.

his original shop, built a couple years before mine, Bobby Weaver placed his windows at a fairly normal residential height (about 34" from the floor to the sill) limiting workbench height, and tool placement, unless he wants to ignore the windows. He did and the one behind the radial arm saw had several panes replaced, eventually, with plywood. He also regrets having used so many windows in his 24' × 40' shop. He had nine, with four in each side wall and one in an end wall, added to two single doors 36" wide and a double door 6' wide. That adds up to a lot of lost wall space, though when he first moved into the shop he felt he had space enough for anything (we all do). Woodworking doesn't work that way. Sooner or later, even the largest affordable shop is going to have its walls hung with clamps and hand tools and templates and patterns and heaven only knows what else. You'll see only a few shots of Bobby's new shop in here, because that old frame shop burned down last summer, thanks to a stray power surge, and he's still building and setting up. Another friend, Dale Toms, built a very large shop, which you'll also see here in part. I was over there earlier this week, and noted that he has just about every tool you might want, but no longer has any extra space in his 32' × 48' shop (with a full basement for the noisy gear like air compressors and dust collectors).

Make allowances, as much as possible, for the increase in your tool numbers. Then think about jig numbers, templates, patterns of other types, and other wall hung items that are going to come along. Too, think of the way the sun rises and falls in your area: At one point during some days,

the light will be perfect through most windows. The rest of the time, it's going to be glaring, shining in your eyes. At other times it's going to be so dim you have to bring over an individual project light if you don't have enough ceiling lights. I prefer placing enough windows for ventilation only, and letting the local power company provide 99.9% of my light from the outset. Even so, I placed one pair of windows without enough thought, catching breezes nicely, but allowing low angle sun to be a real distraction, and possibly a danger, during the winter. The shade has been down on those windows for something over a decade now.

Free standing shops are easiest for getting a good finish on your projects. There's less chance of household activities raising dust to settle on, and ruin, a damp finish. You may select an area and place all your finishing equipment there, keeping it cut off from the rest of the shop to reduce dust problems. Or you may simply clean up and cover up after using the equipment and waiting for each project to dry. Generally, clean-up is far easier to do. Venting of finishing odors is less of a problem in a free standing shop: Place an exhaust fan, and get rid of most of the stink. You don't have to worry about the stench getting into living areas. I suggest, strongly, the use of high-volume-low-pressure (HVLP) spraying equipment, or top quality nylon bristle brushes, and water-based polyurethanes for most wood finishing jobs today. If you must work with volatile solvent-based finishes, you need to work with a spark-free fan and good ventilation.

When selecting basement areas to get ready for shop installation, windows are a nice extra, but aren't essential. If there, use them for ventilation. Light is seldom useful from basement windows, but ventilation during finishing can be a boon.

If you use a basement area for a shop, aim for as much headroom as possible. I don't know about other people, but the biggest problem I find working in basement shops is the low ceiling that can force you into all sorts of contortions to feed anything over six or seven feet long into a machine. There are other possible knocks, including excessive dampness, lack of ventilation, dust problems through the rest of the house, noise problems in the rest of the house, and difficulty in keeping unauthorized people (kids, mostly) out of the shop area. With my freestanding shop, I simply snap the padlock and it's secure until that's unlocked.

Dust problems may also extend to the furnace/heat pump/air conditioning units, overloading filters and getting by filters to create problems. Finishing fumes may be hazardous around any unit that has an open flame, or that is likely to produce an open flame during the finishing. Water heaters are among the worst for this, but my propane furnace, my previous oil furnace and some other appliances like gas clothes driers can also be dangerous.

Basement shops offer limited overhead room, and problems with dampness as their major difficulties. A dehumidifier helps with the latter, as can air conditioning in summer months. The limited overhead room is something you just have to get used to. You have the choice of working with small projects, or being extra careful with long wood for larger projects.

DOORS

At one time, many basements had sizeable entry doors, but in modern homes, that's not always the case. Years ago, I got fed up with the 30" exit door in my basement, and installed a 36" door. Even that is a minimal access size for a woodworking shop (but this basement is not my shop). My freestanding shop has a smaller door based on a full sheet of plywood. After trimming, the door is 45$^{1}/_{2}$" wide by 94$^{1}/_{2}$" tall. It's not fancy, but it has been battered by wind, rain, sleet, snow, people and tools for well over a decade now, and is as sturdy as it was on day one.

If the only door to a shop is a single door, it needs to be at least 42" wide to allow decent in and out movement of materials and projects. You're still limited in project size, but not quite so badly as with a 32" or 36" door (common entry door sizes).

If possible, add a double door to your basement shop. Select a French door style, so that both sides open. Most patio doors open on only one side.

Make certain that there is a good door between the shop and the furnace, with any air transfer going through filters. Do the same for any parts of the basement that are finished and not part of the shop. Use good, tight fitting doors and keep them closed to help keep the dust down.

DOORS FOR FREESTANDING SHOPS

Freestanding shops often use garage doors. As one who truly dislikes the bending and lifting associated with such doors, I find a garage door opener a truly welcome addition. The back strain saved is well worth the cost and the work of installation. Pick a brand designed for easy do-it-yourself installation, such as Marantec or Martin or Liftmaster.

I put in dual sliding doors, using a system Stanley used to make for barns and warehouses. It's easy to install, but very difficult to seal for heating and cooling. The resulting door opening is 7$^{1}/_{2}$' wide by 95" tall. Even that has been a tight fit from time to time. Unloading a palletized 24" Grizzly band saw some years ago, with Dale Toms providing a great deal of help, found us having to lie the saw down on a furniture cart, roll it inside, then stand it up. That's a job that must be done gingerly, because it is possible to really mess up a big saw like that (700+ pounds) by abrupt movements with sudden stops. After my long term experience with sliding doors, my recommendation is that you do as most others have done and go with a garage door. My biggest reason for stating that is that it is a pain in the tail to seal around sliding doors in any meaningful manner, which means heating and cooling are more difficult.

My shop's small door is about 46" wide, by 95" tall.

DUST

A good dust collection system is a need in a basement shop, probably more so than in a well-ventilated freestanding or garage shop. Well ventilated is the operative phrase. If there is any doubt in your mind about keeping dust out of your lungs, WEAR A MASK! I hate masks, goggles, face shields and similar items, and have a great deal of difficulty with all of them, but I now wear them with frequency, unless I'm working outdoors on a windy day. When I wore glasses all the time, they were safety glasses. They saved an eye for me several times. Now, I immediately pop a set of glasses on if I plan to start any tools at all, other than a vacuum cleaner.

In my younger days, I was the dust collection system, with my trusty push broom and a bunch of burlap sacks. The altar factory got cleaned up on a nightly basis, and I was the one doing it. No one, then, took notice of the fact

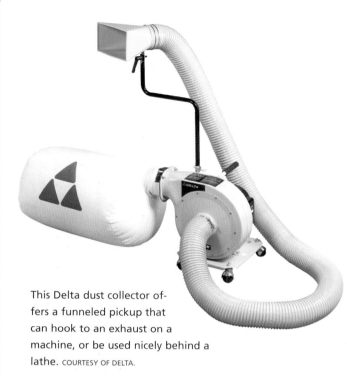

This Delta dust collector offers a funneled pickup that can hook to an exhaust on a machine, or be used nicely behind a lathe. COURTESY OF DELTA.

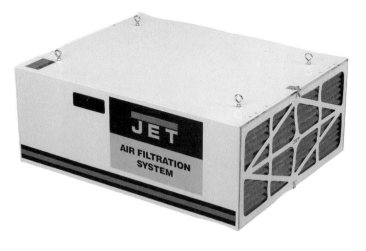

Different from a dedicated dust collector, this dust filtration unit changes out the air in the room, capturing smaller dust particles than a collector. COURTESY OF JET

that a kid learning to work around the shop was choking on dust. Everyone else was, too, when I swept and bagged the sawdust and shavings. Today, I'm paying for that (enhanced by far too many cigarettes, until I quit about 20 years ago). I do have ill effects from that experience. Spare yourself the possibility.

Finishing areas in basement shops need to be ventilated to the outdoors, carefully, and need also to be isolated from the remainder of the house. Moving to an outbuilding to do finishing work is an answer, too, if at all possible. It gets rid of odor problems, and gets rid of any problems with flammability. I also recognize the fact that it's not also always possible. Keep in mind, then, ventilation, and next, water-based finishes. Also, an air cleaner can help get smooth finishes.

If your planning can include space in a garage, you're in great shape. I was probably 16 years old before I knew home garages were mainly for holding cars — and my father was an auto mechanic. Tools, workbenches, and projects seemed to fill many family garages. Our cars only sat inside when they needed work that couldn't be done in the drive.

Garages can lend themselves to fantastic workshop set-ups, or to small, expandable set-ups that come into their own with the family vehicle(s)) backed into the drive, and the tools pulled away from the walls. Even more than a basement workshop, garages lend themselves to mobile tools, and to multi-tools, because the tools can be pulled out and there's enough space to do almost anything with any tool. Some people find space so much at a premium, they are like my old friend, Pete Bade, who stores his little Honda S2000 sports car in his "shop" in winter, with a cover over it.

If you have a Shopsmith, it can go against the back wall and take little more than a 6'-long by 2'-wide space. Even old garages should still accept the family car. Back the vehicle out, pull the tool out, and set up whatever basic tool you wish to use. When the job is done, fold it up, and roll it back into the wall space. European multi-tools such as Felder and Hammer don't fold up quite as tightly, but do offer a tremendous space savings. The Austrian made Felder looks pricey at first glance, but the CF 531, Felder's lowest-price model, includes three motors of 4HP each, a jointing width of 12" with a 59"-long table, a planer, a 12" shaper (four speed), table saw with sliding table and a double miter fence. When you price out the benefits versus the cost of any of the multi-tools, you find they're not quite as costly as they seem at first glance, though all the outlay is up front and in one chunk.

We'll look at several offerings a bit further on in the book.

WHEELS, WHEELS, WHEELS...

Portability and storage also works with individual power tools on wheels. Either after-market or shopmade stands or mobile bases work well. Individual power tools tend to eat more space than a multi tool like a Shopsmith (table saw, lathe, horizontal boring machine, drill press, and 10" disc sander and more). You might not want all those tools, but even a table saw and a drill press tend to eat lots of space. Those two tools alone take up about the same square footage as the Mark V. There are pros and cons for multi-tools, and those are given more room in Chapter Three.

Garages are among the easiest conversions for shops, and double garages are superb. In most cases, you can lay out a pretty darn good shop in a smaller 20' × 20' garage (see Brian Grella's shop, which is exactly that size. Brian

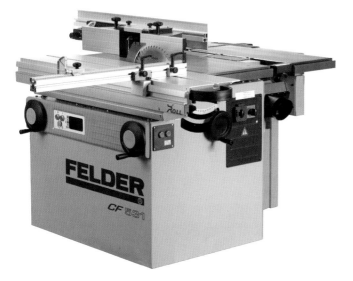

A Felder multi-tool. While not cheap, it includes four quality tools in one, and can offer space saving. COURTESY OF FELDER

turns out some wonderful pieces there.) If there's no need to keep vehicles in a garage, you're well on your way. If half has to be saved for the vehicle, you've still got a decent sized shop, at about 12' by 24'. If the tools need to be moved to allow vehicles in during rough weather (at least), what the devil. You're still better off than most of us have been at many times in our lives.

Though my purpose really isn't to explain the tiny shop with mostly hand tools, even apartment dwellers can enjoy many phases of woodworking. Some tools are relatively small and quiet (band saws and scroll saws, for example) and readily store in a closet. A WorkMate makes a great storable workbench, with accessories that let you do many different kinds of holding (clamping) jobs. In a small apartment, finishing is always going to create problems, from sanding dust to finish odor, flammability and toxicity of fumes. Sanding dust is always with us. Using small hand sanders means you can't use dust collection systems — most of the time. Many newer sanders offer their own sanding-dust catcher, or hoses that can be attached to quiet

Bob Grisso's planer wheels quickly make a big machine mobile.

shop vacuums (as in the Festool series). Those take a long hose that then goes back to fit any standard (metric) vacuum hose, but work best with their own vacuums. It works nicely if you use pre-punched sanding discs that allow the sanding dust to be drawn into the sander, then into the vacuum (use only a shop vacuum for this collection, sanding dust ruins a home vacuum in a shake of a lamb's tail, as my father used to say).

If you want to work with wood, there's not much reason not to do so. It's fun. It's relaxing (sometimes). It may be profitable for some of you. It needs as much space as you can afford to give it, from a patch no more than 3' by about 6' in an apartment to as large as you can afford to construct and fill with tools and materials. Woodworking, though, is not a cheap hobby, and not a definitive way to save money on household cabinets or furniture. You may or may not do the work and save the money, but before you save dime one, you'll invest more than a few bucks.

Read this book carefully and sort out the tips that are most useful to you. You don't need the chapters on framing and flooring and siding if you've got a standing garage to use, nor do you need the chapters on cleaning up as a prelim to setting up a basement for shop use.

SETTLE BACK AND PLAN

Then settle back again, and plan some more. Do floor layouts of your available space, or your intended construction. I've included a couple of mine, and hope they'll help you get an idea or two. Use graph paper if you don't want to work a computer program, or use a drafting table, and drafting machine, or T-square and triangles. Or just do a rough drawing on a pad. But plan it on paper. Layouts are much easier to understand, and to visualize, when viewed from above, in some kind of drawing, no matter how rough.

With a computer and a CAD program, your drawings are more easily changed, but both my drafting programs are difficult to use at the outset; I know of none specifically aimed at helping the shop planner. You really don't need a ton of features, so one of the lower cost programs is fine. I'm not recommending a program here because by the time this book is out, new programs are sure to be out, supplanting old (or making them cheaper), and maybe becoming easier to use (or getting more features, each of which makes them harder to learn for the occasional user).

Follow the codes, and do your drawings on graph paper if you prefer. It has worked for a long, long time. What's important is to get a layout going, make it practical, and to understand in your own mind what you want, what you will get, and how you'll go about getting there. Thus, whether you use the simplest — graph paper, a ruler and a pencil — or the most sophisticated drawing program available is only relevant as long as you realize either is a tool to help you get where you wish to be. Use a cardboard box or an old deck of cards to provide stock for your cut-to-scale mock-ups of top views of your major tools.

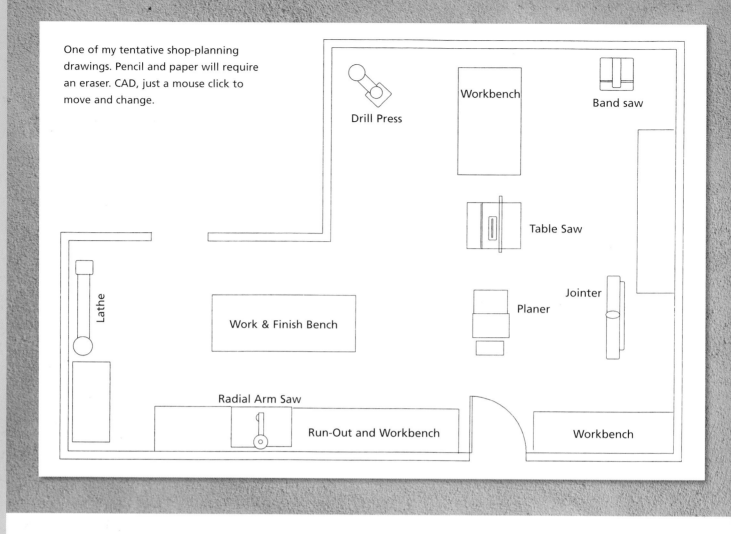

One of my tentative shop-planning drawings. Pencil and paper will require an eraser. CAD, just a mouse click to move and change.

Whatever written planning you do is of help in formalizing your ideas. Start by listing the tools you want in your shop, and then list those you have. Make your choice of shop type from the real-life options available to you, and fit your tool choices to that, making changes as needed.

Know what your woodworking project needs are, and do your best to suit the tools, and the space, and the accessories, to those project needs. But first know what your real life practicalities are. If you live on a 100' × 75' lot with a 65' × 24' house and a 16' × 32' swimming pool already in place, don't expect to fit in a 24' × 44' freestanding woodworking shop as well. If you live in an apartment, don't expect to move in a 500-pound Unisaw and a 15" planer. Dream of the things you can do, not of the sublime — the future may hold more and better woodworking — so dreams are always valuable. If you really intend to set up shop where you are, make those dreams fairly practical.

MAKING CHANGES

It is a lot faster, easier, and much cheaper to make changes in drawings. If changes to a garage, or basement, are extensive you may need some kind of drawings for your local building department. When you're going to erect a freestanding shop, it's almost inevitable that you have some kind of plans drawn up, or draw them up yourself. The department may require the drawings before issuing a permit. Always keep a check going with your local building department. Their codes are based on sensible construction methods, mostly, and are generally aimed at making buildings safer to occupy and use. Too, building codes vary so greatly, as do inspection requirements — I recently discovered that parts of Maine do not require building permits for decks and porches, even though my rural Virginia area does — from area to area. Building codes vary greatly for good reason. What is a more than adequate footing here in south central Virginia is apt to last one season — until the first really hard freeze tosses the carefully prepared and poured concrete up, and drops it back and twists the structure sitting on the foundation — up in Maine. Any place my instructions differ from local codes, go with the local requirements. I've lived in a bunch of places but it is impossible to keep abreast of building codes in more than one or two widely-spaced areas.

WORKSHOP FLOOR PLAN
Based on 6" × 6" pole construction
on 8' centers.

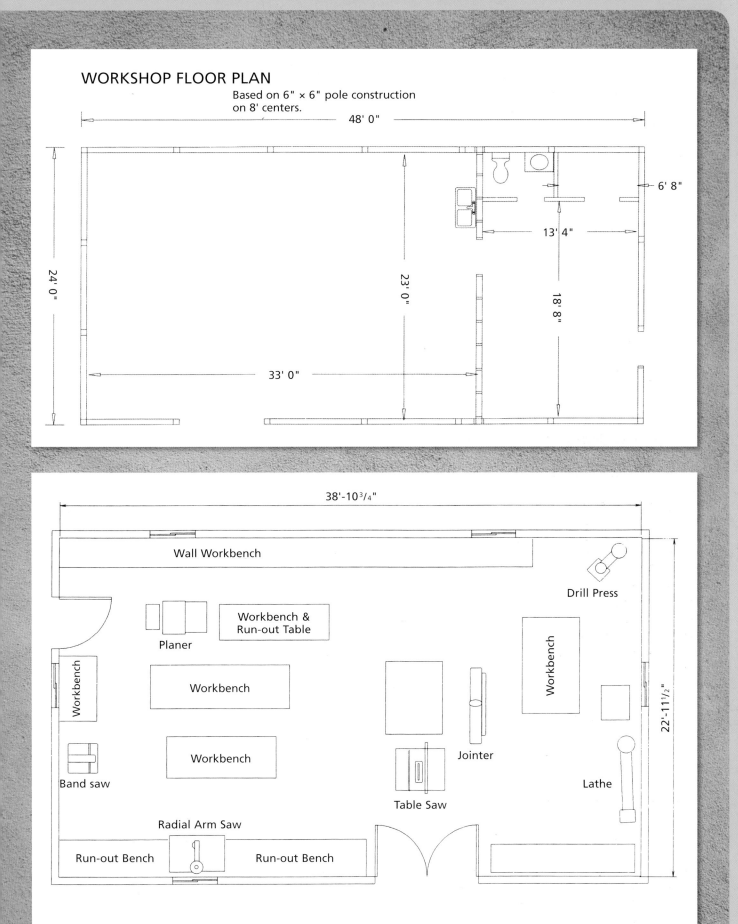

Two other tentative shops that didn't get built, either because of complexity, cost or unsuitability after much thought.

CHAPTER TWO

Space and Its Uses

There are both theoretical and practical layout considerations concerning space needs and general needs for each major tool, and many of the more minor ones. While, for example, table saws and radial arm saws do many of the same jobs, their uses and limitations make space requirements for the two quite different, affecting both tool placement and overall shop shape. Types of projects built, and types of wood used also have a strong effect on layout needs. Those who never use plywood do not need the same space in layouts as those who do, and long-board use demands other layouts. It is possible to design a shop to handle both, but some compromises are needed when space is tight.

Extensive use of plywood requires a shop double the size of one where most of the projects are constructed from boards. You'll find it difficult today to locate solid wood that is more than a foot or so wide, which means you're going to have far different space needs than if you used panels that are consistently 4' wide and 8' long (plywood can be bought in other dimensions, but the 32 square foot panel is by far the most common).

Plywood needs extra storage space, but the most important need is the space to feed that large panel into your machines until it's cut down to manageable size. There's a need for outfeed space for what may be two fairly large pieces, too.

WOOD AND PLYWOOD

Most often, the first tool to be used in a plywood project is the table saw. If you're cutting to the wide side, and aiming at the middle of the board, you need at least 50" on each side of the saw for safety and efficiency.

Once plywood is cut to size, it needs nothing that you don't provide for regular boards, so spacing of tools becomes similar. If you only work plywood, your shop may have limited need for such tools as planers and jointers. Though, again, there always seem to be a dozen exceptions to any rule.

Plan for rough-wood storage, for the most part, outside your shop. Keeping 50 to 100 board feet of lumber inside the shop is a good idea, as is keeping several sheets of your most frequently used plywood immediately on hand, along with a bin of scraps. But storing a large lumber supply indoors can create many problems. Even the massive cabinet and furniture shops don't store more than a few days' supply indoors. It eats space. Space that is floored and cooled and heated can be expensive (heating isn't really needed, of course, but if it's in the shop...).

Wood often carries some passengers as it comes in, including various insects, plus general vegetative debris such as grass stems and heads. If you plan to keep a lot of wood on hand, store only your more immediate needs in the shop. Construct a shed to keep the weather off other wood supplies, or use a tarp, or section of metal roof, to cover the pile. Make sure any outdoor pile is stickered ($3/4"$ × $3/4"$ stickers, cut the full width of the stack and dry, are placed every 2' along each layer). And keep the first layer up off the ground at least 6". Don't ever use lightweight, woven poly tarps for wood storage. First, the tarps transfer color when whipped by the wind, so that they're not much use. Second, and worse, the tarps do not stand weather well, deteriorating to the point of leaking within a short period of time — often as little as three weeks. They're cheap and worth less than they cost for our purposes. Use either a real canvas tarp, coated, or 10-mil black plastic (in my experience, the coated tarps of good quality last about 15 years, while the black plastic is good for one year).

MACHINERY

Tool selection is of exceptional importance to shop design and layout, and actually drives shop layout in general. We place a lightweight 10" or 12" planer in a different manner than we do a 15" or 20" heavyweight planer. This holds true for most stationary tools and many benchtop tools. At the same time, if you want to work with wood in a particular manner, there is no sense at all in creating a shop that works best with wood in another manner. No matter how large, there's always a way to get a job done, even in a tiny shop. You may have to move large plywood sheets outdoors to make preliminary cuts, or do your basic wood planing outdoors, moving the project in as it reaches its smaller, more finished stages. You may, then, find the selection of a lightweight table saw is an imperative. Today's crop of job-site saws provides something never seen before, a truly portable and accurate table saw. No, they are not cabinet saws. Nor are they contractor saws. But they are almost as accurate. Most have easy-lift wheeled stands that make them easy to store and bring out. That means those long cuts and those wide cuts that don't fit in your shop can be easily done in your driveway or yard. Try to find a level spot, of course, for safest working.

My last Unisaw, with accessories, weighed well over 600 pounds, not an inducement to thoughts of portability, but mobility is certainly a possibility. Recently I had a Sears' Craftsman Industrial 10" saw that outweighed the Unisaw, but it sat on wheels and was easily moved as needed.

But you don't want to set up to meet my needs. You want to create a workshop in which you can handle wood in ways unique to you, though using tools and ideas based on those who have preceded you in the field. The first chapter discussed how to select tools to meet your needs, so here I want to help you arrange the space those tools occupy in a manner that will best suit your needs.

Space is always a workshop problem. The need varies according to project types preferred, but no shop ever has enough horizontal flat surface (bench top of one kind or another), and there is seldom enough space for the tools one has, or wants. Rears ago, I rented an $18^1/2'$ × 63' basement for use as a shop. My wife first asked what I'd do with that much space. It took weeks to clean up, paint floors and walls and wire to accept modern loads from power tools. That expanse of gray floor looked imposing while empty. By my sixth month, I was moaning about the lack of space. Frances found the place intimidating because there was little room between benches, tools, stacks of wood, shelves, pegboard hangings, and so on.

WORKING USED

About the same time, a friend started constructing his freestanding workshop, moving from a 10' × 20' basement space into a 24' × 40' frame shop with wood heat. Bobby Weaver is one of the best I've ever seen at picking up old tools and getting them to work, and at finding old cabinets

For plywood and other sheet goods, a table saw with a large top can save headaches — and your back!

and similar items to use in outfitting a shop (using cabinets removed from other places can reduce your fitting time considerably). Bobby bought several, science-building base cabinets, tossed the tops and doors that were in truly rough shape, and added 3/4" plywood tops to provide himself with about 55' of linear flat space. It still wasn't enough, but is better than most of us ever get. Bobby's three table saws were all Craftsman units, varying in age from 15 years (one he bought new, or near new), to one that has a 1929 patent date. His radial arm saws include two Craftsman, bought new, and one Delta 12". Light work goes to one or the other Craftsman, but the really heavy work is passed on to the 240-volt Delta.

Note the number of tools we've already mentioned. Bobby also had two lathes, again Craftsman models. One was a seven footer that he welded up himself so he could make six-foot tall bed posts in a single turning. He had two planers, one an almost antique Parks 12" floor model, and one a Ryobi AP10 10" benchtop model. From there, we can dance around the shop and find a small shaper, a router table, four mid-floor benches (also set up to provide support for outfeeds), two vacuums, two air compressors, a belt sander (about 8' long), a band saw, a drill press, a parts washer (Bobby also does a lot of small engine work)

and the wood stove. Somewhere in there, I'm forgetting something. Suffice to say, that when a few boards are laid in, and one or two or more projects are partially finished — the normal state of affairs — the shop is overcrowded.

The moral: There ain't no such thing as enough space for any woodworker who ever gets serious about things (and many of these machines and tools were purchased used, at a significant savings). While we may never have the room we want, we can try to increase efficiency, safety, and pleasure in our hobby (or small business).

My current set up includes 40' of bench top along one wall, an 8'-long workbench I built for the first edition of this book, and two 6' tables I built for use in a darkroom that I broke down and sold off a few years ago (another benefit of digital photography). I could use more. I tend to rotate through workbenches it seems. I'm working on a new one from Veritas right now. It promises to be a beauty. Another workbench on an entirely different pattern, from a very small company, American Workbench, just came in, and is described in Chapter Four.

When discussing efficiency, I have to talk about mobile bases. One company produces a wide line of mobile bases for woodworking machinery. HTC has, for years, provided wheeled bases for table saws, band saws, drill presses, jointers, planers and other tools. I've used several of them, and have been impressed, as have thousands of others, with the quality, fit and ease of use of these bases. Such bases can make all the difference when you have to have several tools pushed against the walls, or each other, or against benches, rolling them out only when needed. HTC makes many styles and sizes, and sells through a number of the major retail mail-order houses and distributors. You can also get in touch with them for a free catalog, and/or direct ordering information: HTC Products, Inc., 120 E. Hudson , P. O. Box 839, Royal Oak MI 48608. Phone is 800-624-2027 and their web site is www.htcproductsinc. com. HTC has 200 standard models (a number that grows each year), and upwards of 1000 models in all.

Working from the main tool down, we'll start with stationary saws, their size and placement needs for different kinds of woodworking.

TABLE SAWS

The table saw is the basic stationary woodworking power tool in most shops. Not in all — lathe workers often don't use one, or need one, and some general woodworkers use radial arm saws. More unusual, but not really rare, is the woodworker who prefers the band saw to all other saws, and uses it in place of the table saw, though that is a

For accurate crosscuts on smaller hardwood pieces, nothing beats a miter saw. The variety of sizes and features available today is dizzying.

common occurrence with our British cousins. Our needs, though, fit the table saw. Full-size table saws will have a table, or work platform, of about 24" × 36", for a minimum, but rails and fences will add more to that, as will sliding tables. Too, top-grade table saws have much larger tables, often up to 28" × 40", or more. Powermatic's model 66 offers 28" × 38" of table space, but for really great size, you might consider their model 68, a 12" tilting arbor saw, measuring 38" × 48", which is truly immense.

The table saw today is the same as it has been for 70 years, and very different at the same time. Job-site saws essentially jump in between benchtop, super-cheap table saws and the misnamed contractor's saw. The hybrid saw slides in there before we get to cabinet saws. Cabinet saws have changed a fair amount in some ways, but not at all in others.

Steel City recently released the first granite topped table saws to reach the market. According to Scott Box, (a purposefully untitled executive of Steel City — he does whatever is necessary), the primary reason is maintainable flatness. Cast iron is difficult to machine totally flat, and, of course, moves some over its lifetime. It is prone to rust at a wet-eyed glance, and heaven help you if someone sets a leaky drink or coffee container on it. I had some guys installing a drop-down stair in my shop, and came in later to find they'd not only done a terrible job, but had each left a leaky coffee container on my table saw. My pal the contractor saw two deductions on that job, and instructions for those two morons to stay off my property. Granite machines precisely flat with reasonable ease. That's why granite measuring plates are so low in cost. It can't rust. It is a bit more fragile than cast iron in some ways, but the granite used in Steel City's machines is a full 44mm thick (pushing $1^3/4$"), while the cast iron used for saw tables is about $1/4$" thick (it's supported by webbing and heavy lips).

To add to the fun, Steel City also sells a table saw with a titanium coated table. That's a rust preventive, and also helps material move easily over its surface.

Spacing around a table saw is critical for easy, efficient, safe working. Even as a benchtop tool, the table saw needs an acceptable run-in area with a run-out area just as long. If you do a lot of sheet work (plywood panels) you'll find yourself needing greater width at the sides of the saw than otherwise. Long-board crosscuts are generally more easily made with other tools, such as radial arm saws, and power miter saws, but plywood is most easily cut to size, in the hobby shop, with a table saw,

![A full-size table saw that will also protect your fingers!]

A full-size table saw that will also protect your fingers!

door, to the outside, at its front, while the dual set had a medium-sized workbench that could be moved to one side if necessary. The dual set was backed by two workbenches.

The table saw is a primary tool, so is best located near an entrance or an exit so that wood may come directly to it. It is also a tool that works with a lot of long wood lengths, so needs the space, as we've already described, to suit that.

Your working habits may differ. Many people today work with precut wood lengths that are seldom 4' long and not often over 6" wide. In such cases, the above figures should be modified to suit. Certainly, you don't need 9' of run-in space with a 2' or a 4' board. But you do need enough clear foot space around the saw, front and rear, to make handling material safe. If a saw is set in an area full of extension or other cords, air hoses, board ends, or any other kind of clutter, you may bump such junk and end up with a finger or five in the blade. Anything that detracts from you paying complete attention to the work going on, and this is particularly true with the table saw, creates a safety hazard.

Though I well know better, some time ago, I was cutting an 18" square from plywood, with no guards (photos do a much better job of showing what's happening when the lens shows the action, not a guard, so the guards are often removed). I was moving a scrap of wood away with my left foot, when, suddenly, the 18" plywood square came back and whacked my chest with stunning force. Running the blade the standard $1/8$" above the wood, I'd allowed my push to relax a bit while concentrating on the scraps. The wood rode up over the blade which immediately kicked it back, fortunately hitting me on a muscle that is fairly thick.

or a circular saw. You may also get a panel-cutting saw set up but those are single-use tools and are costly.

In general, allow the size of the table saw plus 9' in front of the saw, (for standard 8' board length ripping) with at least 8' clear in back of the rear rip fence support for the long boards to move. That does not mean you actually need a space of about $19^1/2$' permanently clear in front of, over, and in back of each table saw. The saw may be backed up to a door in tight places — or facing a door. The back table may be used for other things much of the time: Both of Bobby Weaver's table saw set-ups, one of which includes two table saws on the same bench, have workbenches set at saw table height behind the saws. One had a standard 36" entry

The insides of the saw shown above. When the blade (while spinning) encouters any flesh, an aluminum cartridge is fired into the teeth of the saw, stopping the blade almost instantly. The result is a scratch, rather than a missing digit.

If you're pressed for shop space, a table saw that folds away and stores in a corner is a great option. COURTESY OF RIDGID

It hit corner first, and I shudder to think what would have happened if it had hit me in my neck, mouth, eye — use your imagination. I have.

The cause had to be stupidity, one hopes momentary, because it surely wasn't ignorance. I've known better for decades. Working without guards needs about 10 times, or more, care. And table saw kickback is rough. I've had small saws — one horsepower hobby models — ram chunks of oak back an inch or more deep into plaster walls. So keep clutter down — and leave the guards on your saws!

Or buy a SawStop® but still leave the guards on. For those who haven't yet heard of the SawStop® it's a remarkably innovative saw that was introduced early in the century. In its essence, it uses a sensor that feels the induction when a finger or other body part is touches the blade. It then stops

A home brew of items from the hardware store will keep your saw's gears clean and running smooth.

the blade, jamming it with an aluminum cartridge, and drops the blade below table level instantly. The replacement cartridge isn't cheap, but, then, the loss of a finger, or worse, is worth the cost. Right now, a cartridge is under $100, delivered, but my bet is you're going to need to replace the blade any time the cartridge is used. I would as a precaution, if for no other reason. SawStop® also offers a contractor's version with the same safety features.

Regardless of brand, minimum table saw space is about 6' wide by 8' deep, though not necessarily in a block that size. You must have room to handle the wood, for rips, but those require only a pass up the center, near the blade, so a cross shape works, if necessary, with the 6' width on the horizontal bar.

Check sizes. My current small table saw, the Ridgid job-site saw, is truly small when stored, and in conjunction with my Craftsman Industrial table saw, it does all I need these days, and gives me portability.

Delta, for its 10" Unisaw with standard fence and table, recommends 6' to the left of the saw, 4' to the right, 10' to the rear, and 10' to the front. Those figures are adjustable to suit, and, as noted, the rear and front spaces do not have to be totally open, only cleared when needed. It's a good idea to remember that companies such as Delta have been in this game a long time and have learned a few things, so when I give their figures for distance, we've got a good working basis. At the same time, let's also remember that there are a great many more mobile bases available from places like HTC and Grizzly than were available when those recommendations were first made.

Bob Grisso's shop provides several examples of shop-made mobile bases. His 20" planer sits on a base he made himself. It is easily the equal of the commercial bases that were available at the time he made it. Bob's shop is a good-sized freestanding garage (at some point in its life), but he has most tools on mobile bases, which eases individual tool-space needs considerably.

TOOL CLEANING

Cleaning table saw gears can be a nuisance, but occasionally, it becomes a needed chore, especially if you buy a used table saw. As a start, clean the gears off with mineral spirits, an old, clean cloth and a toothbrush. Dispose of the rags or paper towels in a closed metal container, water filled. You do not need any fires.

Now go to the auto store and purchase one of those very small tubes of dry graphite. You'll probably have to look for lock lubricant to find it. Next you need some paste floor wax like Johnson's, or Butchers or other mixture that does not contain anything the maker calls a "traction aid". A couple of drops of mineral spirits and a small canning jar for jellies is next.

Fill the jar halfway with wax, add about half the graphite and mix. Add a drop of mineral spirits so the mixture turns evenly black (from the graphite) as you mix it. Aim

Though capable of making rip cuts, radial arm saws are best used for cross cuts and specialty applications. COURTESY OF RIDGID

for the consistency of soft butter, so that the mix spreads easily. Keeping adding wax and graphite until the jar is ³/₄ full and it's dark black, and mix.

Apply to table saw (and other tool) gears needing lubrication. The major benefits start with the wax not attracting dust, as oil or grease does. It is a carrier for the graphite, which provides most of the lube. The wax also lubes, but the graphite does a better job than wax alone.

If you get the mixture in the jar too soft, leave the lid off a day or so. Some of the mineral spirits will evaporate out. If the wax is too hard to apply, add a drop at a time of mineral spirits until it is soft enough to apply easily. When the mix is applied, the mineral spirits slowly evaporates out, the wax sticks to the gears, holding the graphite in suspension to do the lubricating.

I use the mix on all my shop tools, from drill press to table saw and planer. Once mixed, it's easy to apply, and lasts longer than any other lubricant I've tried, adding less mess of its own because it traps less debris from its surroundings. Not much is used on the gears. If any is hanging over the edges it isn't lubricating a thing. Clean it off and have an even neater job. My current jar was mixed when I did an article on waxes for a magazine a couple years ago. It barely shows a dent.

RADIAL ARM SAWS
Radial arm saws have been around a good long time and serve to do a few jobs that don't work too well on table saws. Some

hobbyists use radial arm saws as base saws for an entire workshop, and do very well with them, but most of us use them for special applications such as cut-offs, dentil work, and any form of top, visible dado or moulding work that is necessary. As I've stated earlier in this book, and in many other places, radial arm saws are not the tool of choice for rip sawing. They're basically unsafe, but they can do a good job.

Again, saw size is a variable. Oddly enough, saw cost doesn't always make a difference in table size. Craftsman tables tend to be a little larger than those on some Delta radial arm saws, yet the most costly Craftsman 10" saw is less than half the price of the Delta 12". Still, radial arm saws aren't that hard to place. They're best set against a wall, with a dust collection system placed to draw from the back of the table. For best use in cross cutting and shaping long boards — the jobs at which the radial arm saw shines — Delta recommends 12' on each side of the table, and 3' in front of the saw. These sizes hold for saws right up to 18" diameter.

It's is hard to find a full 27' or so of unused wall space in any hobby shop, and in most small commercial shops. Place the radial arm saw in, or near, the center of a wall that is occupied mostly by work benches, and most of that space becomes available, if your workshop has the overall length. The full length is not essential: Go with what you

This saw is not mobile, but the extra 8' to its right (because of the door) makes up for that. However, it's still hard to clean behind it.

This Delta 20" planer offers a 3-phase, 5HP motor for lots of power and cutting capacity, but it can take up a lot of shop space. COURTESY OF DELTA

can usefully get, and make the saw mobile. With the aid of a couple of supports, you can then move the saw outdoors, or into a roomier area of the basement, garage, etc., and do your extra-long cutting. In fact, those extreme figures are infrequently needed. Most cuts with the radial arm saw are in much shorter stock, so having 6' or less on each side is perfectly acceptable in small shops. The 3' in front of the saw is essential for safe working. I'd also make sure the saw came out from the wall easily. Radial arm saws without dust collectors tend to build up a great deal of dust behind. Make clean-up an easy job and it gets done more often.

PLANERS

Planers are not absolute shop essentials, but in the past couple of decades, (since Ryobi introduced its AP-10 10" portable model for under $400), a number of other companies have come out with lightweight 10" and 12", 13" and even 15" benchtop planers that do an incredible job, allowing more of us to use selections of rough lumber at far lower costs.

Planers, like table saws, require long run-in and run-out space, again depending on your desires for board length.

For tight shop spaces, I'd suggest setting up a planer in front of a door, placing it on a bench or stand that allows you to use the table saw table as a run out area. Bobby Weaver did something similar with his rebuilt, older, 12" floor-model planer. The planer was set up to drop the

boards first onto a workbench (the one mentioned a few paragraphs ago as being movable), then onto the table saw table. His planer ends up with far more run-out space, about 35% of the length of a 40' shop, than is normally needed. In front of the planer was about 10' of open assembly area for large projects, backed by double doors to the outside, so there is unlimited length on the infeed side. And actually, on the outfeeed side as well, as a rear door in the shop is about 6' behind the run-out/workbench set-up for the dual table saws.

Considering the board lengths you purchase will help you site a planer. It's seldom these days that sawmills cut boards over 16' long, and most are in 10' or 12' lengths. You can handle much of the work from one side of the planer. Individual 1×6 or 1×8 boards aren't exceptionally heavy, even in white oak, so working from one side is no real problem for most people. Take your own strength into consideration, just as you do when selecting normal sizes of wood to work.

Planers vary greatly in size, with one of mine, a 13", being only 19" square. That's close in size to most brands of portable 12" to 13" planers, and will extend out to only about 22" × 20" with steel legs, or a 23" × 22" rectangle

Bobby Weaver's new shop internals, along with the Craftsman 12" planer he used for his cabinet stock.

Portable planers will surface a 13"-wide board, run on 110-volt power and can be tucked under the bench at the end of the day. COURTESY OF DEWALT

with a steady, shop-built stand. Lead-in space needs only to allow about an 18"-wide area, so look for lead-in and run-out space of whatever length you expect your boards to be, plus about 20" to 36" for the planer. For stationary planers in larger sizes, the planer head forces you to add 2' to the above figures; most hobby shop planers are going to be 15" and smaller models, so the head is seldom more than 20" deep. Overall, you need a space about 18" wide (plus a bit of a bubble for the planer sides) and 18' to 30' feet long. Most of us can't afford to keep that kind of space free for a single tool that is used only a few times a year. Thus, the portable planer's success when combined with the lower prices: Portable planers are about half the cost of stationary models. It's also the reason behind the success of mobile bases. Most of the hobby shops I know of have their 15" or 20" planers on wheels.

The portable planer space, then, is another cross shape, but this time one crossbar is much longer than the other.

Again, make sure there's plenty of room to work safely. Delta's recommends 12' leading into the planer, with 3' to the adjustment side of the planer. Of course, you need a similarly long space to accept the boards coming out of the planer. That adds up to around 27'.

Planers also turn out an incredible pile of shavings with some rapidity, so you want to have a dust system that sucks it all up; you may also want to wear a mask. I've had shavings pile up and reach the bottom of a planer's stand (about 28" high) after a long session. One of the problems when using a portable planer is its portability. It makes it more difficult to set up ducting and piping for long-term dust and chip removal. Still, your lungs will thank you at some time in the future.

JOINTERS

Jointers are essential tools in power-tool woodshops. That's a truism that is nearly always true. You can make a carriage that does something of the same work on a table saw (getting two edges of a board parallel), but it's not going to give you the planed, finished edge the planer gives. Making chamfers and tapers is far easier on a planer than on a table saw, most of the time.

The jointer is another tool that is prone to kicking back, and it is also a tool where your fingers are working exceptionally close to the turning blades. The guards must be in use, and in good shape. This is one tool where I do *not* remove guards for better photography. If the camera can't get it, I don't shoot it, at least not while the jointer is plugged in.

Jointer space needs are generally small, because most hobby-shop jointers are under a foot wide, with blade widths from 4" to 8", and less than 75" long. Some are light enough to be easily moved, so that they can be placed against another tool, and lifted or pulled into place for use when you need them, though a mobile base is much easier

A common 6" jointer. Cabable of doing a lot of work, but not so large that it can't be pushed into a corner when not in use. COURTESY OF RIDGID

Absolutely no space for a floor-model jointer? This short-bed jointer from Craftsman will store in a cabinet.

on the tool's settings. Like many power tools, though, jointers get more use when they occupy their own slots. Delta's long bed recommendation for a jointer is 6' in front and 6' in back, plus 3' to one side of the jointer, plus, of course, the size of the jointer.

Most material worked up on a jointer is relatively short. Most hobby-sized jointers don't do a good job on material over about 60" or 72". Thus, the run-in and run-out space needed is also fairly short, particularly since almost half the material's length is on the jointer from the outset to the end of the operation. For everything but long doors and similar items, a run-in of about $2^1/2'$ and a similar amount of run-out is sufficient. Less is practical when most of your work is done with boards shorter than 60". Add that to a tool that seldom measures 60" long, and you get a length need of 10', maximum. Many jointers are shorter than 60" and are set in spaces shorter than 10'. The space needs for width also aren't great. You'll need the minimum 12" width, even with 6" blade width jointers, plus enough room for you to stand alongside the jointer and feed the material through. That's going to vary, of course. At one point in my life, 14" would have been sufficient. Today, it's more. Overall, though, you don't need more than 3' for the length of the jointer, plus the board-width space over the blades, seldom more than 6".

For general, light use, a 40"-long jointer with 24" of space at each end is fine, which means less than $7^1/2'$ of permanent space assigned. Jointers are easily wheeled around on HTC mobile bases. Shorter jointers exist, like the Craftsman I'm using in the photo above, or the Palmgren you'll see later. Both are cast iron, durable and small enough to stick away easily, but they are not light.

BAND SAWS

Band saws are exceptionally useful tools, providing an ability to cut modest curves, (for really tight curve cutting, you need a scroll saw and lots of practice) and to resaw fairly wide boards. Depending on the cutting height available, most 14" band saws will resaw a 6"-wide board with much less waste than doing a similar job on a table saw — and much less danger. Some woodworkers believe a band saw can do everything a table saw can. I don't agree entirely. They're lacking in cutting dadoes, use of moulding heads and a number of other operations. Band saws do rip work and crosscutting, in addition to other jobs. I don't believe they rip as well as table saws, nor do they match that saw in several other areas, but for a host of jobs that a table saw cannot do, the band saw is a wonder.

Band saw size is, like that of all stationary tools, variable. The most common band saw sizes for hobby shops are 14" and 16". Delta's 14" band saw, along with Powermatic's, Steel City's, Woodtek's, Grizzly's and a number of others, sit in a space roughly 18" × 18". An overall footprint with the table in place is usually under two square feet.

A good band saw is a power tool that most woodworking shops need. The band saw has so many uses, from

The most common bandsaw (14" cast iron) in any American woodshop. Very capable and versatile.

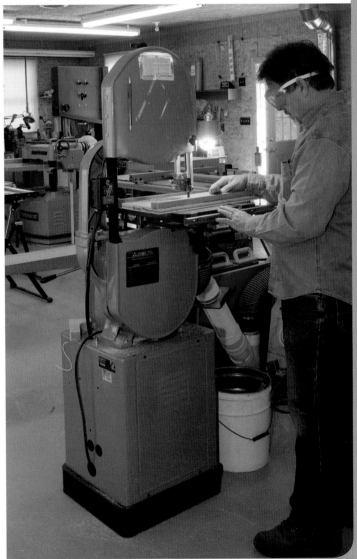

resawing thick boards to pad sawing stacked boards to get identical pieces, plus a lot more, that once you get used to having one, you feel hampered without at least a small band saw. Cutting compound curves for things like cabriole legs is only a starter, as is cutting down bowl blanks so they'll fit onto your lathe, squaring up small logs for use on the lathe or as a source of boards (which are also cut on the band saw), and a plethora of other jobs. You'll see that resawing and cutting logs as if the band saw were a sawmill are limited by saw cutting height — as is ripping boards. The smaller the saw, the lower the cuttng height.

Most hobby woodworking shops aim at the 14" band saw in some form, but some are based on the original Delta model from the '30s. Some of these are excellent tools, some aren't.

The closer they stick to the original Delta design, the better the saws usually are. Most are available with riser kits to jump the basic 6" resaw capacity to 12" (using a longer blade, but the same motor). The larger resaw capacity is offset by the disadvantages one might expect, from possible difficulty in aligning the saw to a lack of power. Often, there comes a time in a woodworker's life when he, or she, feels a need to consistently resaw more than 6", or has to pad (stack) cut boards so often that a 6"-tall pile of $^3/_4$" boards seems puny.

The riser kit then gets added, and the sawyer finds that the original $^3/_4$ or 1 hp motor reduces feed rates to speeds that would lose in a snail race. Though it is unlikely, neck flex might also become a problem in cheaper versions of the 14" band saw. If the riser kit isn't an exact fit, then adjustment problems can jump up and ruin some lumber. The idea of adding a larger motor, say a two horsepower, 220, single phase may suddenly strike one as a great idea. And it may be, especially if you're using one of the open-

Ball bearing blade guides had historically been an aftermarket upgrade. Many manufacturers now offer them as standard.

A sign of a quality band saw — there are two, machined steel trunnions in this Steel City model.

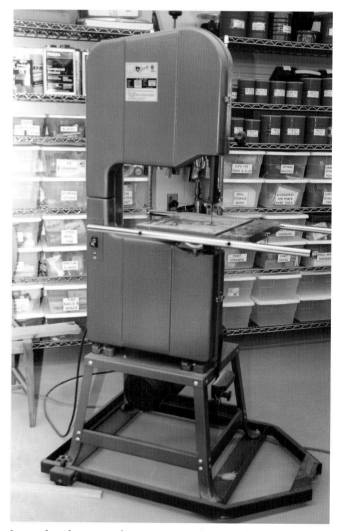

Larger band saws are heavy to move, but a mobile base gives you the freedom to supersize.

stand models produced by many makers, with good, solid basic construction, ready access to the motor, and everything else in top condition. Cost should be reasonable: The motor might run $250, while the old pulley and the old belt may fit right on.

The aforementioned modifications give you a jury rig, though one that under most circumstances provides excellent service. For those who don't want any kind of jury rig, or who lack confidence in even such simple changes by their own hands, there are other methods. The cost is now approaching what you'd spend for a larger, more powerful band saw. When that happens, go for the bigger saw.

BIG BAND SAWS

If you anticipate heavy resaw needs, it may be smarter to buy a larger and more powerful band saw right from the start. The variety of band saws sizes out there now can make it hard to decide the best size for your needs. You can select 15" and 16", 20" and 24", and several companies offer special resaw band saws in larger sizes. If you're a hobby woodworker, or even a small-scale pro, you do not want to know the prices of such saws, some of which are designed to accept power feeders, as well as having a usable blade-width range of 1" to 3" (with 3" blades costing over $100). I'm currently using a 16" Steel City Tools saw that is much better than I expected. One friend has a 24" Grizzly (but uses his 14" Delta for most work because it is easier to set up and run). Another sticks with his 14" Craftsman. As you see shops through this book, you'll see most shops work with 14" band saws.

A mobile base reduces the need for lots of operating space around a band saw. Delta recommends 4' from the table on sides and front of the saw (the column-side may be against the wall, because you can't run material in that direction, unless you're cutting some long, looping curves that run around behind the machine).

Keep interference with your work lines to a minimum, as you always must do with any woodworking tools. You'll then find that for most projects, the band saw needs very little actual space. I used to keep mine rolled up against the wall, hauling it out into mid-floor only when something large had to be cut. In such cases, the space was needed for jigs and supports more than for the band saw itself.

DRILL PRESS

For many woodworkers, there comes a time when the hand-held drill just isn't accurate enough, doesn't have the right combinations of speed and power, and is too difficult to control in precise drilling situations. When that time arrives, a look at drill presses is in order. This is a wide field, with capacities that range from little more than 6" to capacities of over 20" (drill presses work to the center of a circle, so the actual from-the-edge capacity of a 20" drill press really measures 10" from the center of the drill bit to the outside of the post).

Radial drill presses are classed in a similar manner, and provide an inexpensive great way to get extra-wide drilling capacity. A 34" radial drill press measures a maximum of 17" from the drill-bit center to the post, and that gives some woodworkers worry about flex.

Chuck capacity and horse-power are also factors. Most of the smaller, floor drill presses checked have $5/8$" chucks, with power up to a claimed $1 1/2$ hp (amperage is more accurate as an indicator of power).

Some drill presses offer woodworking tables, while others have the classic metal-working styles. The difference is in the slots. In woodworking tables the slots are cut all the way through for ease of clamping with standard woodworking clamps, while metalworking slots go only part way through and accept a different clamp design. The woodworking tables also do not have oil grooves. One final check point is the difference between floor and benchtop models. Benchtop models are always lighter, with lesser capacities. My current Ryobi benchtop model is just about as accurate as my new 17" Delta. The little Ryobi is heavy for its size (12") and type, and offers a laser guide. Quill travel is 3", good for a benchtop model.

Drill presses for the small shop come in two types, benchtop and floor mounted. Both can do what is needed, but space needs aren't

This floor-model drill press offers a table designed for woodworking, great capacity and good lighting. COURTESY OF DELTA

even close to similar. I've got a couple of the benchtop styles, and find they take almost no space — less than 14" square on any bench. Too, they can be set to the back of the bench, or forward to handle longer stuff (with the head reversed). Still, floor mounted 15" and larger drill press can do just about anything any hobby woodworker is ever likely to want. From drilling tiny, precise $3/64$" holes on up to drilling 3'-long, $1/2$"-diameter holes in hardwood lamp bases. The space requirement, even for such a huge tool, is minimal, with a recommended 3' on each side of the drill-press table, plus 3' in front of the table. I wouldn't squeeze this, though a lot of people do stand the drill press at an angle in a corner. I kind of like it at least $5 1/2$' from the nearest obstruction on each side for those times you need to run holes near the ends of 6' boards. Still, placing the unit on a wall so that it's positioned slightly over other tools of similar table height (remember it is the table height that is adjusted on a floor drill press) seems to work.

This is another tool that works well on wheels, and you may want to make your own base, because there is little or no thrust added to create problems with movement against the wheels.

Delta recently introduced a new line of drill presses expressly designed for woodworkers. There are three, and I have the bottom model, the 17", 17-959L. There are also 20" models, with and without a laser guide. A laser accessory seems to be the fate of most tools these days. Like all such lasers, it's mildly helpful and are easily adjusted.

The table is larger than tables on general-use drill presses, with more tilt capacity (right and left 90° and forward 45°), with a $3 3/4$" replaceable MDF insert in the center.

This Dremel scroll saw is easily carried short distances; shown here on my "Common Man" workbench. It comes with a sturdy, steel stand that provides the angle most users like.

The head is new and incorporates a lot of cast iron. I used an engine crane to assemble mine, as I'm getting too old and fat to lift what is close to 200 pounds up to eye level. The $3/4$-hp motor on the 17" is more than sufficient, as are the 16 speeds. The quill stroke is a real bonus at $4 7/8$".

The 20" models have a quill stroke of 6", which is wonderful, but you're paying a lot of extra money for that extra long stroke, at least $200, and as much as $400, because that's the price difference on the 20" machines versus the 17". The $400 difference is for the laser equipped machine. I can see no difference in other specifications between it and the non-laser model.

SCROLL SAW

Scroll saws are delightful tools that provide a great deal of fun on the way to some really intricate work. They're also among the best tools for beginning woodworkers, because, as with the band saw, there's no chance of kickback, and the danger of losing a finger or two is dramatically reduced by the small size of the blades used. That's not to say scroll saws can't hurt you: I've managed to split the ends of fingers several times by not paying close attention. But, they're far less likely to than are table saws, radial arm saws, jointers and a whole bunch of other woodworking tools — including simple chisels.

Space needs for scroll saws are small, while the portability of the tool is probably the greatest among saws listed as stationary. Even most of the heavy-duty industrial models lend themselves to being picked up and carted several feet by one strong person.

Like all stationary tools, scroll saws present different size worries. Many such tools offer a 15" cutting depth, but some go to 24" and beyond. Take this into account when figuring your sizes, but as a rule of thumb, count on 3' on three sides and you're in good shape. Most scroll saw work is small, so you need space, mostly, to move around the saw to get the most effective angle to handle intricate cuts. Many people use stools when working on scroll saws.

Overall, a 24" scroll saw needs about 6' in depth, and $7 1/2$' in width for total clearance. My small Dremel 16" offers a need for less, with an overall length of under 24", and a width, at the stand base, of 22". It fits in any space that allows 5' of depth by 6' 10" in width. It can be used in a slightly smaller space, and weighs very little so it doesn't need a strong person to cart it to any open area with a power outlet.

Bob Grisso runs a Delta C-frame scroll saw in his shop, for much of his intarsia work, while he has another, a Hegner, in the garage for eventual inlay work.

LATHE

A lathe is the essential element to the great craft of turning. The lathe bed is the base of the tool and may be of cast iron, steel tubing, or other material, usually in two parallel rails. Cast iron rails are generally considered better than

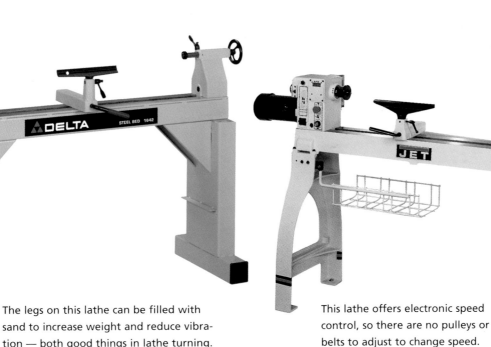

The legs on this lathe can be filled with sand to increase weight and reduce vibration — both good things in lathe turning.

COURTESY OF DELTA

This lathe offers electronic speed control, so there are no pulleys or belts to adjust to change speed.

COURTESY OF JET

tubing rails. The more solid the bed is, the more accurate the lathe can be. Overall, and other things being equal, the heavier any lathe is, the more precisely you can turn with it. Weight dampens vibration.

The machined parts of the bed, on which the tool rest and the tail stock move, are the ways. Whether the bed is tubing, cast iron or other material, accurate machining and great strength are necessary ingredients. Cast iron is the preferred material for accurate work.

At the left end of the bed is the head stock, which may also contain the motor housing (the motor may also be hung on the outside of the head stock). The driving center, with spur, attaches to an arbor that holds a pulley that attaches, through a series of belts, to the motor. Swap the belts from pulley to pulley and you raise and lower driving-center speed. Driving speeds on lathes range from 500 to 3000 rpm, depending on pulley size, arrangement and other factors. Some newer lathes do not use belts, but provide an electronic speed control that is both faster and safer to use (some turners have a tendency to not always wait for the pulleys to stop moving before starting to move belts). I've used several, with most experience on the Craftsman 15", which I like a great deal.

At the right end of the lathe is the tail stock. This part can be moved along the base rails to vary the distance between the back center (on the spindle, at the top inside left of the tail stock, facing the driving center) and the driving center so different length materials can be turned.

The tail stock has a spindle lock and a spindle advance to help in locking pieces in place for turning, and there is a tail stock lock, usually located under the tail stock between the rails. The spindle on the tail stock holds the tail stock center.

Utilizing a steel rod rather than a cast-iron bed and stamped steel legs, this lathe is a departure from traditional lathes, but still very functional.

COURTESY OF RIDGID

Bob Grisso's lathe is firmly planted in the center of his shop. No mobile bases here.

Between the tail stock and the head stock is the tool rest. This adjustable platform, in miscellaneous shapes (straight, long, short, "S" and "V" are just some) is where the turner rests the tool as it shaves away material. The tool rest has a tool rest lock, for height and distance from the work for the tool rest, plus a lock that holds the rest in place on the lathe bad.

The lathe sits on a stand or a heavy bench. The heavier the stand or bench, the more precise your turnings can be.

FITTING IT IN

Lathes are another tool that can often be backed close to a wall and left in place. Bobby Weaver had a 3'-capacity lathe, plus one that has a 6'-length capacity, along the same wall. He uses the long lathe, which he designed and built from two Craftsman lathes, for making cannonball bed posts. Bob Grisso has his lathe near the center of his shop. It is one of the few tools in his shop that isn't on a mobile base or wheels of some kind. Lathes are improved by extra weight and a solid stance, so mobility is far less desirable than with other tools. Dale Toms uses the alcove formed by the stairs to his shop basement to hold his Delta lathe.

Delta recommends 4' to the left (at the head stock) of a lathe, and 3' in front for the operator's stance, along the entire length of the bed. Since most hobby lathes are not much longer than 3' at the bed, and about 5-6' overall, you need a space of 9' or 10' along the wall. You also need some way to gather up shavings. The shavings are thrown in a large area, so some light plywood or sheetmetal work to duct the waste to a dust collecting system is best.

If you're using a massive bowl lathe, you have to do some figure conversion, because the bowl lathes may have no actual bed, but do have a truly immense throw that lets you to turn large-diameter bowls. Most spindle lathes have a throw of 16" or less. With bowl lathes, you'll have to move out from the wall to allow yourself access around large bowls. I suggest stationing such a lathe at least 4' from any wall on the working end. You may want to butt the other end against a wall, but a lot of working space in a block is needed at the spinning end.

A friend is using his large Delta lathe for pen turning, but most people buy and use what some call a mini-lathe for that particularly hobby. A mini-lathe requires some operational space, but is essentially a benchtop tool that can be put away (under a bench) when not in use. Most work on a mini-lather requires minimal movement, so the 3' front clearance and a foot at either side is fine.

SHAPERS AND ROUTER TABLES

The router table has just about taken the place of the shaper in today's small shop. It tends to offer a few extras, though until recently it was harder to adjust and clean.

This 3-hp shaper offers a decent size table and excellent fence adjustment. Adequate for most shops. COURTESY OF POWERMATIC

If your shaper will see lots of work, this 5-hp model with an oversized table top may better suit your needs. COURTESY OF DELTA

Routers are not designed to work upside down, which means many of them do not react too well to the stuff that drops into their cases.

The space needs of both are similar. You need space behind and around the tool to make adjustments, bit changes and to check things out. You need space in front of the tool for yourself. You often need a long run-in and run-out space. At one point in my life, I worked in a factory that manufactured church furniture and we spent a great deal of time using a shaper for long runs (pew backs, choir loft rails and similar items). There wasn't anything unusual in running an 18'-long piece of oak through the shaper to form a rail. That takes run-in and run-out space. Even there, though, other machines were shut down, so the operators weren't in the line of the long piece, coming in or going out. It is seldom possible to leave quite that much space at each end of a tool. Today's mobile bases allow for easier space adjustment for a shaper. Commercially made router tables have gotten much more sophisticated and costly. Jessem, one of the leading manufacturers, makes tables with inserts that turn any router into an easily-adjusted unit.

You don't need 20' at each end of a shaper or router table. Such occasions are infrequent, and the space can usually be cleared if it becomes necessary, or the tool moved. For large shapers, or router tables, in industrial situations, or near-industrial set-ups, leave 6' of working space for the operator, plus 8' from the table on each end. That covers anything. The large operator movement area is needed because both router tables and shapers are often used to mould pieces that extend towards the operator a considerable distance — door panel tops, sides and bottoms, for instance.

On first look, it appears there's a possibility of a knock-down-drag-out contest between shapers and jointers, with small shapers vying for the utility title over router tables, with 3 or 3$^{1}/_{4}$-hp routers.

What actually happens, though, is a lesson in symbiosis. The tools are enough different that having one of each, assuming a need for the specific different features, may not be a bad idea.

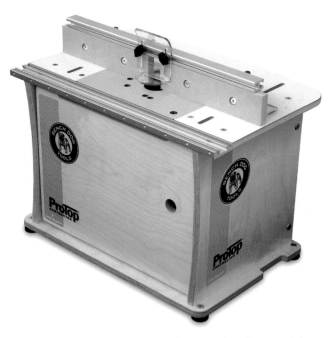

For most woodshops, a benchtop (as shown) or floor model router table will be the tool of choice. COURTESY OF BENCHDOG

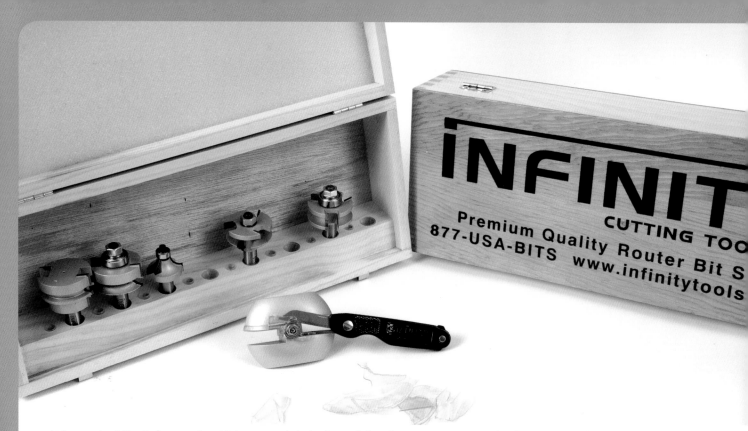

Using router bit sets for occasional joinery needs (raised-panel doors) can save money and still produce professional results.

POOR MAN'S SHAPER

The router table has long been called a poor man's shaper. Tain't necessarily so. Jessem and Bench Dog router tables are definitely not cheap, coming close to being about a wash on price when compared to a basic shaper. Argue until the dawning of the Apocalypse about the lower power figure for a router, but the fact is these motors are pretty close to equal, with an edge going to the lower rated shaper. The low-down, grunt-and-go power of the shaper motor wins every time, even tough it turns the spindle at only about half speed compared to the router.

Shapers generally have two speeds, around 7,000 and 10,000 rpm, and use an ampere reversible, single phase motor to get to and hold those speeds. Motors are totally enclosed fan cooled (TEFC) types. Bearings are shielded and have permanent lubrication. They are induction motors, providing plenty of speed and power for modest-sized shaper cutters, though rotational speed is nothing like that of the router's universal motor. Shaper motors are, though, far more durable under heavy loads than universal motors.

The variable electronic speed router has soft start, so there's no torque kickback, which is far more important hand held than it is table mounted. But one of the router's advantages is that it can be dismounted from the table and used handheld.

BIT AND CUTTER COMPARISONS

Router bits normally have two cutting edges, while the shaper bits use three. In addition to the extra cutting edge, which actually increases cuts per rpm to 30,000 with small cutters and 21,000 with large, the shaper cutters have much more mass in cast iron. Well made and balanced cutters run more smoothly than do lighter cutters and bits. As a test, I ran several shaper cutters from Freud and Amana. Both brands proved excellent and gave nearly glass-smooth cuts in MDF, ash, oak and cherry. Router bits I tested came from Amana, Freud, CMT and Infinity. Again, all proved well made, and gave very good to excellent cuts with the test woods.

The primary difference between cutters and bits is weight and the amount of carbide (size of actual carbide tips). Within one maker's line, the carbide is usually the same grade for both router bits and shaper cutters. But the more massive cutters for the shaper, along with their larger carbide inserts, tend to wear longer, sharpen more times, and thus offer greater life for those who do a considerable amount of shaping. In other words, if you're going to raise 10-15 panels for kitchen cabinets, the router table is king, because the lower cost bits are also easier to insert and lock in place. For those doing 20 or more (up to hundreds), the shaper is king, because the cutters hold their edges longer (large edges, plus more of them, mean longer life, all else being equal).

There is a considerable difference in cost between router bits and cutters. In general, shaper cutters cost as much as 150 percent more than router bits for similar uses, but the choice of profiles available is much wider, and the cutters are more durable than the bits.

Many, maybe most, smaller shapers offer an accessory router collet spindle, which allows the use of router bits

Incremental above-the-table height
adjustment is a huge benefit.

Aftermarket router lifts can bring shaper performance (and extreme adjustment
accuracy) to your router table.

with the shaper. Again, a generality: Router bits, with only two cutting edges, are intended for high speed use, so when used on most shapers, with lower maximum speeds, the results are not as good as those possible when the same bit is used in a router.

PERFORMANCE

Usually, a router table is handy even if you have a shaper. The shaper does everything the router table does, including (with the optional router collet spindle) blind work, but it doesn't handle two-cutter router bits as well as the router does. If you've never used a shaper, and don't do a lot of raised panel work, or moulding production, you'll never miss it. Once you get one, you'll miss it if you get rid of it. If you have a 3 hp or larger shaper already, then a router table is almost essential for other shop work.

Some advantages for routers include higher speeds (some routers hit 25,000 and more rpm). Higher speeds produce a much better cut finish with two-edged bits. The slightly higher cost for a complete router table with qual-

ity router life can be mitigated by buying it a piece at a time — router, table, legs, fence (not necessarily in that order), or by building your own (which allows for constructing a top, legs and cabinetry that are optimum for your personal needs and desires). Many router table inserts can be modified with Porter-Cable style guide bushings to allow template work. My Jessem came in five packages, at least two of which could have been dispensed with at the outset, and added later (legs and fence — though I'd hate to lose that fence).

SHAPER ADVANTAGES

Pluses for shapers start with the heavy-duty motor that provides lower rotational speeds, but much greater grunt, meaning, usually, a longer lasting machine. Induction motors used on shapers are quieter than the shrieking universal motors on routers. Magnetic switches used on most small shapers are safer than the switches on most router tables should there be a power loss. Cutters last longer than bits, which is an overall shaper advantage, even though the cutters usually cost considerably more. Changing and adjusting a cutter is easier than changing a router bit, and getting it set for height. A Router Raizer will eliminate this advantage, but at a cost of an additional $90 or so. Today, though, many routers, including my Triton, come with built-in raisers. Shapers have cast iron tables, which are flatter (at least in theory) than the laminate tops used for router tables. Highly polished cast iron tables are easier to work with than is a laminate surface, and, in essence, doesn't wear, though wear is seldom a problem with hobby-use of a router table. The standard shaper fence has guards, guides, and often, a decent dust collection attachment set-up (router table dust removal systems do continue to improve). The reversing switch on shapers allows some more complex work, including feeding backwards into a reversed (top to bottom) cutter to get varied profiles.

A huge advantage for the shaper is the number of stock cutters available, even for $3/4$" spindle machines. For larger shapers with 1" and $1^1/4$" spindles, the variety is even greater. There are also shaper cutters that hold individual high speed steel cutting knives that can be ground to any shape desired at modest cost (anyone with a modest amount of time to practice can produce his own profiles, basically using a grinder). Or buy already cut profiles.

That sounds as if the shaper is the ideal tool, even for the hobbyist woodworker. Unfortunately, the cost of that great variety of cutters keeps it from being as great as it might be (and there doesn't seem too easy a shot at cost reduction, because of the size of the cutting devices involved; the size is an advantage that becomes a disadvantage when overall use is considered).

FINAL JUDGMENT

Any woodworker thinking of getting either a shaper or a router table needs to take into consideration, after the age old question of affordability of the basic machine, how great a variety of profiles he or she expects to cut over the years, and how large some of these profiles are. If the primary construction is boxes, and box joints are a near daily use while raised panels only come along a couple times a year, the router table, with the versatility of the removable router, is the certain choice. The shaper is overkill, and the small, straight bits used with box joint jigs don't cut as cleanly at lower speeds on the shaper as it will at higher speeds on the router table.

If things go the other way, and the hobbyist is determined to outfit the entire neighborhood with arched raised panels for kitchen and bath and recreation room use, then the shaper is the way to go, with acceptance of the fact that getting a wide range of cutters may take longer because of cutter cost.

For the average woodworker who has space and money for only a single tool, the router table is the way to go. For the advanced woodworker who expects to produce lots of raised panels, stile and rail doors, and large mouldings, the small shaper may be the sensible starting point. Our discussed small shaper is at least $1^1/2$-to-2 horsepower, no more than two. For those who do so much moulding that a stock feeder seems a good idea, a step up to a three horsepower unit is in order.

The Tormek Sharpening System owes its origins to a bench grinder, but goes well beyond a grinder's abilities.

GRINDERS

Grinders may be mounted on benches or on pedestals. Size variations here are fairly small, but you need a few feet on each side of the grinder, plus 3' in front for the operator. Delta recommends 3' from the wheels for each side of a 7" or 8" pedestal grinder, and a foot on each side for a 6" bench grinder.

Horizontal wet sharpening systems are growing rapidly in popularity. COURTESY OF DELTA

The newest sharpening systems use interchangeable abrasives and glass plates for support. COURTESY OF WORK SHARP

Using a vented disc and abrasive sheet (above), you can actually watch the workpiece as you sharpen (below). Perfect for gouges and lathe tools. COURTESY OF WORK SHARP

Much depends on location: I've had pedestal grinders set in close, with about a foot on either side, but the pedestals, and the grinders, were light enough to be pulled out and the grinding wheels dressed or changed as required that way. There's little other reason to work with 3' on each side, though many people do use the flats of the wheels for some grinding (not recommended by most wheel manufacturers: Side grinding is a good way to explode a wheel).

It's simple to make a grinder pedestal using two flat pieces of 1/4" plate steel, one 29" × 3" OD mild steel tubing, and an old 15" or larger light truck or car wheel. One piece of plate needs to be about 6" square, while the other is 10" or 12" square (depending on the grinder base size). Center the tubing on the 6" square piece and weld it in place. Drop it through the center hole on the automobile wheel, and weld the tube assembly in place. Weld the 10" piece on the top of the tube, adding, if you like, a couple of L-brackets for bracing. Drill holes for mounting the grinder and mount.

With today's prices for already-built grinder stands, I'm not sure the effort and cost for the above is really justifiable, unless you already have an old wheel and a piece of tubing on hand, as well as some kind of welding machinery and the skill to use it.

This type of simple pedestal is stable, but can be tipped and rolled out of the way fairly easily. If it doesn't seem stable enough, add an old tire to the wheel, and fill the old tire with concrete.

The sharpener-grinder is a relatively new innovation. Tormek produces the most famous, with its base grinder that takes accessory jigs for just about ever woodworking tool, or other tool, we might have. Unfortunately, by the time a Tormek sharpening set-up is complete, the cost is over $1,000. The Delta wet grinder shown at left works well, but I've got a Work Sharp 3000 that does just about anything you can want with chisels, many turning tools and plane blades (though it's not great for sharpening long planer knives) and similar tools. You'll still need a grinder for your turning gouges and carving tools. I'd hesitate to

take a grinder to carving tools. Stick with slipstones. I've just gotten a new Ryobi 8" grinder. It's similar to my older Ryobi, except for better protection against flying sparks and small bits. The Work Sharp, though, is a delight, with its tempered glass wheel that can have different grits (pressure sensitive adhesive) mounted top and bottom for different stages of sharpening. The Edge-Vision™ slotted wheel actually lets you see what you're doing when you

A quick way to extend the life of drill bits is with a Drill Doctor. COURTESY OF DRILL DOCTOR

A thickness sander can make easy work of wide panels, maintaining accurate thickness across the whole board. A sanding drum (above) is powered by a separate motor than the feed belt. COURTESY OF DELTA

sharpening from the underside. For final touch up, there's a leather honing wheel.

All the Work Sharp 3000 wheels are mounted on a $^1/_5$ hp motor that is gear-reduced to 580 RPM. The standard tempered, float glass wheel is sturdy, long lasting, and easy to change. There is an underside angle guide that is precise, giving 20°, 25°, 30° and 35° settings. The upper side of the wheel can be used with or without an adjustable tool rest for freehand sharpening. It is a dry system, with the low speed wheel preventing burning of edges and loss of temper (too much heat build-up is still possible, but using the correct technique keeps it from happening).

The Work Sharp comes from the people who also brought us the well-thought-of Drill Doctor.

After years of using oilstones and waterstones, I'm delighted to be using a dry system, and one that's easy to use.

SANDERS

There are so many different kinds of sanders used in workshops today that describing space needs for all of them is an impossibility. In most shops, a 6" × 48" belt sander with, or without, a 9", 10" or 12" disc will be present, and needs specific space. The DeWalt I used to have was fairly easy to move around, so I always had at least the 3' to each side of the disc, plus 4' behind the machine and 4' leading into the belt. Currently, I'm using a Craftsman benchtop model that has a 2"-wide belt and a 6" disc; that works well simply clamped to a WorkMate. Pieces that can be worked on these sanders are of moderate size, so you won't need long run-ins and there's no need for long run-outs. Assembled or partly assembled boxes, birdhouses and so forth, along with the occasional parts of a cabinet frame, door or panel are the types and sizes of things most often worked on such units, though they also work nicely to clean up the rockers on cradles and rocking horses.

Belt/Disc sanders offer two-for-one economy.
COURTESY OF CRAFTSMAN

Though more of a specialty tool, a spindle sander will pay for itself quickly if your projects involve sanding interior curves.

Drum, disc, belt and other sanders exist in profusion, and you should always try to allow sufficient space to be comfortable working at the machine — usually figured as at least 3' for you to stand and move around in — plus plenty of space for the work pieces you expect to feed into, and receive from, the tool. Again, most sanding is done on narrower stock, but there are large panel sanders that will handle material as much as 3' wide. These are often used to sand down countertops and tabletops, and the length of the feed, and run-out, then becomes important. Most hobby shops will not have such sanders, but they're great labor savers when available. You get a real good look at what a flat surface can be (as you do on countertops and benchtops run through a 25" wide planer). Dale Toms' shop provides a good look at the top-end amateur's shop. Dale built his shop when he was in a high-pressure sales business. He used the shop to relieve the pressure, and, in the process, has gotten a great deal of enjoyment from it. He has a wide belt sander — not a drum: He tried one, hated it, returned it — that requires much more space than usual. It is set up very much like his 20" planer. Dale's shop is 32' × 48', though, so there was room to play with when planning tool layout. He also has a full basement,

which provides a secure, out-of-the-weather place for the noisy gear, including his air compressor and dust collector.

The now venerable spindle sander is in another incarnation from Triton. It has a cast iron table, with a 3" maximum spindle size. The Triton offers the same rotating and oscillating action that other brands have had, along with onboard storage of almost all the items that get changed, from sanding sleeves to the drums and inserts (six, ranging up to 3" from $1/2$"). If you have much curved sanding on small items to do, these tools take little space and really do the job well. Dust collection is decent, the motor is a low draw at $31/2$ amps, and table size is $141/2$" × $113/8$" in a kind of oblong with a flat back. The unit fits on a bench about 16" × 20", and works well on a bench top, with little extra clearance other than space for small items being sanded and the operator's body.

AIR TOOLS

Air tools in the wood shop once were confined to a compressor driving a spray gun, though they also drive other tools that are useful (air tools provided the first random orbit sanders. It took electric tool manufacturers many, many years to figure out how to get that to work at a rational cost and reasonable weight). Personally, I do very little high-pressure spray finishing, but I find the staplers, finish nailers, and various sanders, provided by air tools so handy I won't be without one.

If you want to have a compressor, you need to make room for it. If the tool is to be stationary, a vertical tank model is probably the best buy for most woodworking shops. The choices are extremely wide. For a stationary set-up, use a 60 gallon tank, and a 5 hp compressor (beyond that and costs rise considerably). You can go larger without going to three phase, but, generally something like Porter Cable's $71/2$ hp, 80 gallon model is more than enough. But when you get into two stage compressors for higher pressure, you quickly find prices rising appreciably: A quick check of prices shows a 7 hp, 60 gallon Porter Cable compressor should currently be available most places for around $550; to jump up to $71/2$ hp, (believe me when I note there is an immense amount of difference in these two motors) 80 gallon, two stage, and the price is going to be around $1,600. If spraying and sanding aren't in the cards, almost any one horse pancake or hot dog compressor

This 80-gallon compressor will handle all of your shop's air needs, including finishing.
COURTESY OF PORTER-CABLE

does fine. DeWalt offers some real wonders for a middling high price, while Grizzly brings in good tools for well under $200. Craftsman has some excellent compressors at really rational prices. Over the years, I've had very good luck with their air tools, especially the nailers, staplers and other small drivers.

Not much has changed in the large air compressor area in a decade, except for a few brand names. Looking at three old-line names, Craftsman, Maxus (from Campbell-Hausfeld) and Porter-Cable, (ranging from 5 to $7^1/_2$ hp, I found impressive quality added to plenty of power and features. All three had 80-gallon tanks, with pumps that can readily keep up with reasonable demands, and some unreasonable ones.

A general recommendation for a small woodshop specifies one of the above, or a similar model from another maker. A two stage air compressor with a minimum of a 5 hp motor, and an 80-gallon tank suffices in most shops that don't need a true production-line process. The Porter-Cable is the most powerful of the three above, while the Craftsman is the lowest cost and the lightest, a possible factor when being moved by one person (and getting by whomever controls the purse strings). The Maxus is mid-range all the way, but is sturdily built.

If you plan to do HVLP finishing, or any spraying really, you need one of the 5 hp models, at a minimum. A bigger tank, at least 60 gallons, is also needed.

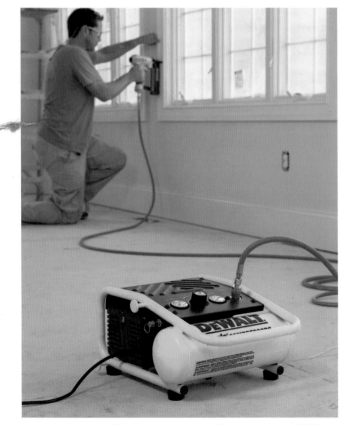

For short bursts of high-pressure air and excellent portability, a small compressor unit is just the ticket. COURTESY OF DEWALT

Because that covers maximum shop needs, or nearly so, for most shops, is there a need to even look at portable models? Necessarily a lesser tool, starting with weight, going through power, and including storage capacity. But prices start at or near $150, and all of them drive a single air nailer, several brad nailers or staplers, and the heavier ones, like the Maxus I mentioned, may do small finishing jobs. For a small amateur woodshop, a portable compressor such as one of the pancakes may be all that is needed.

Of course, finishing touches can all be nailed by hand, and most nailing is easy enough, but using an air compressor and air nailer, speeds the nailing process and eliminates the need for nail setting. Also, on small projects that need nails or brads, there is a tendency for the projects to bounce as you nail, which may create difficulty. That bounce is eliminated with air nailing.

The biggest evolution in the past decade or so has come in the realm of take-along, or pull-along, air compressors available for installation and finish jobs and for callbacks. The old tire-pump-capacity air compressor is now available in ratings from a single horsepower on up to about three, with the biggest selection dropping in at $1^1/_2$ to $2^1/_2$ hp. Ratings move from oil-free lightweights on up to oiled heavyweights (A take-along air compressor that weighs over 75 pounds is a heavyweight. Several of the compressors checked exceeded that, and the Maxus was over 100 pounds). Most of the heavier air compressors have wheels. Ridgid's offering is a wheelbarrow style, while the Maxus is the old horizontal 20-gallon tank configuration, with wheels. The Husky we looked at has a vertical tank and wheels. The DeWalt is a newer configuration, with the wheels nearly hidden by the cage and the tanks. The portable Porter-Cable I checked out was a lightweight, easily handled compressor that was also the lowest in cost of any of the compressors.

The Porter-Cable C2002 provides an excellent starting point. It weighs 34 pounds, possibly its finest feature at the end of a long day. In addition, it provides 2.6 cubic feet per minute of air at 90 pounds, using a no-maintenance oil-free pump, driven by a 10-ampere, 120-volt motor.

Is moving to air driven tools cost effective? With a hammer and nail set, you're looking at several actions before getting to the putty, holding the moulding with one hand, which also holds the finish nail or brad. Your other hand holds the hammer. A couple taps, maybe three, and the nail is in position to be set. You then place the nail set and tap the head of the nail below the surface.

Using air, you hold the moulding in place, set the tip of the nailer where you want the nail and squeeze the trigger.

The main points are air delivery and amperage and voltage. For general portable work in the United States, the motor must use 120 volts and must draw less than 20 amperes, with a max of 15 being better. That requirement is set by the basic electrical installation in the average home, and can't vary on the high side.

A NOTE ON OIL-FREE/OILLESS VS. OLD COMPRESSORS

There is a weight difference, a noise difference and a durability difference between the two types. The oil-free air compressor, generally, is part of a lighter unit, and does not last as long as the oiled unit. It is also considerably noisier, though some work with shrouds, as on the Husky vertical model, has reduced that difference more than a little, dropping it to 75 decibels at the light duty setting, growing to 79 dB at the Medium Duty setting, then moving up to 85 dB at the Heavy Duty setting.

James Vintzel, of Porter-Cable, notes, "We measure decibel levels on all of our compressors, and only recently have they been advertised on actual performance labels. This can be tricky, as lower pitch is more pleasing to the ear, but it does not translate as lower noise. In general, oil-lube is in the lower 80's in dB, due to the fact that the oil in the crankcase has a dampening effect. On oil-free pumps with a universal motor, dB can run from the upper 80's to the lower 90's, depending on shroud and pump speed. Oil-free pumps with induction motors will be about 90 dB."

The DeWalt 55146 uses its shrouding to reduce noise levels to an ear-easy 78 dB. Both of these are oil-free compressors, the DeWalt fairly expensive, and very much an industrial level tool, while the Husky is less expensive (and comes with a plethora of non-cabinet related tools). Each shows its worth over time.

WHEELBARROW COMPRESSORS

Wheelbarrow units have long been popular among contractors. Put down a single plank and you can run them anywhere, regardless of surface conditions. They fit easily through doors and can be tilted to high enough angles to get around almost anything. The only thing more portable than a wheelbarrow air compressor may be the hand-held pancake type. Ridgid's 90150, 9 gallon wheelbarrow has twin 4.5 gallon tanks, a 2 hp motor, comes set up for 120 volts, but is easily changed to 220 volts for those who need or desire that, and produces a maximum psi of 150, with 5.5 SCFM (standard cubic feet per minute) at 90 psi. It is an oiled unit, with belt drive, two quick fittings, and two gauges. The impression of solidity is great. Like the Maxus, this one is built to outlast most woodworking shops in normal or heavy use.

Furthering the wheeled revolution is the Craftsman 0916778, a 5 hp, vertical-tank unit with large wheels and a 25 gallon tank. This two-stage unit offers 175 psi, and 5.1 SCFM at 90 psi. It is also oil-free and relatively low in price. I had one for several years and found it very useful and easy to handle.

While we work our way through some of these models, it might be a good idea to remember that the listed air compressors are just those we were able to check, not the only models in anyone's line, nor the only lines available. You can supply your own favorite manufacturer or distributor that has been left out. Campbell-Hausfeld has plenty of models in lower priced lines than its Maxus.

Porter-Cable has a good array beyond the two we looked at. Those were picked because they spanned the line, with

Portable, but powerful, wheeled compressor (either vertical, or, horizontal, wheelbarrow type) will handle most compressed-air needs. COURTESY OF HUSKY

the pancake model at the very bottom and the two stage, 80 gallon, 7.5 hp, vertical tank at the top.

DeWalt offers a range of portable air compressors, as does Craftsman, while Maxus, too, has lighter duty models than those we selected. Jenny has several more hand-carry types, and wheelbarrow models, plus dual-wheeled portables that offer two-stage compression.

There's quite a price range in these portable compressors, ranging from a low of around $175 on up past $600. There are a few around at under 100 bucks: In a very few cases, those prove to be a good buy, those cases being for shops where you're certain of nothing but light duty work.

Otherwise, that's enough money to make an examination of shop needs a sensible idea. Most of us don't put $300 and up to work or play without some extra thought. Too, according to Porter-Cable's James Vintzel, cost is harder to figure when durability and other factors are considered:. He states, " Life of an oil-lube is about 1,500 hours, but performance drops off gradually over time. Life of an oil-free is about 500 hours, but there is an upgrade kit for about $25 that will give an additional 500 hours. Generally, the oil-free units are less expensive versus oil-lube at the original retails."

In essence, don't pay more than about two-thirds the price for an oil-free unit that you would for a similarly powered and featured oil-lube model. With the kit, you'll get two-thirds the use. Other considerations still apply. Weight: The oil-free compressors are generally lighter. Wheels, though, reduce or eliminate a disadvantage caused by weight in most cases. Noise: The oil-lubed models start out quieter, but shrouding and other work these days actually has brands like Husky down in the same range as the oiled compressors.

Putting wheels on a small air compressor, along with a decent handle, makes even 100-plus pound units easy to handle. I must admit, though, that carrying the handheld units isn't any real strain, even at the end of a long day. Almost all the brand name portable air compressors are able to drive two or more finishing nailers at the same time. None of them drive air sanders well. A basic dual-action sander takes 8 SCFM, at 90 psi, while the largest of the above tools turns out 5.5 or 5.6 SCFM. Reversible air drills (1/4") take about 4 SCFM, so are usable with many of the more powerful lightweights, but those have mostly been supplanted by cordless driver/drills and drivers.

If you get this book in a later year, the model numbers and prices will be different, but the specs, and quite probably most of the manufacturers, will be the same.

HVLP

For many years, high volume low pressure sprayers (HVLP) were the province solely of the cabinet shop and the production line, arenas where original cost is sometimes outweighed by other factors. Those factors include lower material use, greater speed of production and fewer problems with air-borne contaminants. Recently, prices of low-end HVLP spray units have come down.

Production HVLP units start at about $500 and go upwards quickly. If you expect to do a lot of spray finishing, they're well worth it. For infrequent use, probably not.

For those with an air compressor on hand, high pressure spray wins on an equipment cost basis: You can buy a good high pressure spray gun for about $120, and add in a line filter for another $35 or so. You also need a much better respirator mask, and some kind of very efficient ventilation system, which is a problem in many home shops. It is, in fact, necessary to have good ventilation even with low VOC (volatile organic compounds) and HVLP systems in use: Replacing oxygen in the air with glop, regardless of how volatile, just isn't a great idea for breathability.

The best feature of the HVLP spray units is simply the fact that the reduction in overspray means less film on my glasses, in my lungs, and far less wasted material. Application of material with HVLP sprayers brings 70% or greater adhesion versus somewhere around 30 to 35% with regular high pressure spray equipment, used expertly. This is transfer efficiency; the reason it is so high with HVLP units is the low pressure, which makes the unit need a special turbine. Most HVLP units work with 4-5 psi, while the standard high pressure spray guns need 40 psi or more (often as much as 50 psi) to work.

VOCs floating in the air are reduced, reducing problems with respiration even when using solvent-based materials. When using water-based materials, even fewer air contamination problems exist. It's still probably a good idea to wear a decent respirator, but you'll find yourself changing filters with a greatly reduced frequency.

HVLP spray guns bounce far less material off the surface being finished than do standard high-pressure spray guns. As a result, they are both different and easier to use, though at first they do seem a little weird, if you're used to high-pressure sprays. One major difference comes in coverage: With more of the material sticking to the object

FUJI XT-2 TURBINE SPRAYGUN

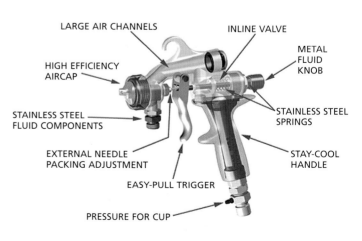

LARGE AIR CHANNELS

INLINE VALVE

METAL FLUID KNOB

HIGH EFFICIENCY AIRCAP

STAINLESS STEEL FLUID COMPONENTS

STAINLESS STEEL SPRINGS

EXTERNAL NEEDLE PACKING ADJUSTMENT

STAY-COOL HANDLE

EASY-PULL TRIGGER

PRESSURE FOR CUP

HVLP sprayers offer less overspray, conserve finishing materials and offer professional finishing results. COURTESY OF FUJI

being coated, your finishing material goes further (in my experience, you use about 40% or less of the material you use with high-pressure sprays), so coverage is faster. That needs care, particularly on vertical surfaces.

HVLP spray units for production use or home shop use are not designed to lay on heavy materials, such as latexes. They splatter and clog and make a mess with heavy solutions, unless those solutions are thinned so much there's little benefit in spraying them.

If you've got a superb project just coming to a close, say a bookcase for the kids that needs to look great, but that is also going to get well pounded over the years, start considering finishes and application systems. Tung oils and other nut oils are fortified with polyurethanes. There are solvent-based polyurethanes, combination stain and polyuethanes, shellacs, lacquers, water-borne polyurethanes, acrylics, enamels: All hanging in there, each offering what its makers class as the greatest finish of its type. Most provide an excellent finish, with minimal labor, though the traditional shellacs and lacquers may be a bit too fragile for use in the kids' room.

Each of these finishes works well, too, with most delivery systems, but there are more hassles with systems for laying the finish down than there are in some other areas: I've never had much luck with foam brushes, so I quit using them many years ago; fine varnishing or lacquer brushes do a good job, but have a tendency, with many finish materials, to leave brush marks. Any bristled brush has a tendency to drop the occasional bristle into the finish on the project, often without the bristle being noticed until after the finish is dry. High-pressure spray outfits require oil-free and water-free air, which means adding a special filter to the line. Then there's the bounce-back (overspray) problem. You need 75% or 100% more material to coat a project with high-pressure spray finish than you do when using a brush. HVLP units reduce overspray to as close to nothing as you'll find, reducing materials needs (you'll still need more than you needed with a brush). On top of all, HVLP guns are as easy to clean as spray units get, because the finish goes only through the gun.

Where HVLP units shine is in the application of finishes like polyurethanes, stains and most water-based polyuethanes. Water-based finishes and HVLP units seem almost invented for each other; each adds a great deal of ease to getting a top-quality finish with only a rational amount of practice.

Use a drip stick or a viscosity cup to test the material: For drip stick testing as I did, the need is for a single second between drips. If the liquid drips faster, it's too thin. If it drips more slowly, it's too thick.

Save shirt cardboards and old boxes so you'll have plenty of cardboard on hand for test spraying.

You can adjust the spray gun to offer a round, horizontal or vertical pattern: Use whichever pattern you feel will logically cover the best for your work. The gun also has a material-control knob, which is turned to increase or decrease the flow of material. Air flow may also be controlled with an air-flow-control knob.

Practice. And practice some more. Use different weights of finish material so you'll get used to different application rates. The odd thing about HVLP systems is that they're easy to use for the novice, but respond well to increases in experience and skill. The more experience you get, the better the results are going to be.

Keep running tests: You'll use up a couple quarts of finish and mess up a lot of cardboard and spare wood that way, but when the time comes, you'll be ready to spray almost any project with great results.

Clean-up is easy. Start by spraying solvent through the gun. The guns disassemble quickly and are then sloshed in suitable cleaning solvent. You can sit the whole disassembled gun in a bucket of water when using water-borne materials. Slosh, remove and shake partly dry. Let air dry and reassemble. Even with uneven or multifaceted surfaces can be sprayed quickly. That's hard to beat — as is HVLP.

CHAPTER THREE

Harmonizing Tool and Work Needs

The most pleasing and enjoyable woodworking comes when you harmonize your desires for shop use with the needs of and for different tools. This harmony blends with the space and shapes available to let you determine the best tool and shop pattern for your uses. Unlike the Colonial era shop shown in this first photo, today's shop is less easy when it comes time to get all parts working together because of the extensive use of power tools.

PHOTO COURTESY OF COLONIAL WILLIAMSBURG

SawStop introduced the first table saw designed to avoid injury. The saw uses a mechanism that senses electrical current in the human body. When it senses that current near the blade, an aluminum cartridge (below the saw table) fires into the blade, stopping it almost immediately. PHOTO COURTESY OF SAWSTOP

TABLE SAW

This is the basic power saw of use in almost all woodshops. The variations available today are far greater than ever before, combining some affects of technology, along with the simpler, but no less important directives of many years of experience. The possibilities range from a 10" benchtop table saw that weighs under 50 pounds to huge 12" blade models that weigh well over 10 times that amount. Along the way, there's a table saw for almost everyone who needs one in a woodshop application. Most of us would like a table saw along the lines of the SawStop or the Felder combo machine shown in these photos.

Wood is usually best worked to within $1/64$", maybe $1/128$", and not in microns, or thousandths of an inch. Thus, you need, at most, a saw that will work to within $1/128$" for greatest accuracy, and one that will repeat such accuracy as often as you need it to. That is where the differences fall: Repeatability over time. If you're only going to make a dozen or two cuts a week, with required accuracy in your own projects limited to $1/32$", or even $1/16$", then the least expensive, lightweight saws are all you need until your project requirements change. Even lightweight saws offer good to excellent accuracy, though, and at reasonable prices. Ryobi's BTS21 (shown on page 54) is a good example.

If your need is in the middle, a range that most of us occupy, with repeatability of $1/32$" and a hundred or so cuts weekly most of the time, and the occasional project needs a full $1/64$" accuracy, then you have the widest selection possible.

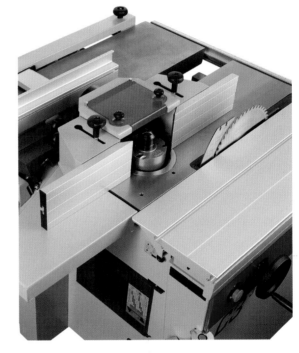

A Felder table saw is much more than just a saw. These multi-function machines often offer a sliding table for easier handling of large panels. The one shown at left also offers a built-in shaper. Blending more than one function into a single machine can save shop space, but it does come at a price. PHOTO COURTESY OF FELDER

If your need is hundreds of cuts weekly, week after week, with $1/64$" accuracy and a wish for more, then you have a smaller, and more costly, range from which to choose. But you still have a range.

BENCHTOP TABLE SAWS

The basic benchtop saw has changed greatly in the last few years: Actually, it has partly gone away and been replaced by a much better tool, the job-site saw. This is a true contractor's saw, generally easy to move, but heavier than the old benchtops, with some newer models weighing in at well over 110 pounds (my Ridgid, for example). These saws present a good solution for the basic woodworking shop,

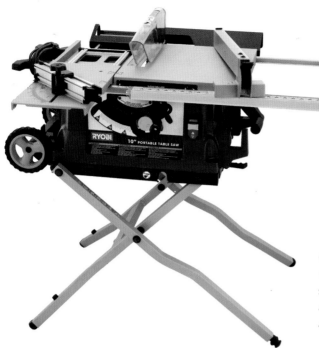

Compact and portable job-site saws have many of the features you expect from a table saw. In fact, some you wouldn't expect, such as the sliding table at the left, and blade storage, shown on the right. COURTESY OF RYOBI

and the price is right (usually under $400). All are supplied with 10" blades, and provide good accuracy within their cutting limits. None have the capacity to take larger fence systems and they're not particularly well suited to larger shop-built accessories such as sliding miter tables. But they work well. As our first category of table saws, these job-site saws endure a good amount of use without losing their basic accuracy (remember, we're working here to a max of about $1/32$", with durability extending over a few dozen cuts per week, with little desire for any form of production or framing construction work) and generally hold up well.

I like to have one or more of these saws on hand for times when the standard shop saw is locked up on other jobs. It may also be handy to have a relatively low-cost tool set to one side of the shop with a dado head in place so that specialty cuts may be made without breaking down the set-up on the big saw.

A portable table saw can handle plywood, but without extra support, half a sheet is probably the maximum. COURTESY OF RYOBI

Lock everything down, collapse the stand and store your saw vertically in the corner to save space. COURTESY OF RYOBI

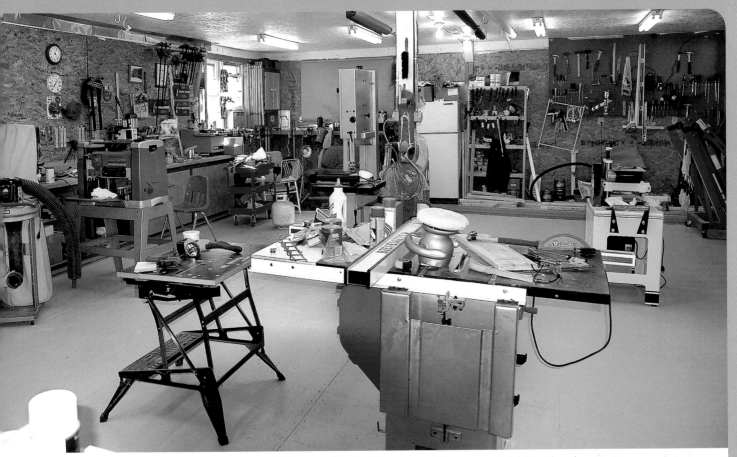

My hybrid saw (shown in the foreground) has a fold-out outfeed table to support longer material. Very handy.

HYBRID AND LIGHTER-WEIGHT SAWS

There is a new category of table saw to consider these days, too. The hybrid saw seems to have been a DeWalt invention, some 10 or 12 years ago. The detail is simple. Using a lighter motor and pulley system (one belt instead of two or three as in a Unisaw and other cabinet saws), the hybrid saw also uses cabinet-mounted trunnions to hold and position the table. This makes adjustments easier and the saw more stable. It also makes the saw somewhat cheaper than a full-blown cabinet saw, as well as lighter.

Another aspect of the hybrid category is the suspension of the motor inside an enclosed cabinet. This offers two benefits: Better tension on the motor pulleys (the weight of the motor is a benefit and also keeps the cut square when beveling the blade) and the enclosed cabinet dramatically improves the dust collection on these machines.

To date, every major saw manufacturer has its own version of the hybrid saw. I used the Craftsman hybrid $1^3/4$ HP model for several years and like it a great deal. It is now in a friend's shop, continuing its work.

In the contractor saw category, many older models had extension tables with grids. I've heard a number of people say the grids in these tables need filling, as you're likely to catch your fingers in them, which, I imagine, might be rough on the fingers. Dropping pencils and other tools through the grid was also a common complaint. In general, the open-frame tables are a thing of the past.

Looks like a cabinet saw, but priced to please. A hybrid from Craftsman.

COURTESY OF CRAFTSMAN.

We come to my basic complaint about lighter weight table saws: The blasted table inserts all take several operations for change. In most cases, you must back out, and sometimes remove, one or two small screws. Any operation that has small parts, especially fasteners not easily replaced from shop stock, floating about where piles of sawdust may be building up is a nuisance, for obvious reasons. Such operations are also time wasters. Nothing beats the Unisaw insert system: It drops in place. All others should, but that requires the inserts be made thicker, more precisely fitting, and the insertion space be cut more deeply and precisely.

This contractor (a term that is outdated these days) saw from Ridgid has a solid table top, an excellent T-style rip fence and an easy-to-use mobile base that quickly disengages to provide a solid footing while cutting. Easy-to-read beveling scale and a handle placed to not bang up your knuckles are all advantages. COURTESY OF RIDGID

It's a lazy man's complaint, I guess, but I find the Unisaw insert is also easier to level with the table's surface, and it's less likely to tilt up on one end and down on another. Too, the insert is heavy enough that it is never going to warp or twist, sometimes a problem with less costly saws. Aftermarket inserts are available, improving the fit and adjustment, but you shouldn't have to upgrade a new saw.

CABINET SAWS

At this point, we step up to the next level of table saw, the light-production cabinet saw. The Delta entry in the field is the Unisaw, and it more or less sets the standard, as it has for many decades. These saws are definitely not portable. Once set up, they are best left in place, as their exceptional accuracy is better maintained when the saw isn't jerked around. Properly designed mobile bases can be used if mobility is forced on you by tight quarters, but this should be the exception. The Unisaw weighs in at about 400 pounds in its most basic form, and each step up in equipment carries more weight. Motor covers are not standard equipment on some cabinet saws, but other features may be far more important: The miter slot is a T-slot (with the horizontal slot on the bottom), so the miter gauge is held more accurately. There is a magnetic motor starter available — and I recommend it — as it keeps the motor from restarting without permission if power is cut off from any place other than the switch. The trunnions that hold the

table on the cabinet are truly massive, and rack-and-worm gears elevate and tilt the blade mechanism. Power? It's pretty much up to you, but standard power is a 3 hp motor, with a 5 hp, three-phase unit available.

In my unabashed opinion, three-phase power has no place in the home shop. It is too complex — if you don't believe that, get three professional, industrial electricians, or electrical engineers talking about it. The overall confusion and expense elevate things to an industrial level very quickly. I remark on this in part because there is a continuing temptation to buy discarded tools from industry and school sources. Such tools are sold long before the useful life is finished, but almost all are for three-phase power. Not really a good buy unless you've got a low-cost source of electrical motors of the right frame types, or are into building or buying phase convertors (Grizzly sells a couple, with the rotary convertors over $800 delivered for the smallest, 5 hp mode). Static phase convertors are less expensive and should work well for most home shop operations. They give 90% of total power for as much as 15 minutes per use. A 5 hp (actually, 3 to 7) is about $200 delivered. That static convertor also weighs less than five pounds, compared to over 100 for the similar-output rotary convertor.

Delta is not the only maker of cabinet saws. The list is longer than it used to be, with the addition of models from Jet, Craftsman, Grizzly, Woodtek, Steel City and others. Powermatic has always provided a superb saw that is strong competition for the Unisaw. Too, a Canadian company, General Manufacturing, turns out a lovely Northern version of the 10" tilting-arbor table saw. There is also the SawStop™, with its cartridge and safety capability.

As a rule of thumb, it's possible to say that Powermatic saws are going to run just a touch more than the Delta products (about 5% to 10%), but offer a slight design change for that slight extra cost. Quality is on a par with the Unisaw. General matches the pride of product, and the features, but presents a few problems with pricing — being tied to the Canadian dollar, not the U.S. The saw is worth it if you can find one.

Steel City Tool Works, based in Tennessee and Pittsburgh, is putting out some superb Taiwanese-made tools. I have one of their 16" band saws and am solidly impressed with features like cast iron trunnions, in a tool area that often gets cast zinc in that size and price range. Machining is also excellent, and the finish is unusually good. This seems to be a common trait amongst the Steel City Tool Works line, which continues to expand. If you check the price and features on Steel City machines you'll be pleasantly surprised.

Larger table saws (such as cabinet saws) also offer the power to use specialty cutting accessories, such as the two types of Freud blade sets shown below. The 6" dado set

The average woodworker would be ecstatic to have the space and opportunity to have a 12" cabinet saw such as the one shown here from Craftsman. A 12" saw is often a luxury and most woodshops will do nicely with a smaller (10") version of this type of saw. PHOTO COURTESY OF SEARS/CRAFTSMAN

cuts as deep as 99.9% of us ever need, and swings easily on almost any good table saw. The box joint cutters save a lot of time and hassle of set up, reducing problems of getting correct width of cut to almost nil. Every shop should have one or both of these. The dado set, or one of equal quality, is close to an imperative.

FENCES

One other advantage of better table saws is the ability to swap off fences. A properly aligned rip fence helps you

Specialty blades are better and more useful than ever. A quality dado blade (left) is indispensible. A newer addition, a dedicated blade set for making box joints, takes much of the setup out of the equation. COURTESY OF FREUD

Three brands of T-style rip fences, from left-to-right: Biesemeyer, Delta's Unifence and an HTC model. All offer excellent accuracy and repeatable settings. Once a luxury, these fences are now standard on most cabinet saws and many contractor saws.

turn out precise rip after precise rip, with never a hair out of place. Well, almost anyway. The hair gets displaced when you work with larger, heavier pieces of wood, regardless of the worth of the fence.

The ideal fence, aftermarket or stock, has an easily set, precise measurement on a quickly-read scale. It then locks down to that measurement without moving, and stays there no matter how hard it is bumped, until the lock is released. That ideal fence can then be returned to the same mark to produce more rips of the exact same measurement, even after a long period of time and much other use.

The ideal fence lifts off the rail(s) with no wild gyrations or tools needed and is replaced just as easily. The perfect fence moves along its rail(s) smoothly, even slickly, and sawdust build-up doesn't interfere with that movement.

Any adjustments needed to get the fence parallel with the blade are easily made, and just as easily repeated if needed, but do not need frequent repeating. Some commercial fences go months, even years without adjustment for parallelism once correctly set.

The ideal fence is fairly simple, extremely durable, and, unfortunately, can be fairly expensive. The fence must be sturdy enough to suffer through the whacks of 4×8 plywood and 10/4 cherry being trimmed for smaller jobs, while also being precise enough to allow consistent ripping of $1/8$"-thick strips. The perfect fence also has to be easy to use with jigs, either riding on the fence or fastened to it. And, certainly, the ideal fence is fairly easy to install on a wide variety of machines.

Incra set-ups are popular but, for some reason, I have never used one. I have a good friend who uses one frequently, and you'll see in Bob Grisso's shop that his table saw is fitted with an Incra system. He loves it.

The Accusquare fence is a Canadian effort that works well, though it is smaller and lighter than most of the other fences included here. From Mule Cabinetmaker in Newmarket, Ontario, this fence uses a star wheel handle to twist and lock down its clamp, rather than a lever, as do most of the others. The Exaktor is its kissin' cousin, with the differences being mostly in the colors anodized onto rails, the fence body and clamp. The Accusquare is gold, the Exaktor is silver. The clamp base is steel and sturdy.

The fence is an aluminum extrusion, square ($2^1/2$" on a side), 35" long (plus the clamping section). The clamp section is 10" long, with adjustment screws on the back that rest on the rails and are easy to use. Overall, installation on any brand of saw is easy. These are well made, nicely designed, low-cost aftermarket fences.

We found the fence to be very easy to use, though the fence's shortness took a little getting used to after working with the Biesemeyer, its clones, and the Unifence. Still, most European woodworkers work daily with fences that stop at the blade, so that's nothing more than a habit.

Jigs can ride over the fence, or can be inserted (with T-slot bolts) in the three T-slots designed into the fence extrusion for just that purpose.

This aluminum extrusion is the end of an Accusquare fence. Accusquare fences install easily, are easy to use, and are low in price, probably lower than any other top-notch fence.

The readability of the scale on your saw is critical. Many include a magnifying lens to help with viewing, but this can shift the reading. It's best to determine if the scale works for your eyes before purchasing.

Overall, this fence adjusts easily, its accuracy is dependent on your placement of the tape, and adjustments are easy. The plywood test — setting up for a cut, whacking the fence lightly with a shove on a 4×4 piece of ³/₄" plywood — could be done hard enough to jar the fence but the setting didn't change. You must tighten carefully with any fence. The job seems a bit harder with a turning handle than it is with a lever; the twist-and-lock feature is effective. The rails are aluminum, and are easier to damage than are most of the others used.

This is a well thought out fence that is nicely made and should prove durable over the long span in a home shop, and in a small commercial shop where people care about tools. It is so easy to install that it makes a really great project/present for those who want their tools to work with little fuss. And it's inexpensive.

The Biesemeyer Commercial sets the standards for all T-square fences. Actually, its design strength and overall sturdiness combined with accuracy and relatively easy installation sets the standard for every aftermarket saw fence. If it doesn't match the Biesemeyer at or around the same price, another brand is not considered worth fooling with by many woodworkers.

The rail is very heavy steel, as is the 42" fence tube, with a 3" × 2" cross section. Biesemeyer is still using the many-ply side plates, with internal fastening done at the factory.

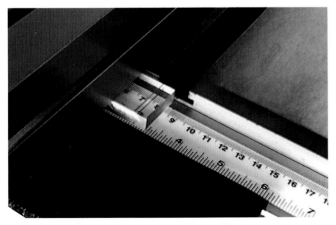

Scale readability on the Accusquare is excellent.

The Biesemeyer moves slickly along its rail, and the 16"-wide clamp assembly makes for easy side-to-side adjustment, while providing more than enough surface for solid clamping. Nylon glides aid slick movement. The fence lifts off easily and is returned just as easily.

Durability of Biesemeyer fences is legendary. It takes a severe accident or a fire to damage one badly enough to take it out of use.

On an overall basis, the Biesemeyer has to rate very close to the top of the list of commercial new or replacement saw fences. It is easy to install, slick to use, and readily accepts almost any jig that rides over the fence. It has become a legend for very good reasons.

Craftsman Align-A-Rip XRC Fence System: There are certainly more Craftsman table saws on the planet than there are any other brand. Probably 95 percent, maybe more, came with original fence systems that are politely described as inaccurate and hard to use. Most use a sheet metal fence on a couple of cheap chunks of angle iron, with front and rear clamping by a threaded internal rod, to do the job. They do it, but without precision and without much in the way of real durability. Repeatability is horrible.

Newer Craftsman saws have better fence systems, including the Align-A-Rip. It uses a complex aluminum extrusion to accept the clamp section of cast aluminum. The fence itself offers three T-slots for jigs, with entry into those only from the rear of the fence. It is well shaped for jigs that need to ride over it. I mounted an Align-A-Rip in a friend's shop, on a six- or seven-year-old Craftsman table saw. It was easy and quick, with the rail for the fence going on square head bolts in already-drilled and -tapped (factory) holes. The rear rail, a smaller, less complex extrusion, goes on in a similar manner. These two rails must be parallel, because the Align-A-Rip locks front and rear. A separator channel extrusion keeps rail ends apart.

The biggest hassle, for some people, will be the 30" limit on cutting width with this fence. Longer rails are not available. Instructions are clear, with good-sized drawings used instead of photos.

The hairline indicator can be installed on either side of the fence's clamp head and has a micro-adjust feature.

The fence extrusion has plastic caps at both ends, is 36" long, $2^1/2$" wide and 3" tall. T-slots are on both sides and the top for easy jig attachment. Repeatability was good and the fence itself aligned easily with the saw blade. The fence lifts off easily and is easily returned, up to and including the point of repeating a measurement after lifting the fence off.

Overall, the Craftsman is a good fence that is a good replacement for cheesy fences on earlier Craftsman table saws (there's no real reason this fence cannot be fitted to other saws, with a bit of drilling and tapping). It is fairly durable, but the complex-form extrusions and base are vulnerable to damage from swung and dropped lumber, possibly more so than fences such as the Exaktor, which use steel for the T-part of the clamp assembly. Installation and affixing jigs is easy.

A few years ago, HTC popped up with a unique answer to replacement fences for those who already have tube rails installed. Their Multi-Fence System fits nicely on Biesemeyer, Xacta, Accufence and most similar rails already in place, lowering the cost and hassle of replacing a fence that is worn out. In most cases of wear, the fence body and probably the clamp, are battered and no longer accurate. Simply buy the HTC, drop it on the rails already in place and you're ready to go. Both contractor's and commercial systems are available, with 30" and 50" rails if those are needed, or the fence alone.

Fence facings are dark green UHMW (Ultra-High Molecular Weight) material, and there is a unique tap-on replacement system for the facings. Clips are used to hold the fence in place, so that a solid tap from a rubber mallet removes the old facings, and a quick exchange of clips onto the new face and pop, you're back at work. The really great part of this is the fact that clips are available separately, ($7.95 for a pack of eight), so you can set up auxiliary fences and have them ready for immediate installation.

The hairline indicator is installed on the right of the fence, on the clamp, and adjusts over a reasonably wide range (necessary when using other companies' rails). The plastic grip on the clamp handle helps make lockdown easy. This fence locks only on the front rail. As an additional boost, and to reduce the tap-tap-tap needed to adjust many fences precisely, HTC has added a micro adjuster. It works well and easily, with a full turn of the knob equaling $1/16$". According to HTC, an eighth of a turn equals $1/128$", close enough to true micro for most of us.

The contractor's (HTC-800) unit measures $37^1/4$" along the $5/8$" thick UHMW facings, and its fence tube is $1^1/2$" by 3" by 36" long. The clamp is 14" across and the main fence lock is $1^1/4$" × 2", screwed onto a $3^1/4$" shaft. The commercial version, the HTC 900, uses full $3/4$"-thick UHMW, $41^1/4$" long × $2^3/8$" high. The fence tube is 2" × 3" by $39^1/4$". The main fence lock knob is $1^1/2$" × $2^1/2$" on a $4^1/4$" shaft.

Overall movement, on its own rails or on both Biesemeyer and Jet Xacta rails, is excellent, smooth and easy. Accuracy with its own rail is much easier to attain, but a short tuning session with rails from other makers dials the measurements right in. With the heavy steel construction, expect long life and few problems. Should you have problems, HTC has a lifetime warranty on both models.

Jet's Xacta fence offers a fat load of features and great durability, along with reasonable ease of installation and pricing similar to that of the Biesemeyer. Available in different rail lengths, the Xacta II, is more sophisticated than

The Unifence (standard on many Delta saws) can be removed and flipped to the other side of the fence guide.

its predecessor, with HDPE (High-density Polyethylene) sides, vertical (side) adjustment, and a hair-line indicator. The locking system is said to assure perpendicularity while the fence is moved along the guide tube. Pads are graphite impregnated, which assures a slick movement along the tube. The alignment screws work nicely, too, and the powder paint really looks great.

The Xacta II fence installed easily on the Unisaw, with supplied instructions. Hole drilling to match up on non-Jet saws is done in the flat rail onto which the tube fits, after a guide mark is made and measured 8" to the left of the right side of the saw blade. Sounds confusing, but the drawings make it easy.

Movement is slick and sawdust build-up wasn't a problem. Lock-down with the lever was quick and there was no movement as the fence was locked down (with any fence, this takes a little care on the part of the operator, but the top makers make it easy). The hairline indicator is viewed through a magnifying section of the holder, mounted to the right of the fence body, on the clamp base. Stand directly over that indicator or parallax will be even worse than it is without magnification. Lifting the fence off the saw and then returning it presented no problems.

The HDPE sides are easily removed for replacement (six brass Phillips head screws hold each side in place). Too, shimming for flatness of the HDPE is easily done because of the screws.

Like the other T-square models, this is a top-grade fence, with some added attractions in the form of the HDPE, and easy adjustment of verticality as well as of parallel to the blade. It works well and should keep working well for an indefinite period of time (upwards of a decade).

Overall, the Jet Xacta II is a sleek looking, slick working fence. The fence HDPE is $41^7/8$" long × $2^1/2$" high × $1/2$" thick and the clamp is 16" wide. The actual box beam is 2"

high × 3" wide and $40^1/8$" long, with a plastic end cap. It has plenty of adjustments to keep fidgety types busy, but is so sturdy that adjustments are going to be infrequent.

Woodstock's Shop Fox line has two versions, but the Classic is their reproduction and treatment of the T-square fence. This fence may have begun life as a clone, but it has progressed nicely beyond that. The fence sides are HDPE on a heavy steel tube welded onto on a wide (16") clamp base. Brass Phillips-head screws hold the HDPE in place and allow shimming for flatness.

Mounting is a straightforward matter with either the short or the long fence, but be advised that long fence, as are the long fences on all of these saws except the Exaktor and the Accufence, is a two man mounting job. I've done several of these by myself, and it creates an inventiveness with the vocabulary that has to be heard to be believed.

Woodstock's clear manual presents three different ways to drill holes if the saw's original holes don't line up with those on the rails. The same system should work for any similar fence: Drill and tap mounting holes in the saw table, through holes in the table or drill holes in the rails. Given a choice, go for drilling the rails.

The optional 7'-long rails for this fence bring the possible cutting width to 54".

The hairline indicator is clear and easy to read and can be placed on either side of the fence clamp base.

The fence rail (left edge, front rail) is predrilled with holes for the saw's switch.

Woodstock recommends adjusting what they call lead on the fence so that the gap is $1/64$" wider at the rear of the table than at the front. Some people prefer this to true parallel — this writer is one. The lock handle has a round, plastic ball end and the lock is smooth and easy to work. The Shop Fox lifts off the saw and is easily returned The fence didn't seem to notice the 4×4 plywood-whack test.

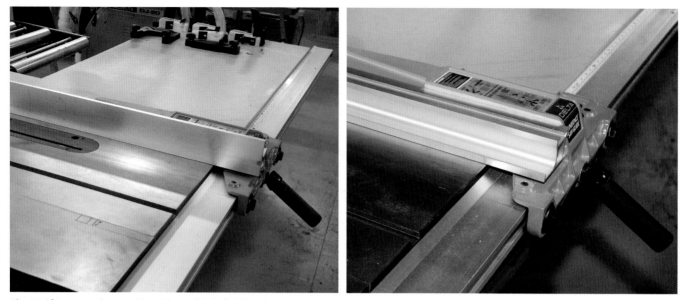

The Unifence can be used in either a high (left) or low position (right), depending on the material being cut.

The overall length of the fence is 41⁵/₈", and the Shop Fox Classic fence stands 1⁷/₈" tall × 2⁷/₈" wide (the box beam). The walls of the box beam are extremely heavy, a full ¹/₈" thick. A glide strip rides on the rear rail and handling is smooth and slippery.

There is an extension table available for the longer rails that comes with a free set of legs. The fence lifts off and remounts without a care.

Unifence by Delta sticks with aluminum, but in a totally different category. There is no way to not consider the Unifence a professional rip fence. It is feature-laden, close in cost to the T-square styles, but almost entirely different in execution. The cast aluminum clamp housing has a rotating (with strict limits) steel section that clamps itself inside the very heavy aluminum extrusion rail. Lifting off and returning the fence to the saw is simple: Twist the handle to remove, pull the fence back towards oneself, twist the handle again to reinstall, getting the steel section even with the slot in the rail, insert and twist.

There are two knobs on the right side of the fence clamp/base. Turning these loosens or tightens the fence on a steel tongue. The fence can then be moved back and forth to more conveniently work, as needed. Too, the fence can be turned on its side, placing the low side of the fence on the table, and cutting the gap between the table and the fence. This position is suitable for cutting laminates and veneers; the hairline indicator has a special position to show the sizes being cut when the fence is laid down.

Delta also has a 12"-long section of fence extrusion, which works as a cut-off jig.

It is in jig use that the Unifence falls short in some minds: Because it is not rectangular or square, ride-on accessories jigs don't do well, but it's not all that hard to make a jig that allows the use of ride-on jigs. Too, there isn't any reason on earth not to drill holes in the fence so it's possible to quickly mount sacrificial boards, as well as boards to which jigs may be attached.

The Unifence installs easily, adjusts quickly and works well. It is professional looking, with appearance that seems to speak of complexity, which is there in the design, but not in the use. Both 30" and 52" versions are available, with, as is always the case, the 30" version costing less.

Overall, this is a top quality fence, with extra features that are of a specific help to anyone working a lot of laminate or veneer, and general features that do everything else well. It is durable, easily passing the lockdown test whack with the 4×4 plywood, and repeatability is superb.

RADIAL ARM SAWS

Back in the 1922, when Ray DeWalt invented the radial arm saw, there was no electronic wizardry, nor was there much beauty, but the saw did the work for which DeWalt intended it. In recent years, Black & Decker has transferred the DeWalt name to its line of high-quality, portable power tools, and dropped radial arm saws from their line, whether under the DeWalt name or the Black & Decker name. That leaves fewer makers, with Delta, Sears Craftsman and Ryobi bearing the brunt. I was told that it was a liability "issue" in today's parlance. When did problems become "issues?" They're not magazines.

I feel it is more a matter of adjustment versus price. In other words, cheaper radial arm saws don't hold their basic adjustments well if they're moved off their center (90°) position. The massively-built Original Radial Arm Saw, similar to some older DeWalt models, and the high-end Delta saws escape this problem, but the prices are stunning compared to a similarly-capable table saw. Not many of us really want to pay $4,000 for a hobby saw.

The basic advantage of the radial arm saw is in cross cutting. It will rip, but is not as safely, nor is it as accurate

A solid tool for crosscuts (shown above), a radial arm saw can be adjusted to create simple dadoes. COURTESY OF RIDGID

as the table saw. The crosscut width on some of the larger Delta saws is 29". It takes a large sliding table to offer that kind of crosscut width for a table saw, which then runs the table saw into the stratosphere of price.

Several of today's radial arm saws also accept router bits on an accessory shaft, and, of course, they do all sorts of dadoing and similar work, with the cut visible to the operator: Table saws do the same work, but the cut isn't visible until it is finished, which tends to complicate set-up a little bit. Radial arm saws also shine when squaring up the ends of long stock and when making miter, bevel and compound cross cuts in long stock. Placed correctly, the radial arm saw has no limits on the length of the material it can cut. In practical circumstances, it isn't all that difficult to make sure you can trim either end of a 14'-long board; about the longest standard length you're going to find today.

At one time, the radial arm saw was touted by some experts as the perfect saw for the one-saw shop. It isn't, but then, no saw is.

Radial arm saws can be finicky to tune and to keep in tune, so that needs to be kept in mind when selecting the basic saw for a shop. I won't use a radial arm saw as

a basic saw. It is a superb supplementary tool that does a great many things more easily than does a table saw or a band saw, but it is not a replacement for a table saw and most certainly can't replace a band saw. With some quick adjustments and a few accessories, the table saw (basically a rip-sawing machine) can be made into a superb cut-off machine as well, but it is never going to be truly fantastic, except with a sliding table, at making crosscuts. The Delta 14" radial arm saw isn't going to lose its adjustment easily.

I like the radial arm saw for two reasons. First, you can get extreme depth in dadoes, if such is needed (a 10" radial arm saw will operate an 8" dado set, while a moderately powered 10" table saw will not run more than a 6" dado set. (A $1^{1}/_{2}$ hp table saw shouldn't run anything more than a 6" set.) It will run the 8", but not to maximum width and depth of cut. Most of us never need a dado deeper than the 6" will make anyway. A 12" radial arm saw can easily run a 10" dado set, assuming you have enough power. Secondly, but in the same area, using a dado head or a moulding head, you can get some fine multiple cuts and shapes going because you are able to view the cuts as you make them. Too, it is fairly easy to set up to make multiple dadoes as you do when creating dentil moulding.

Radial arm saws can take up a lot of space, so fitting them into your plan early is advised.

A 14" cast iron band saw from Delta. One of the most common (and useful) designs found in shops. COURTESY OF DELTA

BAND SAWS

This is one of the saws that tends to fall under the "other tools" category in many shops. But the band saw offers capacities and capabilities that many of us need to remember. You cannot cut, no matter how slowly, 6"-thick wood on your table saw or radial arm in a single pass, but you can on most 14", and even some 12", band saws. You hope you can't cut curves on table and radial arm saws, but gentle curves, and with some special techniques some fairly short-radius curves are readily cut on the band saw.

The band saw lends itself, because of the thickness of cut, to production cutting of complex parts in a process known as pad cutting. This is important in any kind of production scheme — even if what you're doing is cutting identical parts for toys for half-a-dozen grandchildren.

Most band saws have available accessories to make ripping and cutting circles easy: The band saw is just about the only tool of choice when cutting round tabletops of any size. Blades are available that make near-scroll cutting easier ($^1/_{16}$"), as are blades that make ripping operations easier.

In fact, many sawmills use band saws, which waste less wood than massive circular saws (and are less dangerous to use, easier to make portable, and a host of other good things). Band saw blades, in resawing operations (long rips on the wide part of the board) have a tendency to follow the grain in many woods — special tooth designs help reduce this problem.

The traditional band saw runs its blade around two wheels, one above the other, giving a specific neck depth for wheel size, thus increasing the cost a great deal to take a step up. More or less standard are the Steel City, Jet, Delta and Powermatic 14" light-industrial models, and the Craftsman 12" versions, of which there are several. Woodworker's Supply offers one in their Woodtek line, and Grizzly has three at this time.

Steel City, Craftsman, Dayton, Palmgren, Laguna, Grizzly, Shop Fox, Woodtek (Woodworker's Supply), Delta, Powermatic, General, and others offer 16" or 17"

Larger steel frame saws (of European lineage) are gaining popularity in many shops. COURTESY OF CRAFTSMAN

An excellent safety feature on many newer machines is the oversized off switch. If things get hairy, the last thing you want to be doing is fumbling for the off switch.

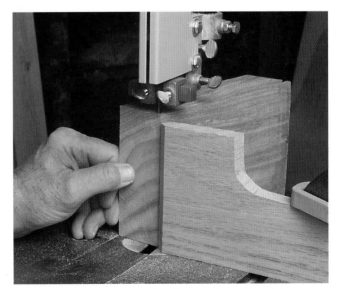

Many useful accessories can be shop-made, such as this resaw guide, shown in use.

band saws, with prices ranging all over the lot. These are all European pattern (squared shaped) saws. As noted earlier, I have the Steel City 16" band saw and I am truly impressed with its features.

Band saws are versatile tools that, I believe, need to be in every semi-serious woodworker's shop in one version or another. You may not use your band saw on a daily basis, but sooner or later we all need to cut a curve, and it is often at a time, and in a place, where a bayonet or jig saw will not work. When that task occurs, you'll be glad you have a band saw. Techniques such as pad cutting can be put to many uses. When cutting oak strips down to shingle size for doll houses, I made up a simple jig to hold the strips, stacked them about 6" high and cut many in a single pass. The strips were $1/8$" thick, so a 6" stack, with allowances, gave me about 40-45 shingles per pass, a lot faster than a single cut at a pass.

SCROLL SAWS

For intricate work, there's nothing like a scroll saw. Bob Grisso does intarsia using his two saws: An ancient Delta he reconditioned right down to the proper color paint and a much newer Hegner saw. Scroll saws start as unusual

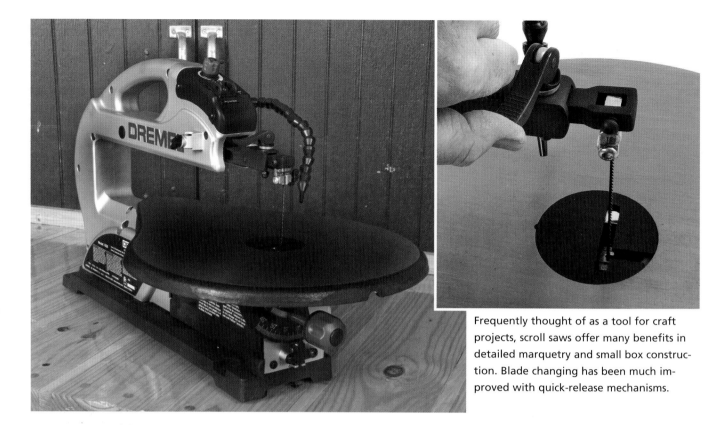

Frequently thought of as a tool for craft projects, scroll saws offer many benefits in detailed marquetry and small box construction. Blade changing has been much improved with quick-release mechanisms.

tools and go on from there. The blade action, considering the force/direction of an electrical motor, is weird. That blade moves in the vertical, straight up and down (or close to it), powered by a device that is spinning in a circular motion. There are several different ways that this is done, none of which is going to get described in any detail. Often, the connecting device is nothing more than a cam with an eccentrically- mounted spindle shaft that provides an up and down action — in the same manner as a camshaft in an auto engine moves the valve shafts up and down — a blade holding clamp moves with the cam spindle action. These are usually fixed-arm scroll saws, with power provided through the upper arm to drive the blade downwards, after which a compressed spring returns it to its position. Constant tension saws use a rocker action on a C- or U-shaped frame, with the tension on the blade more nearly constant than with the cam-spindle type. Another type offers parallel arms that rock in unison, but are not a single unit.

The constant-tension models are considered more modern, but there are still some fixed-arm types available. My new Dremel 1830 is a parallel-arm, constant-tension type and is hard to beat for a saw on the lower end of the price scale. This is the most expensive scroll saw Dremel has ever made, but still is about $1/3$ or less the price of the top-priced brands. I've used an old 24" Craftsman walking beam, parallel-arm type that was quite good. I've also got a Ryobi that is low cost and decent.

Among the fancier tools, I've seen the Excalibur at work, though the one I saw didn't look a whole lot like the

ones I see today (at least an 18 year lapse). I admit to being extremely impressed, both with the saw and the skill of the operator. The RBi scroll saws are also impressive tools, in a price range similar to that of the Excalibur models. My stepson uses an RBi Hawk and loves it. When we talk of RBi, top of the line Delta, Excalibur and Hegner scroll saws, we're into the deluxe areas of scroll sawing. You can spend as much as $1500, and not any less than $550 for these tools.

The new Dremel provides a good example of features available. It takes pin and plain-end 5" blades, draws 1.8 amps, has a $3/4$" blade stroke, cuts 2" at 0°, and offers table tilts to 45° left and 5° to the right. It also has a light-duty blower to keep the cut line clean, a front-mounted, quick-

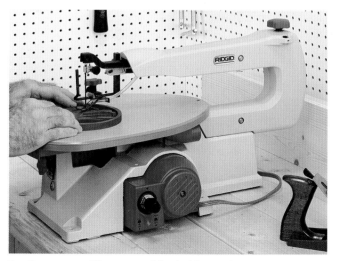

Scroll saws are still very good for hobby work.

An improvement on scroll saws was moving all the controls to the front of the machine for easier access.

release lever for blade tension and a blade-storage door. A vacuum hook-up is under one side of the table to eliminate the small mess these saws make.

The best scroll saws are nearly vibration free, and pass the nickel test: Stand a nickel on edge when the machine is running and it won't fall over.

Scrolls saws do intricate fret work go from there to being the only saw that, with any kind of ease, can do pierced, interior cutting. Simply drill a hole in the work, remove the blade and thread it through the hole and reinstall the blade. This takes only seconds to do. The only other common stationary tool that does the same job is the band saw, and it needs a blade breaker and a blade welder to work, while still being unable to do the truly intricate cuts that a top notch scroll saw can make.

A scroll saw is superb for anyone teaching youngsters the craft of power woodworking because it offers a modest powered tool with no kickback problems, and one that you have to almost ram body parts into to get cut. It can be done, and I've done it (I cut nicely into a fingertip some years ago, while running my mouth and not paying enough attention), as have many of my friends, but you can sensibly keep children under your eye, and usually you can react before there's any injury. You can't do that with a table saw, shaper, radial arm saw or jointer.

For your own work, if you build a lot of toys, or like to cut intricate patterns in projects, then a scroll saw is almost inevitable. Prices range from low to wild, as you've probably noticed.

JOINTERS

Jointers are truly necessary for most woodshops where the woodworker doesn't wish to get heavily involved in hand woodworking. (Using hand planes to joint boards, or to face them, can be a tremendous amount of work, though it is almost supremely satisfying when you successfully join your first 10 or 12 foot long oak or maple or cherry board.) For most of us, the need is to square up and smooth two sides of a piece of wood before we can carry out further operations with any accuracy. Short of buying all wood cut to size for each project (you can, but the price is incredible), or, at the very least, surfaced four sides, you need a jointer. Jointers come, as do most other power tools in a wide array of types, sizes, power requirements, capabilities and price.

The light-duty models are benchtop styles from Sears and other companies and offer a 4" blade width, a table under 2' long and a modestly-powered motor. A step up from those finds 6" jointers available from Craftsman, Woodworkers Supply's Woodtek, Grizzly and other makers getting into the lightweight (around 50 pounds) low-cost jointer area. Ryobi's lightweight 6" jointer with electronically variable speed was the best I've ever seen at producing a finish that almost appears shined. Ryobi called it a jointer-planer, but it's not a planer, and be glad of it. The JP155 was the only variable speed jointer I've seen, with a range of 16,000 to 32,000 cuts per minute. The table is short for a 6 1/8" jointer, as are all those above, possibly the shortest of all, but there was an accessory set of extensions

A 6" jointer is capable, but limited in size for some woodworking applications. COURTESY OF RIDGID

67

that work very nicely to expand stability. The tool does not offer a rabbeting ledge, which the current cast iron models do. Overall weight is about 27 pounds, and even with a steel stand, it was well under 50 pounds and didn't need much dedicated floor space. The cast iron models are readily available today, but Ryobi apparently quite producing their aluminum jointer some years ago. Too bad.

Delta's 6" jointers are noted throughout the industry, as are those from Powermatic. Steel City is right in there slugging with their new models, and, of course, Craftsman Industrial (6" and 8") jointers are tough and well made.

Powermatic's table length is 48", while Delta's model is $55^{1}/2$". Grizzly brings in a 6" × 47", 1 hp model that appears to be quite nice. The Craftsman Industrial $6^{1}/8$" jointer lists the motor as $1^{1}/2$ hp, with a stalk-mounted switch. The Craftsman jointer works well, has a rabbeting ledge and is reasonably priced. The larger 8" model has more hp, a longer 72" table and a larger fence, with controls mounted on the base.

All these companies offer significantly larger models, (including Delta's $16^{1}/2$" × $102^{3}/8$", 5 hp model) but a larger 8" jointer will please all but the professional woodworker. Depending on your woodworking needs, any of the 6" jointers is likely adequate. In a small shop, you may do best with one of the Craftsman, Grizzly or Woodtek 6", small-bed jointers. It's nice to have the biggest and best of everything, but it is not always necessary. The extra money might be spent on wood to work.

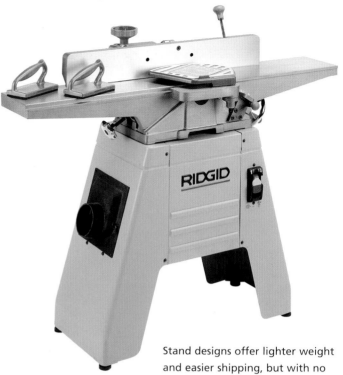

Stand designs offer lighter weight and easier shipping, but with no loss of stability. COURTESY OF RIDGID

PLANERS

As mentioned, the invention of the portable planer started many woodworkers on the road to lower cost, more accurately fitted, and, generally better, use of more kinds of wood. The planer reduces wood costs in any shop and makes it simpler to get the precise thickness of wood you need without forcing you to depend on local sources for planing to hit-or-miss standard sizes in hard and soft woods. Too, you can buy, as I do here, locally available hardwoods and allow them to air dry, planing them after a year or so, and reducing my costs considerably. For a few cents per board foot, you may even be able to locate an outfit in your area to finish-dry your stock in a kiln. Add

An 8" jointer (left) offers excellent capacity, but many operations are also possible on smaller benchtop machines.

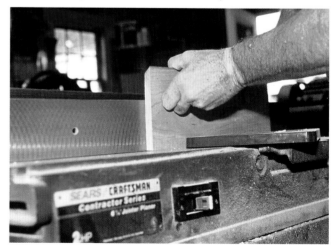

The infeed and outfeed tables on this Delta planer (left) offer excellent support. The Craftsman portable planer (below) offers convenient storage. COURTESY OF DELTA AND CRAFTSMAN

that to custom planing and careful jointing, made possible by having the appropriate tools in your own shop, and you can do more work at lower cost — in the long run — than ever before. Original set up is much cheaper than it used to be, but it isn't free.

Most 12" to 15" portable planers are considerably cheaper than are 15" stationary planers. Grizzly's prices are accounted low, but even the Craftsman benchtop planers are little more than a quarter the price of Craftsman's Professional 15" planer. Grizzly's 12^1/$_2$" portable planer is about a third the price of the their 15", GO453. Grizzly has slipped in a neat feature, a built-in mobile base, that can be a real help in any-sized shop.

Now, like a lot of you out there, I'd dearly love to pop my walnut and oak through a Delta or Powermatic 24" planer, but in this life, it ain't likely. Even a mortgage wouldn't bring the money — and no true need exists. All are three-phase and the weights are incredible, with the Powermatic at 2,885 pounds with the motor and the net weight of the Delta is 1,675 pounds. If you're wealthy enough, go to it. Grizzly's Extreme Duty 25" is only about $8,500 delivered. It weighs a fairly solid 2,267 pounds at the loading dock. I'd hate to imagine what size dust collector you'd need when you fed wide stock, or a lot of narrow stock, through this one.

The rest of us will select from a portable 12^1/$_2$" to 13" or a stationary 15" planer, if we get a planer at all, and be glad to get it. We'll also be proud of the results it gives.

The portables are true high speed machines and give a more polished finish to the wood because of the high speed motors used. They also have a tendency to snipe the ends of the wood as it comes out of the planer. Snipe is a cupped cut at or near the end of a board, and the only real defense with these planers is to make sure the board has an additional foot overall so you can cut off the snipe and use it for kindling in your wood stove. Making sure your portable planer has four posts and a locking head to help keep snipe down. You'll never totally eliminate it. Cut a few inches extra for each end as a scrap allotment.

Decide whether or not a planer is for you, and then whether or not you've got the space for a 15" or even a big 20", 3hp (240 volt). This latter planer is probably the final step for the hobby or small pro shop and doesn't cost a lot more than smaller (15") planers from other sources. Grizzly's G0454, 20" will sit in your driveway for under $1,500. But it's heavy at 920 pounds shipping weight, so get three or four pals to help you move it into the shop. This Grizzly also has a mobile base, but you might need a helper to move it around your shop anyway. For many of us, something like the pictured DeWalt (page 70) will fill most of our planing needs.

SHAPERS

Forget it. My simple comment on shapers for the hobby shop is not going to make some tool importers or manu-

Some of the newest features in portable planers are a wider cut (13") and stance, plus two-speed capability for a cleaner final pass. COURTESY OF DEWALT

ROUTERS

There are so many routers on the market these days, that an attempt to describe more than a few would take the rest of this book. I'm currently using three routers. First is a Porter-Cable 690 with a D handle, one of the actual old classics. I've had this router nearly 20 years and am going to make it, or the motor, the base motor for a new Jessem router table. Unless you're doing an extensive line of raised panel doors or something similar, a $1^1/_2$ hp router is plenty. My second (current) router is the Bosch 1617. It, too, is a

facturers happy, but in all honesty, beyond an easier time setting up (reduced severely with the new raising mechanisms for routers), I can see no justifiable rationale for a shaper in a hobby woodworking shop. The router table with a good $1^1/_2$ hp or stronger router does as well over a wider range of shapes, often at lower cost. Jet has one of the top lighter-duty shapers (shown at right) on the market, a good buy if you need or want a shaper. Others come from all the major makers, from Delta to Woodtek.

In lieu of a shaper, a good router table will suffice. You don't have to start with the best router table. Start cheap. When you're ready, move up to more power easily by just changing the router. Or move to a more precisely adjustable table like the Jessem models.

That's an option not open with shapers. You move up in fits and starts, from a low of $1^1/_2$ hp, on up past 5 hp if you wish. You can get into tilting arbors and sliding tables and this and six that's, including multi-spindle shapers. But these tools are far beyond what even the most advanced hobbyist is going to want.

Too, router bits are considerably cheaper: Even top-grade bits from Freud, Eagle and others cost less than comparable shaper bits. Yes, the shaper bit cuts hundreds of feet more than a comparable quality router bit, so on that basis, the economy is simply one of size, not scale, but the woodshop I use doesn't pass enough hardwood through a router bit to wear it out quickly, so a shaper would be overkill.

Specialty router bit sets offer good economy and quality.
COURTESY OF INFINITY

Plunge routers offer safe cuts in the center of a piece of wood.
COURTESY OF CRAFTSMAN

non-plunge type, 2 hp and uses a magnesium motor casing that tends to discolor from oxidation, but otherwise an excellent router.

I also have a $2^1/4$ hp plunge Triton that has, as the Aussies who designed it might say, all "mod.cons." The case contains, as well as the usual wrench, a table winder handle for raising the collect to an accessible distance, a series of seven guide bushings, a table spacer, a half inch router bit and some other items. The router features a turret stop and depth-stop lock knob, good dust extraction and a collet lock. It also has a plunge lock release that is unusual: It's a button in the handle. Lock and set is easy. The table winder accessory requires drilling a $1/4$" hole through the table insert, after which you can adjust the unit from above the table.

One more word on routers. You can spend a fair amount of money buying bits to outfit these tools. I suggest starting with a decent-quality multi-profile set (10 pieces), then add individual bits as the need arises with any new projects. You'll have a great selection of router bits in no time at all.

SANDERS

The variety of available stationary power sanders for small shops is large. There are 1" belt sanders, 4" belt sanders, 6" belt sanders, disc sanders from 4" to 12", flap sanders, drum sanders to 36" wide, short and long edge sanders, and upwards and onwards. Much depends on your needs and shop size, but for full-scale shops, one of the 6" × 48" belt sanders, with a 9" or 10" disc is a good way to go. Later, add a 1" belt sander for finer work when you have time. Unless you're planning to do huge amounts of countertop or similar building, the wide-drum sanders aren't necessary — or cheap — but they are sure nice.

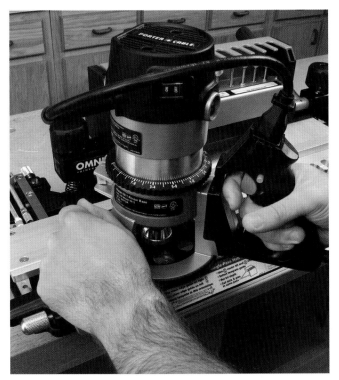

Fixed-base routers (D-handle in this case) work well for template work, with the switch right at your finger tips.
COURTESY OF PORTER-CABLE

A belt/disc sander is a terrific two-in-one tool.

COURTESY OF CRAFTSMAN

MULTI-TOOLS

The multi-tool is a different thing in the European concept than it is in the American. The Shopsmith Mark V, in its present incarnation, typifies the American all-in-one shop, but there are several almost typical European products: I looked at the Hammer and the Felder; both impressive machines.

Shopsmith has been around for a long time, now, and there have been a few lower-cost versions offered over the years, mostly made in Asia to almost the same patterns. I'm going to describe what I like and don't like about the Shopsmith, with which I am much more familiar.

The Shopsmith line of multi-tools is a series of moderate-cost hobby tools for use in shops where space, or money, is severely limited (and where there's no desire to work with used tools). The basic tool includes a table saw, lathe, drill press, horizontal boring bar and disc sander.

Additions are available, driven from the same power unit, as are additions with separate power units. You may add a 6" × 48" belt sander, a band saw, a scroll saw and a planer as desire and cash flow permit.

The tools work with some limitations, but also have features that some people prefer: The tilting table on the saw is something a great many woodworkers dislike, but that others swear by (the distance from the edge of the table to the front of the blade at any particular height setting is the base limit of cut-off width, since that's where the miter gauge starts its stable run: this can be modified with technique and jigs); the table needs three adjustments to get the wings at the same height. I do not like the height of the table myself, as I am used to table saws that are much lower.

The lathe is said by some to be whippy, though I never found it so. My turning with Shopsmith tools was limited to work under 6" in diameter and less than 24" long, but more recent reports indicate that the lathe is actually very good.

The drill press and horizontal boring bar are essentially the same tool, turned on end to become the drill press. It is effective, reasonably accurate and has a decent quill travel length.

The disc sander is a plate that attaches to the arbor, which is a feature available for virtually every table saw.

For wide material, a thickness sander can be invaluable.

COURTESY OF CRAFTSMAN

The arbor is 1" diameter, instead of the standard $5/8$", reducing the selection of blades and accessories such as moulding heads and dado sets. You can get some manufacturers — Forrest comes to mind — to custom drill any of their blades or dado sets. It may add to the cost.

Set-up and changeover to one tool or another is a pain in the tail, compared to having separate tools waiting and ready. There is always the chance that you'll do as I do, and forget to cut or drill one piece. Returning to your original set-up is less fun than many things.

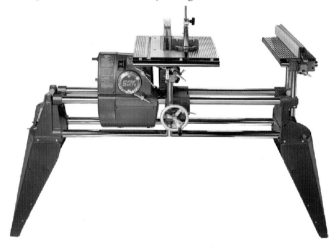

A stationary multi-tool, the Shopsmith Mark V can be many different machines, using the same motor. It can take a little time to switch between tools, but the space saving is undeniable. COURTESY OF SHOPSMITH

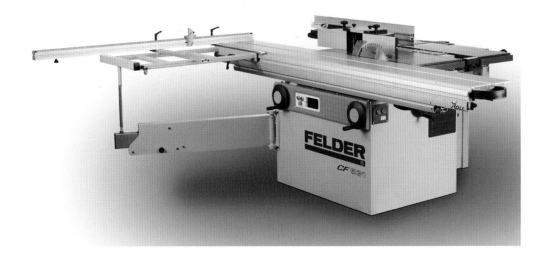

A European multi-tool such as this Felder model is likely one of the only ways the average woodworker can justify the quality provided — having four machines in one. COURTESY OF FELDER

On the pro side, you get a good, useful array of tools of good quality in a Shopsmith Mark V. Developments are continuous, and the company has been around a long time in one form or another, so you can update and upgrade easily. The tools work well, and set-up takes only a minute or so, going from, for example, the table saw to the lathe. From table saw to drill press is seconds longer, but not much. The more you make the changes the faster and easier the changes get.

Further on the pro side, the entire unit is on wheels, and is easily stored at the end, or side, of a garage that must house a vehicle or two. Too, it slips under basement stairs pretty easily (overall, the unit is about 6' long by about 2' wide and 42" tall when not in use).

The boring bar\drill press controversy isn't necessary. The machine does the work well, and each position has its use at one time or another, though most of use are less familiar with boring bar use — try finding a horizontal boring bar to use the next time you plan building a 24" or taller table lamp. It's far easier to accurately drill the cord hole.

The sanding plate set-up may be available for most table saws, but most owners don't bother to set the machine up for such use. It is very handy for some kinds of shaping work, and, as are all disc sanders, for end grain sanding.

It has been some time since I've used a Shopsmith, but I enjoyed the experience of at least partly building most of the projects for my first project book with a Mark V a long time ago. At that time, I was using a parlor for my workshop and the Shopsmith was close to ideal there.

So, the Shopsmith can be a boon, and may allow you to have and use a woodworking shop in spaces that otherwise are not suitable.

EUROPEAN MULTI-TOOLS

European multi-tools span fewer actions — none I know of include a lathe or boring bar — but are much more sophisticated in engineering and finish. They are also pricier, but as with the Shopsmith, it's necessary to keep in mind that you're not buying a single tool, but a system. The three most prominent names in the field right now are Laguna, Hammer and Felder. I managed closer contact with Felder and Hammer than I did with Laguna, but the variations are on a theme, not from a different opus. When noting prices on these machines, it is necessary to remember two things: They are not made anywhere on the Pacific Rim; they are absolute top quality.

Hammer and Felder are both made in Austria. Let's start with what might be the least likely low-end tool around, the Hammer, in its most basic model.

The Hammer B3 basic offers two motors of 4 hp total, with a saw and shaper. The sliding table is 31" long (48" and 81" are available), rip capacity is $27^{1}/_{2}$", and the dado capacity is $^{3}/_{4}$". Price is about $6,200 in the original set-up.

The next step up, the B3 winner, provides a 49" sliding table and a fence with a round tube, among other changes. Rip capacity rises to 31".

Getting more inclusive, we find the C3 31, which might be everyman's tool, if everyman is well funded. The C3 31 includes a compact table saw assembly with a very intriguing fence, the usual European crown guard and riving knife, a small sliding table, a neat crosscut fence and generally slick and easy adjustments all around. There is a scoring blade (with its own 1 hp motor) and dado capacity to $^{3}/_{4}$".

The shaper spindle runs at three speeds, 3,000, 6,000, 8,000 and 10,000 RPM, while the jointer-planer cuts to 15" wide, with a 55" long table. Those are the basics. The tool has three motors, in single phase with a 4 hp total. That's the basic C3 31 package that runs about $8,000.

Available upgrades include a 78" sliding table for the next step up.

Felder is even higher up the scale. The Felder CF 531 offers three motors, totaling 4 hp, with a 12" jointing width. The jointer table length is greater, at 59", using a special two-knife cutter head, and a 24 foot-per-minute feeder. Shaper tilt is from 90° to 45°. Planer height range is $^{1}/_{8}$" to $8^{5}/_{8}$" (12" width). Shaper speeds are the same as on the

Hammer, but the shaper fence is designed to allow tooling up to $8^{1}/_{2}$" in diameter. The sliding table is 39" long and there is a double miter fence. That is the basic Felder woodworking system and it currently sells for $10,800. Additions are possible, with available sliding tables up to 98". The next step up, the Professional, offers all the above, except that the fence for the shaper allows a full 9" swing while the sliding table is 81" and there is an outrigger table with a telescoping arm to aid working with the sliding table. The crosscut fence is 102" long for the outrigger table. You're getting into some bucks here, with a current price of $14,200.

The next Felder system is the CF 741, which is probably out of bounds for any amateur shop, with a base cost of $17,000 (it goes up over $21,000 full loaded).

These are superb machines, right on top of current metallurgy and other technology, but even the lower cost models are expensive, so it is a good idea to make sure you are going to be engaging in woodworking for more than a single shot before you pop for even the Hammer B3. At that point, I'd get to thinking hard about the C3 31 basic package instead, but that's me.

DRILL PRESSES

A drill press is that fortunate major tool that requires very little space of its own. It is safest bolted to the floor, but the variable height table means it seldom gets in the way of nearby tools. A good, precise drill press is a need in any complete woodshop, but is also a tool that is often put off until late in the process. I now have two, Delta's new 17"

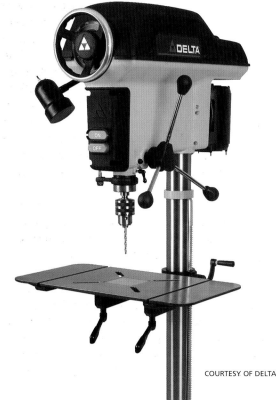

COURTESY OF DELTA

laser model and a Ryobi 12" benchtop. Neither is portable. I thought Ryobi might be, but it's heavier than expected, so rests in one position on a countertop. The Delta is the most useful, as you would expect. It has a long quill travel, letting me easily drill through two 2×4s or similar material, and the laser is helpful instead of being a gimmick as is too often the case.

SHOPPING AROUND

Equipping a shop doesn't come close to stopping with a selection from the preceding power tools. The photo at right shows a spacious, well laid out shop, designed for several people to use.

There are many hundreds, probably many thousands of hand tools, with varied woodworking aims. If you prefer total handwork, you need to aim at a layout that includes more free benchtop space, plus a good bit of extra vise availability. You may be more interested in a European style workbench as a main bench, with its multiple array of excellent clamping devices, bench dogs and other top-of-to-the-bench accessories.

For a woodworking shop, combine tool spaces to see what can profitably (from a standpoint of safety, work efficiency and space efficiency) be overlapped and what cannot in the selection of tools needed to carry out your basic woodworking desires.

Overlap the feeds for table saw and the planer in one direction, and all may work well, but do it in the other direction, and problems crop up. Basically, the planer may feed into the front of the table saw as an end result after at least 8' of run-out space, but it is probably best not set to run into the table saw from the rear. It can overlap its feed with the table saw from the sides, needing only the blade run down and the rip fence removed to make the saw a handy helper.

Planers and table saws do best placed near the main entry door or doors, because they are the machines you're most likely to be feeding long stock into with frequency. Make it easy to get the stock to the tool and you save time, and energy, thus creating a shop where you rush less, and don't get extra tired. Taking one's time and being well rested are foundation stones of workshop safety.

Placing a planer so that its outfeed table runs the finished stock over a table saw table depends on two things: First, the tables must be close to the same height, with the table saw lower than the planer, if there is a difference; second, you must set up so the chips and dust from the planer do not foul the table saw. The planer turns out more waste in the form of chips and dust than does any other tool, a fact that always needs consideration.

Using planned in-feed and out-feed overlaps, you can design a shop with many tools with relatively small space needs. Bobby Weaver's shop, though large for a hobby shop, had a lot of tools, and most were placed so as to allow outfeeds over unused — at that moment — work-

While a different variety of woodworking than most of us routinely practice, boat building is a good example of the careful need for space planning in a shop.
COURTESY OF WOODENBOAT SCHOOLS

benches, or over other tools. Otherwise, he'd be unable to afford space for three table saws.

Bob Grisso uses a different approach, making his tools mobile—just about all except his big lathe—so he can move them where infeed and outfeed is easily controlled.

Dale Toms uses an even different concept, but he has by far the largest shop of them all, at 32' × 48'. Too, Dale had a good chance to learn from my mistakes, and did. His tools all sit right next to their dust collector outlets, thus are permanently in place. He uses a combination of roller top outfeed stands (or side supports) and a couple of rolling tables he has built as outfeed support. Even then, his main table saw, a Unisaw, is directly in line with the garage door that serves as his large shop door.

All Bobby Weaver's table saws fed onto workbenches built at exactly the same height as the saw tables (which

are placed on stands Bobby designed and built). None of Dale Tom's or Bob Grisso's saws feed into any other tool.

No matter what size shop you create, there will be a need for some space-saving. Real life. Even if you could afford to construct an aircraft hanger, you'd eventually fill it. Check the sizes of all your tools, and of the tools you plan to buy. Draw a diagram on $1/4"$ graph paper close to scale, and make cardboard cut-outs of the various tools and their placements. It's probably best, on major stationary tools such as the planer, table saw, jointer and band saw that you make the cut-out of a size to include the in-feed and out-feed needs of the tool (run-in, run-out). Too, mark the height of the tool's table, if known.

Most band saws have considerably higher tables than do table saws, scroll saws, sanders and so on, so are readily and easily placed close to benches at the saw's rear, and one side, as long as there's sufficient working room for the operator. Lathes are easy to place and require little room, but that room cannot safely be impinged upon. Three or four feet to the left (headstock side) of the lathe to make adjustments. Even Dale Toms' cubby hole/niche for his lathe leaves plenty of adjustment space for him to work. There must be 3' along the full length of the lathe to work the materials without worrying about bumping into things. There's no fun, and less safety, in working a long spindle on a lathe, doing some rapid turning along the entire length, and bumping into a bench leg, project part or something else sticking into your path.

Leave yourself enough free space to concentrate on doing your work safely, regardless of which tool you're placing. Don't waste space, though, for too much space between tools can be almost as bad as too little.

Try to envision your working habits, based on the projects you now build or intend to build. If you start with raw wood, you want a protected area to store the drying wood, and an even better-protected area to store wood that's finished drying. You want easy transfer from the first to the second, or to a vehicle if it is to be taken and kiln dried after air drying. The seasoned-wood stack needs to be close

Above, Joe Zeh's workbench offers lots of space on top for working with handtools and lots of storage space below.
COURTESY OF JOE ZEH

At right, Grizzly's workbench offers a handy drop open storage area for easy access to tools. COURTESY OF GRIZZLY

by the door that leads directly to your planer. From there, go to a radial arm saw (possibly) or a miter saw to cut the wood to length. Next, you need a jointer, and, only then, a planer and a table saw. Beyond the table saw, or beside it, you want your drill press and band saw. If you do a lot of lathe work, park that near the table saw, but beyond a gluing bench where you glue up sections for turning (if you do such glue-ups).

Finally, there's the finish area. Most hobby shops are, and will probably remain, light in the finishing area. Finish is stored under a bench, and the brushes are kept covered under the same bench. Everything is brushed or blown clean before finishing is started, and the entire shop ceases availability for other projects when that one is drying.

While spraying finishes gives the smoothest and best coverage, it isn't suitable for all projects. A good air compressor, tank and spray equipment is going to cost hundreds of dollars and eat some shop space. I find them invaluable but know many others who don't use them.

Your finish area may need some enclosure to protect it from dust, and to protect other areas from overspray and fumes. If you enclose your area, use a spark-free fan to exhaust air to the outside. I toss painter's film (very light plastic sheeting) over the tools that are the dustiest before I clean the shop for a finish job, if I'm spraying. I then clean the shop and go away for at least two hours — cleaning makes me want to lie down — but in this case, it's to

let the dust that cleaning has floated into the air settle out. These days, a few microfiber dust cloths and all is well.

In most small shops, spraying is moderate, and special venting may not be needed. Good shop ventilation is a requirement anyway, with the few windows installed placed so as to give good cross-ventilation.

Otherwise, the construction of a small, benchtop spray booth to hold small projects can reduce overspray and fume problems and helps to keep airborne dust off drying projects. These are simply made, of 1/4" plywood and a light frame, or of 1/2" or thicker plywood and no frame. Simply make a 3-4'-long box 2-3' high (depending on your needs) and at least 18" deep. You may slant the top and sides so as to have better access around a piece. Put a small turntable in the middle when you're doing a lot of small parts and want to get all sides of each one fast.

It works nicely, and a cup hook or two placed in the top of the booth lets you hang small pieces and spray all sides in one operation if you don't want to work with a turntable.

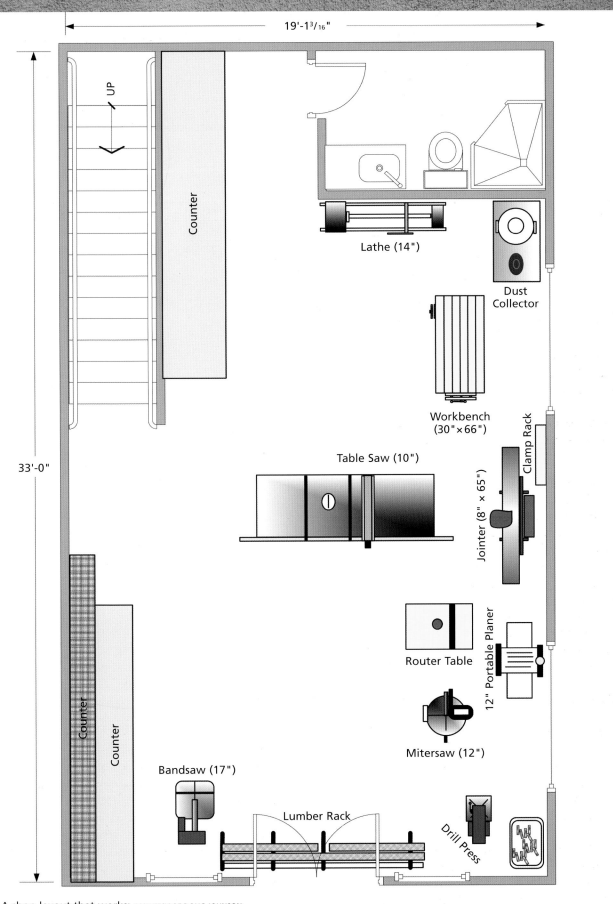

19'-1³/₁₆"

33'-0"

UP

Counter

Lathe (14")

Dust Collector

Workbench (30"×66")

Table Saw (10")

Clamp Rack

Jointer (8" × 65")

Router Table

12" Portable Planer

Mitersaw (12")

Counter

Counter

Bandsaw (17")

Lumber Rack

Drill Press

A shop layout that works: COURTESY OF DOUG JOHNSON

CHAPTER FOUR

Workbenches

I can barely even begin to discuss the full range of benches available, that you can build from plans, such as the below reproduction of a bench by 18th century French woodworker Andre Roubo, built by author Christopher Schwarz (*Workbenches*, Popular Woodworking Books, 2007), or that some company at some time or another has built. On my own, I figure I've used at least 100 types of benches over the years. Bobby Weaver has used all those, and some more, and once had five types in his shop. And the sizes varied all over the place, as noted in our earlier chapter. Pick what suits you and then place it as suits you.

Currently, I've got three WorkMates, plus two 8'-long benches of my own construction, and along-the-wall workbenches over cabinets that are very handy.

Placement needs to feed into your work habits. I like at least one bench placed in the center of the floor, so that all four sides are easily accessible. That means, with a 24" wide bench, a space of at least 8' wide × 14' long (my shop-built workbenches tend to run long, with the shortest at 8'). My second bench goes up against the wall, and is 22" wide. WorkMates go anywhere and get shoved and stacked and hung out of the way when not in use. Bobby Weaver prefers to use wider benches when all four sides are accessible. One of his was a full 48" wide. Bobby also garnered a lot of school-lab cabinetry rejects and placed them around much of three walls of his shop, giving him a huge amount of flat space. There's still never enough horizontal space, but that's the case in any workshop. Whatever there is gets occupied quickly.

Try to leave yourself 3' of working space around sides of any benches that are intended to be accessible. You can often get away with 30", but more is better in this case.

LEE VALLEY WORKBENCH

This bench comes in two distinct models, one with heavy-duty cast iron legs and the other with heavy-duty wood legs. I'm assembling the model with the wood legs — I had hoped to have it done in time to photograph here but that won't happen. The slab tops are in two parts, each about 12" wide × 6' long. They are made of laminated maple and are drilled for Lee Valley's round bench dogs. The design accepts a center trough and your selection of vises: I've got an old Jorgenson standard woodworker's vise for a side vise and a new Lee Valley twin handle for an end vise. Eventually, I will build cabinets to go underneath, which is the primary reason for getting the wood base. The entire unit, including a front vise, is available, with either type of legs and the twin screw Veritas end vise. The end vise is chain driven and easily allows cocking of the vise plates around any item it is holding, but returns quickly to parallel when that's desired. This is close to an ultimate bench. Check it out at www.leevalley.com.

AMERICAN WORKBENCHES

A few years ago, John Zirpola decided that a low-cost workbench styled to general, American woodworking, needed a solid place in the market. So, he designed and started building a couple of models, one of which I now have. This is an excellent workbench for power-tool woodworking, less so for hand-tool woodworking, but, then, John designed it for the modern woodworker. It fits. According to John, my American Workbench model is a new design called "The Common Man". It is a suitable name for a workbench that is 50" × 30" × 1⁷⁄₈". Legs are 3¹⁄₂" × 3¹⁄₂". It comes in three

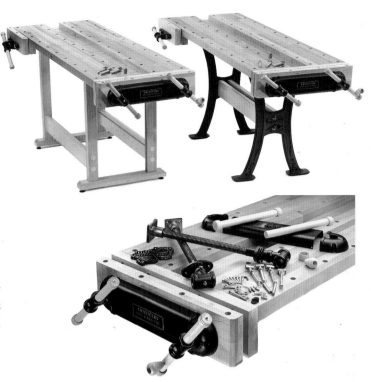

A look at the well-constructed bench-with-trough from Lee Valley, with wood base (top left) or cast iron legs (top right). Directly above is the excellent, chain-driven, twin-screw vise, also from Lee Valley/Veritas. COURTESY OF LEE VALLEY

An American Workbench that I own, makes a great stand for a variety of benchtop machines.

John Zirpola's American Workbench can be bought with extensions and other add-ons. This bench is in John's shop.

packages, with 16 lag bolts to hold it together and a neat little three-pocket assembly that attaches to hold smaller tools and supplies. This model is one up from my model.

Suitably enough, it is nearly ideal as a base for benchtop woodworking tools, such as planers and jointers. It also is handy as a site to do sanding, drilling or other woodworking operations. Price is low (as this is written, it is under $270, plus shipping). You supply our own vise, or John may have one that you like. He offers a large, reasonably priced vise, installed and ready to go.

As stated above, the Common Man workbench can serve as a base for benchtop tools, which makes it a great base for the small workshop, one that has to be stored in little room, and used in not much more. Stack a Palmgren 6" benchtop jointer on top, slip a DeWalt or other benchtop planer on the shelf, and stand a Ridgid job-site table saw next to this unit, and you're ready for most reasonably sized woodworking projects. As you work, start with the jointer, go to the planer, and then size your materials on the table saw. Space for storage is about 6' long × 4' wide. Space for use depends on the materials being worked..

You can find this workbench in Charleston, SC, but to save driving, check out www.americanworkbench.com and see what you think. For the price, and the amount of handwork that goes into the bench, I have to wonder if John Zirpola is making much money on his benches. It is a worthwhile investment.

PLAN BUILT

Tom Watson is a cabinet and furniture maker from Gulph Mills, Pennsylvania (right outside Philadelphia). Something over 20 years ago, he needed a bench, saw a set of plans in the Garrett Wade catalog that he felt made sense for him and ordered them.

Tom says, "I built this bench in about 1985 from a set of plans from Garrett Wade. That plan was for a 6' bench and because of the kind of work that I was doing, I scaled it up so the top is 102" with the end vise closed and 113" with it open. It is 25" wide."

According to Tom, that length was nearly essential, because he was often working on ceiling-height cabinets, which in most homes are 96" tall. He says, "The bench dog arrangement lets me hold the side of an 8'-high cabinet without protruding above the working face."

Even after more than two decades of use, the rock maple bench is still solid as Gibraltar, with almost all of its original beauty shining through the patina of work and age.

Tom no longer recalls whether the vises are Record or Marples, but, he says, "I still have the catalog and could look it up." At this point, it doesn't matter since neither is available any longer so I didn't take him up on the offer. He does offer the following, "The vises are quick opening so that you give a sharp turn to the left and you can open them close to what you need, then turn right and tighten." Look for easy open screws on whatever vises you buy.

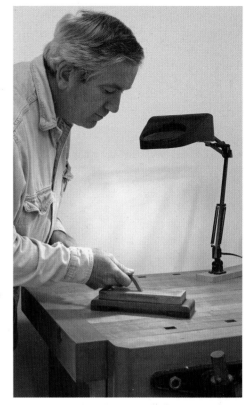

Tom Watson's workbench has seen a lot of wood move across its surface in something over two decades of professional woodworking use.
COURTESY OF TOM WATSON

Tom is using the bench as a sharpening station. COURTESY OF TOM WATSON

He states, "The hold-down is Marples and the bench dogs have no name on them."

For additional utility, Tom says, "I built two carriers for wheels that the bench just sits on, no screws. When I do carving I usually lift the bench off of the wheels."

He followed what is a good, standard procedure for smoothing tops when you don't wish to spend the time and effort hand planing them: "After I glued the top up I took it to a larger shop that had a Timesaver wide-belt sander and gave them fifty bucks to run it through a few times."

Tom Watson feels strongly that a good bench is essential and he very much likes this one. He says, "I'd build this same bench again. I've been offered a thousand bucks for it and wouldn't sell."

IMPORTS

Grizzly has begun importing European-pattern workbenches in several styles. Tops are as much as 4" thick and both major models feature end and front vises; with the end vises being shoulder style. They are holed to accept square

Bench dog, saw sharpening vise and Marples hold down. COURTESY OF TOM WATSON

Grizzly's imported workbenches have many of the features of the European standard but are made in Asia.

based dogs. The are priced well under European imports, with 84" long tops made of laminated birch. Tops are 24" wide. The unit (shown above) with nine drawers weighs over 360 pounds as shipped.

Several European bench manufacturers seem to be wobbling, on the market on year, not there the next, back again, gone again. Prices are well up there. Deifenbach (www.diefenbachworkbenches.com/ModernAmerican.htm) seems well sustained, though very costly. The benches are gorgeous and so is their construction. There are photos and information on the web site.

Sjoberg has become the popular version of the European workbench these days, primarily because they make versions priced in a range similar to the range American Workbench is in. Sjoberg's more expensive workbenches, though, are in the price range of the Diefenbach benches. I had one small Sjoberg for several

Drawer slides of good quality and felt drawer linings add to the usefulness of the Grizzly bench.

years and liked it well enough. In fact, at times I miss it and its leg supports for material being jointed with a hand plane, even though it was far too light for such use. Those are typically European features, but a brace and bit can add them to almost any workbench that has wood legs. Drill 3/4" holes at least 3" deep. Use dowels about 6" long to serve as material supports.

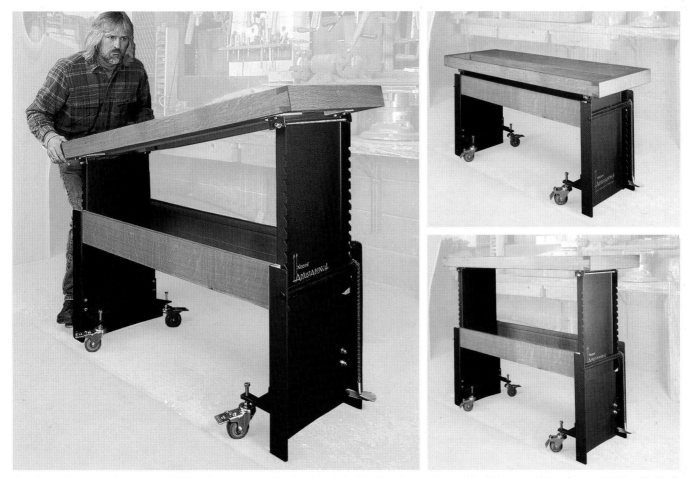

A unique design, and a great addition to any shop, the Noden Adjust-A-Bench can be used in it's low position (around 28" with top) or extended through a range of stops to a height of around 45". If you need an angled bench, it works that way as well. The legs are sold separately, so the size of the bench is determined by your needs. COURTESY OF ADJUST-A-BENCH

NOT AN IMPORT

For anyone who needs more than a single workbench height, the only real solutions I've seen involve two benches, or the Noden Adjust-A-Bench. The Noden uses two steel trays with a ratcheting mechanism to move its top up and down to suit the job at hand. The heavy ($1/8$") sheet metal is stable, so the bench can work with heavy loads. Standard vises attach in standard ways. Overall, this American-made bench qualifies as unusual and exceptionally useful.

The Noden inner tray slides over a range from $26^{1}/4$" to a height of $42^{3}/4$", with 12 ratchet locking steps along the way. A foot pedal releases the locking stops for security and easy adjustability. It thus becomes useful for fine detail work where you want to essentially be eyeball-to-eyball with your work (as in carving). It is also heavy duty enough to be useful when doing some work as hand planing, a notoriously demanding chore for workbenches.

It's also touted as a workbench that can be readily shared with another woodworker who is either taller or shorter, or who is doing a different kind of work. For full details, visit www.adjustabench.com.

Another workbench concept that I like is one that appeared in *Popular Woodworking* magazine. Published originally in 2001, the workbench, built by editor Christopher Schwarz, added as much bang for the buck as possible. The result was a bench that originally priced at $175. In 2005, Chris redid the bench, adding some features and kicking the price up to $235. Still a great bench for the money, and with the magazine's blessing I've included the plans and steps for the bench here.

Chris is an admitted workbench enthusiast, and you'll find more plans for a variety of workbench styles on the magazine's website at www.popularwoodworking.com.

$230 Workbench

by Christopher Schwarz

When I built this bench in 2000 my mission was to construct the best bench I could for just $175. When I completed the project, my plan was to take it to my shop at home to replace my grandfather's workbench. Plans, however, change. The bench turned out to be so useful that I left it at work and built a similar one for my shop at home.

Like anything in an active woodshop, the workbench evolved during the following four years. My work habits changed—I use hand tools even more now. And my knowledge of what makes a good workbench has deepened.

As a result, what you see here is the product of more than four years of tinkering and experimenting. I cannot say this is the ultimate workbench, but I can say it is a flexible design that can be easily altered as your work evolves.

THE BENCH'S FEATURES

The following is going to sound like a description from a woodworking catalog, but keep in mind that the price is about one-fourth of the sticker price of a commercial bench. It's a good deal. This bench features a simple—and yet versatile—system for clamping large or odd-shaped pieces. You can secure an entryway door in this bench. You can clamp a round dining room tabletop on the benchtop with ease. A planing stop on the end of the bench allows

you to plane material that is monstrously thick or even ¹/₄"
thin. The stop is an easy modification.

The bench is 34" high, so it can be parked as an outfeed
table behind most brands of contractor saws and cabinet
saws—and 34" is an ideal height for most planing and
power-tool operations.

The bench is stout, heavy and designed for the long
haul. The base is built like a bed with a system of bolts and
nuts so you can tighten it up if it ever wobbles (I've had to
do this once in four years).

And it is a tremendous value. When I first built the
bench it was $175 in materials. With inflation, the price
has risen to $184. However, a few years ago I replaced the
original wooden face vise with the metal one shown here. I
am so glad I did; this vise is much more stout. If you build
the bench in this configuration (which I recommend), the
price is $230. And that's still a good deal.

LET'S GO SHOPPING

First a word about the wood. I priced my lumber from
a local Lowe's. It was tagged as Southern yellow pine,
appearance-grade. Unlike a lot of dimensional stock, this
stuff is pretty dry and knot-free. Even so, take your time
and pick through the store's pile of 12-foot-long 2 × 8s. Tip:
Don't be tempted to use 2 × 4 stock for the legs and top.
The 2 × 4s generally have more knots and twists.

To find Southern yellow pine in your area, visit south-
ernpine.com. Fir and poplar also will work.

Here's the story on the hardware: The bolts, nuts and
washers are used to connect the front rails to the two ends
of the bench. Using this hardware, we'll borrow a technique used by bed makers to build a joint that is stronger
than any mortise and tenon. The Bench Pup and Wonder
Dog will keep you from having to buy an expensive tail
vise. Using these two simple pieces of hardware, you can
clamp almost anything to your bench for planing, sanding and chopping. The face vise goes on the front of your
bench and is useful for clamping and holding with the
assistance of the sliding deadman accessory.

PREPARING YOUR LUMBER

Rip and crosscut your lumber. You've probably noticed that
your wood has rounded corners and the faces are not glass-
smooth. Your first task is to use your jointer and planer

When you glue up your top, you want to make sure all the boards line up. Lay down your glue and then clamp up one end with the
boards perfectly flush. Then get a friend to clamp a handscrew on the seam and twist until the boards are flush. Continue clamping
up towards your friend, having your friend adjust the handscrews as needed after each clamp is cinched down.

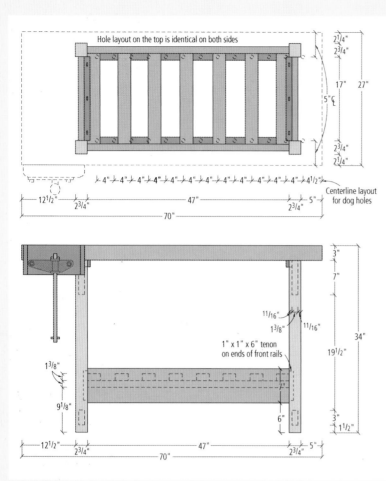

Hole layout on the top is identical on both sides

2¼"
2¾"
17"
27"
5"
2¾"
2¼"

4" 4" 4" 4" 4" 4" 4" 4" 4" 4" 4" 4" 4" 4½"

12½" 2¾" 47" 2¾" 5"
70"

Centerline layout
for dog holes

3"
7"

11/16"
13/8"
11/16"

1" x 1" x 6" tenon
on ends of front rails

34"
19½"

13/8"
9⅛"
6"
3"
1½"

12½" 2¾" 47" 2¾" 5"
70"

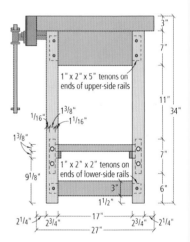

3"
7"

1" x 2" x 5" tenons on
ends of upper-side rails

1/16" 13/8" 11/16"
13/8"

11"
34"

1" x 2" x 2" tenons on
ends of lower-side rails

7"

9⅛"
3"
6"
1½"

2¼" 2¾" 17" 2¾" 2¼"
27"

SHOPPING LIST

8	2 x 8 x 12' Southern yellow pine boards @ $9.57 each	76.56
8	³/₈" x 16 x 6" hex bolts @ $.51 each	4.08
8	³/₈" x 16 hex nuts @ $.07 each	.56
16	⁵/₁₆" washers @ $.03 each	.48
1	Veritas Bench Pup (#05G04.03)	7.95
1	Veritas Wonder Dog (#05G10.01)	24.50
1	Veritas Front Vise (#70G08.02)	69.50
	Total Cost	$183.63
1	Quick-release steel vise (#10G04.13)	$115.00
	Total cost with steel-jawed vise:	$229.13

SUPPLIES

Lee Valley Tools
800-871-8158 or leevalley.com

Prices as of publication date.

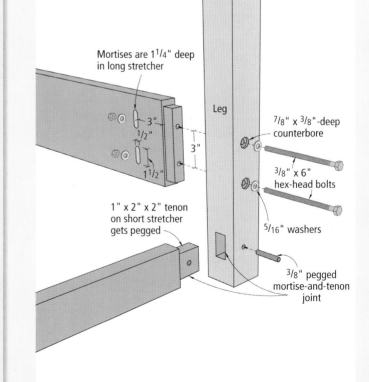

Mortises are 1¼" deep
in long stretcher

Leg

3"
1/2"
3"
1½"

7/8" x 3/8"-deep
counterbore

3/8" x 6"
hex-head bolts

5/16" washers

1" x 2" x 2" tenon
on short stretcher
gets pegged

3/8" pegged
mortise-and-tenon
joint

After you cut your tenons, lay them directly on your work and use the edges like a ruler to mark where the mortise should start and end (above). Use a 1" Forstner bit in your drill press to cut overlapping holes to make your mortise (left). Now square up the edges of the mortise using a mortise chisel and a mallet (right).

to remove those rounded edges and get all your lumber to 1³/₈" thick.

Once your lumber is thicknessed, start work on the top. The top is made from 1³/₈" × 3³/₈" × 70" boards turned on edge and glued face-to-face. It will take five of your 2 × 8s to make the top. Build the top in stages to make the task more manageable. Glue up a few boards, then run the assembly through the jointer and planer to get them flat. Make a few more assemblies like this, then glue all the assemblies together into one big top.

When you finally glue up the whole top, you want to make sure you keep all the boards in line. This will save you hours of flattening the top later with a hand plane. See the photo below for a tip when you get to this point. After the glue is dry, square the ends of your assembled top. If you don't have a huge sliding table on your table saw, try cutting the ends square using a circular saw (the top is so thick you'll have to make a cut from both sides). Or you can use a handsaw and a piece of scrap wood clamped across the end as a guide.

BUILD THE BASE

The base is constructed using mortise-and-tenon joinery. Essentially, the base has two end assemblies that are joined by two rails. The end assemblies are built using 1"-thick × 2"-long tenons. Then the front rails are attached to the ends using 1" × 1" mortise-and-tenon joints and the 6"-long bolts.

Begin working on the base by cutting all your pieces to size. The 2³/₄"-square legs are made from two pieces of pine face-glued together. Glue and clamp the legs and set them aside. Now turn your attention to cutting the tenons on the rails. It's a good idea to first make a "test" mortise in a piece of scrap so you can fit your tenons as they are made. I like to make my tenons on the table saw using a dado stack. Place your rails face down on your table saw and use a miter gauge to nibble away at the rails until the tenons are the right size. Because pine is soft, make the edge shoulders on the upper side rails 1" wide. These deeper shoulders will prevent your tenons from blowing out the end grain at the top of your legs during assembly.

Now use your tenons to lay out the locations of your mortises. See the photo at right for how this works. Clamp a piece of scrap to your drill press to act as a fence and

Drilling the ³/₈" holes for the bolts is easier if you do it in this order. First drill the holes in the legs using your drill press. Now assemble the leg and front rail. Drill into the rail using the hole in the leg as a guide (left). Remove the leg from the rail and continue drilling the hole in the rail. The hole you drilled before will once more act as a guide. You still need to be careful and guide your drill straight and true (right).

chain-drill the mortises in the legs. Make your mortises about ¹/₁₆" deeper than your tenons are long. This will give you a little space for any excess glue.

Once you've got your mortises drilled, use a mortise chisel to square the round corners. Make sure your tenons fit, then dry-fit your base. Label each joint so you can reassemble the bench later.

BED BOLTS

There's a bit of a trick to joining the front rails to the legs. Workbenches are subject to a lot of racking back and forth. A plain old mortise-and-tenon joint won't hack it. So we bolt it. First study the diagram at left to see how these joints work. Now here's the best way to make them.

First chuck a 1" Forstner bit in your drill press to cut the counterbore in the legs for the bolt head. Drill the counterbore, then chuck a ³/₈"-brad-point bit in your drill press and drill in the center of the counterbore through the leg and into the floor of your previously cut mortise.

Now fit the front rails into the leg mortises. Chuck that ³/₈" bit into a hand drill and drill as deeply as you can

through the leg and into the rail. The hole in the leg will guide the bit as it cuts into the rail. Then remove the leg and drill the ³/₈" hole even deeper. You probably will have to use an extra-long drill bit for this.

OK, here's the critical part. Now you need to cut two small mortises on each rail. These mortises will hold a nut and a washer, and must intersect the ³/₈" holes you just drilled. With the leg and rail assembled, carefully figure out where the mortises need to go. Drill the mortises in the rails as shown in the photo at far right. Now test your assembly. Thread the joint with the bolt, two washers and a nut. Use a ratchet and wrench to pull everything tight. If you're having trouble getting the bolt to thread in the nut, try chasing your ³/₈" holes with a ⁷/₁₆" bit. That will give you some wiggle room without compromising the strength of the joint.

BASE ASSEMBLY

This bench has a good-sized shelf between the front rails. Cut the ledgers and slats from your scrap. Also cut the two cleats that attach the top to the base. Now plane or

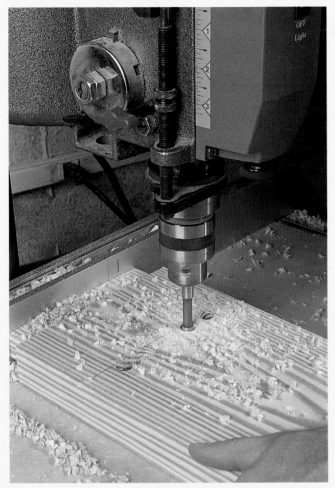

The mortises in the front rails are also made on the drill press. Make them 1¹/₄" deep to make sure you can get a washer in there. If you can't, try clipping an edge off of the washer.

Drilling your dog holes may seem like hard work using a brace and bit. It is. However, you get an amazing amount of torque this way – far more than you can get with a cordless drill. Sadly, I had cooked my corded drill, so this was my only option.

sand everything before assembly – up to #150 grit should be fine.

Begin assembly by gluing up the two end assemblies. Put glue in the mortises and clamp up the ends until dry. Then, for extra strength, peg the tenons using ³/₈"-thick dowel.

Screw the ledgers to the front rails. Make sure they don't cover the mortises for the bed bolts, or you are going to be in trouble. Now bolt the front rails to the two ends (no glue necessary). Rub a little Vaseline or grease on the threads first because after your bench is together you want to seal up those mortises with hot-melt glue. The Vaseline will ensure your bolts will turn for years to come.

Screw the cleats to the top of the upper side rails. Then drill oval-shaped holes in the cleats that will allow you to screw the top to the base. Now screw the seven slats to the ledgers.

FINISHING THE TOP
Before you attach your top, it's best to drill your dog holes and attach the vise. Lay out the location of the two rows of dog holes using the diagram. I made a simple jig to guide

a ³/₄" auger bit in a brace and bit. The jig is shown in action in the photo at right.

Now position your vise on the underside of the top and attach it according to the directions from the manufacturer. I added a wooden jaw to my metal vise, which extends its clamping abilities and is easy on my workpieces.

Now you are almost done, but first you must flatten the top. Use "winding sticks" to divine the problem areas in your benchtop.

Winding sticks are simply identical, straight lengths of hardwood. Put one on one end of the top and the other on the far end. Now crouch down so your eye is even with the sticks. If your top is flat, the sticks will line up perfectly. If not, you'll quickly see where you need work. Use a jack plane to flatten the high spots. Then work the top diagonally with a jointer plane. Finally, work the top along the grain. Rag on a couple coats of an oil/varnish blend on the base and top.

With the bench complete, I was pleased with the price and the time it took, which was about 30 hours. When you complete your bench, don't be afraid to modify it. I'm sure that my bench still has some changes in its future.

CHAPTER FIVE

Basement to Shop Conversions

Conversions of existing space in basements are sometimes be the only way to create a practical workshop for shaping wood of any real size. Framing of basement partition walls can isolate regular basement and home spaces from sawdust and sanding dust. Entry may create some problems and may cause a woodworker to examine project selections with great care, as changing some basement features to allow enough space for entry and exit of large projects may be totally uneconomical.

Pictured at left, the American Workbench, Palmgren 6" jointer, DeWalt 13" planer and Ridgid 10" table saw make my point about small shops. Tool selection is critical, but is easier than ever today.

Ryobi's easily-stored job-site saw is a type that has replaced junky benchtop saws for the most part. COURTESY OF RYOBI

Certain tool advantages exist today, so that a wide array of individual tools, such as stationary belt sanders, table saws, band saws, radial arm saws, planers, and jointers may be easily fitted into a relatively small workspace.

Of course, the multi-tools also fit into small areas, and provide many now-classic solutions to limited shop space. With benchtop tools, there's less of a differential in price for the basic tools than there was some years ago, but overall, multi-tool advantages for small shop and limited budget needs still exist, though today the emphasis has to be more on the small shop area than before.

On a personal basis, if I had to work in a small shop area, I would select one of the 10" job-site table saws, and then select two of the benchtop tools I consider to be the most useful. For the basic shop, I'd probably stack a Palmgren 6" benchtop jointer with a 13" DeWalt 735 planer. This way, you can end up with a decent or better table saw, and three of the most useful tools you will find for a workshop. If you have the space, a small drill press completes the array. The basic three power tools, though, have a current cost of about $1,200 for a power woodworking shop of great capability, in a small space.

With space conservation in mind, you begin working on your basement. Start with graph paper — or a drawing board or a drawing program on a computer — and measure the basement carefully, taking note of doglegs, lally columns, windows, current lighting, outlets, etc.

Make a rough drawing with rough dimensions and determine the basic area that you can allow for your woodworking space.

For greatest efficiency in living, as well as in working, close off the woodworking shop from the rest of the house as well as possible. That may mean installing a partition with a door or simply installing a door. If you keep noise and dust from filtering through the house, the shop stays a welcome addition.

Partition walls in such spaces are not installed in quite the same manner as they are in other areas. For a regular wall, partition or otherwise, in an area that has no present ceiling, you build the wall on the floor, and tip it into place. In a basement, you first make take note of any pipes and wires running along under the joists. You next construct the wall without its sole plate (there are other ways to do this, but I prefer this one), place the sole plate and then

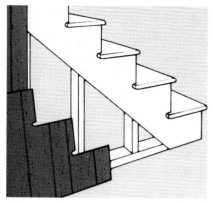

Stairs may be totally enclosed in this manner to help prevent dust infiltration. COURTESY OF GEORGIA-PACIFIC CORPORATION

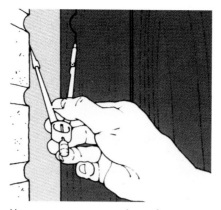

Use a compass to trace irregular surfaces onto wall board and cut with coping or scroll saw. COURTESY OF GEORGIA-PACIFIC CORPORATION

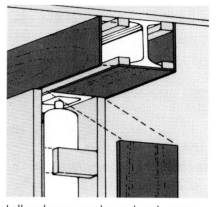

Lally columns may be enclosed, as may metal beams. COURTESY OF GEORGIA-PACIFIC CORPORATION

Cut out for electrical boxes. Coat the lips of the box with paint or chalk and tilt the already cut wall panel against the box. That marks the back of the panel, so you can drill all four corners and mark to cut on the front. COURTESY OF GEORGIA-PACIFIC CORPORATION

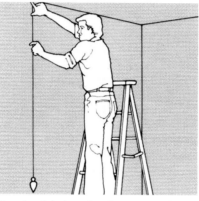

Use plumb bob or level to assure plumb of the all-important first panel. COURTESY OF GEORGIA-PACIFIC CORPORATION

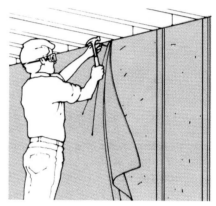

A vapor barrier helps control basement moisture. COURTESY OF GEORGIA-PACIFIC CORPORATION

set the constructed wall in place on the sole plate, setting each stud on its mark. The entire job is eased if you run a slightly diagonal 1×4 brace across the wall to keep studs from spreading too much (nail at each stud, with a 10d nail driven in most of the way, but leaving at least $^1/_2$" sticking out so it can be pulled easily to remove the brace when the wall is up).

Use a double top plate on partitions, and a single sole plate. If the basement floor is concrete you can use cut masonry nails or other concrete anchors to hold the sole plate. Mark for each stud, placing studs on 24" centers (these are not bearing walls). The simplest way to do this is to measure from the edge of the sole plate (or the top plate), and mark a straight line down, using a combination square set at $3^1/_2$" depth. At $25^1/_2$", mark to the edge side of that line and you have a 24" center for your second stud. At the edges, mark in $1^1/_2$" and use the combination square to draw a line at that point. Place an X, in pencil, to

the edge side of the line in both cases, marking where the stud end will go. Continue pacing down, measuring 24" on center and marking the penciled X where every stud end will fall. Match the top plate to the sole plate: This is most easily done by continuing the sole plate mark up $^1/_4$" or so onto the edge of the 2×4, and then placing the top plate on the sole plate. Mark the top plate. Use the combination square to draw the line and mark the required X. This sounds like a lot of extra work, but saves mistakes and the problems mistakes bring. Do this with each and every sole plate and lower top plate. Studs are measured and cut and nailed through the top plate and into the stud end. Once that's done, nail on the second top plate, place the brace, and tip the assembled wall into place. You may toe nail the studs to the sole plate, or you may use framing anchors (if you don't have a lot of experience toenailing, then the second method is much easier: You can get around your lack of toenailing experience by starting the toe nails before tip-

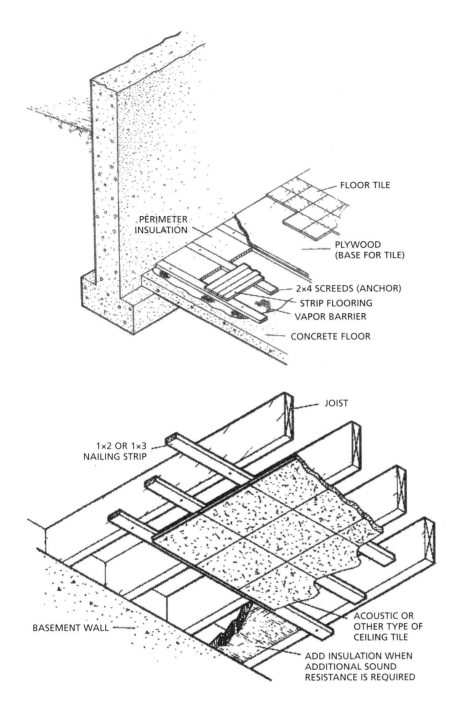

FLOOR TILE

PERIMETER
INSULATION

PLYWOOD
(BASE FOR TILE)

2×4 SCREEDS (ANCHOR)
STRIP FLOORING
VAPOR BARRIER

CONCRETE FLOOR

JOIST

1×2 OR 1×3
NAILING STRIP

BASEMENT WALL

ACOUSTIC OR
OTHER TYPE OF
CEILING TILE

ADD INSULATION WHEN
ADDITIONAL SOUND
RESISTANCE IS REQUIRED

Lay out sole and top plates together
for accurate fit. COURTESY OF GEORGIA-PACIFIC
CORPORATION

Make any basement partition wall 1"
shorter than floor to ceiling distance,
tip into place, plumb and wedge
tightly. Then nail.

COURTESY OF GEORGIA-PACIFIC CORPORATION

ping the wall into place, and then finishing nailing after the wall is in place. Jam your foot against the stud on the side opposite the nails to keep the angle nailing from causing it to skitter away from its proper place. (We'll hope you've gotten the nails in at a near correct angles — about 45° — because too shallow an angle has two results here, one of which is painful as one or more nails is driven into your instep. The other result is a weak wall). These days, most everyone uses pneumatic nailers. They cost more than hammers, but can save a tremendous amount of time and effort.

For concrete basement walls — block or poured — you have a couple of choices. Simply paint the walls with a good grade of concrete paint, or furr them out, insulate and cover with paneling or other drywall, including pegboard. Pegboard sheets may be hung directly on concrete and concrete block walls, too.

Furring strips go on easily, usually with cut masonry nails and a touch of construction adhesive. Place them on 24" centers. Insulate between furring strips

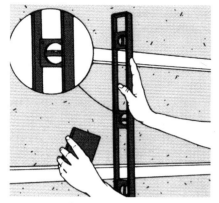

Keep a careful check on plumb as you shim out rough walls.

COURTESY OF GEORGIA-PACIFIC CORPORATION

Continue to check on plumb.

COURTESY OF GEORGIA-PACIFIC CORPORATION

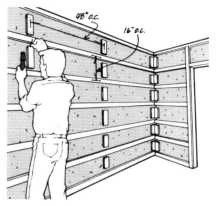

Furr walls and shim to plumb on 16" horizontal centers, with nailer blocks on 48" centers. Use 1" × 2" ($3/4$" × $1^1/2$" $1/2$") furring strips or $1/2$" × $1^1/2$" CDX plywood strips.

COURTESY OF GEORGIA-PACIFIC CORPORATION

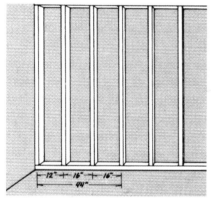

Vertical studs or furring may be used.

COURTESY OF GEORGIA-PACIFIC CORPORATION

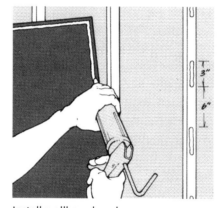

Install wallboard as shown.

COURTESY OF GEORGIA-PACIFIC CORPORATION

on exterior walls if you wish, using a foam board insulation the same thickness as the furring strips. You may also add a vapor barrier to the warm side of the installation (always install vapor barriers on the heated side of insulation).

After that, install paneling or other drywall as you would in any installation, nailing according to manufacturers directions.

For an optional furring method, used primarily when a vertical installation of narrower planks, instead of large sheets of material, is nailed up, apply furring strips horizontally on 16" or 24" centers.

To properly place furring strips (plumb), use a chalk line with plumb bob attached (the case on most chalk lines can be used as a plumb bob). Mark the 24" centers high on the wall and drop a line from that point.

Make allowances for all electrical wiring as you place furring strips. When furring strips cross over, or are cut out around cable, you must protect that cable with inexpensive steel plates carried at most building supply stores. Surface wiring on concrete walls must be protected with conduit, either plastic or metal.

Ceiling installations in basements vary from none to fairly fancy fiber-

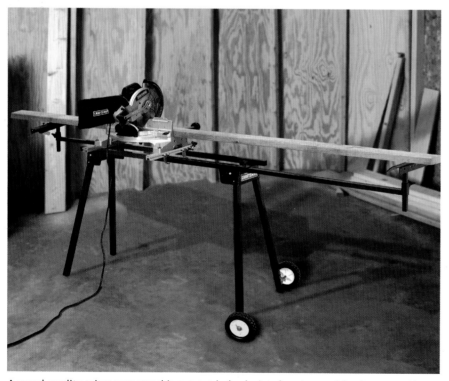

A good quality miter saw stand is a great help during framing and furring operations, supporting longer pieces of material with ease.

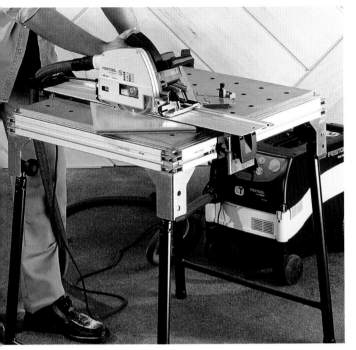

Festool produces what is close to a shop in a pack with their tools. The circular saw is using one of their guides, on one of their worktables with its own Festool dust collection system.

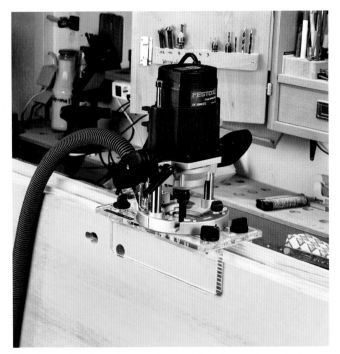

The Festool router offers a wide variety of jigs, plus a dust collection system.

glass insulated drop ceilings. I'm not sure of my own preference here, as my current basement ceiling is fairly fancy, with a short drop (at my height, any drop is too much, though), and looks great until I move a board too fast and gouge a chunk of the vinyl overlay off the stuff. As far as insulation goes, something under an inch of fiberglass does keep heat from rising to the upstairs — but so what. It's already warmer up there than down here. Where the insulation shines a bit is in preventing extremes of sound from rising — the floor thumps come through pretty well down here, but the reverse isn't true. Certainly you can hear a router or table saw, but the piercing edge does seem to have been peeled off. Check out the ceiling tile types at a local supplier, and follow the manufacturer's directions for installations. There are so many systems and methods of installation, it serves no purpose beyond padding for me to cover them in this book. Most are fairly simple, including drop ceiling installation, requiring little more than care in measuring and installation of the original support strips.

Floor problems in basements are created by concrete. Most basement floors are concrete (regardless of what the finished floor appears to be, if you have any kind of a finished floor in a basement, nine chances out of ten the subfloor is concrete). Concrete floors, as I've noted earlier, are not the greatest for woodworking shops because they're hard on feet and legs, hard on dropped tools, and not at all nice to projects that get dropped during assembly or at other times. Still, concrete beats pounded dirt, and can be covered with vinyl tiles, vinyl sheet, sleepers and wood,

Internally or externally, this plunge router is a major tool, useful and clean operating.

paint and many other substances. Too, if your feet really ache, you can get one of the industrial-type mats and place that in front of your most occupied work space. Check out local farm stores for prices on rubber sheet called cow or horse mats. These are usually considerably cheaper than floor mats from a woodworking tool supplier. Currently, a

5' × 8' horse stall mat is going for about $60 at a farm supply chain called Tractor Supply. Local farm stores may or may not do better than that.

The easiest flooring job is laying sheet vinyl or tile, and is best done by following the manufacturer's directions. A test is needed before you get started: If your floor doesn't pass moisture through, place any good, below-grade rated vinyl tile or sheet with the appropriate adhesive (some are self-adhesive and much sheet material doesn't use adhesive). Do a good, tight job and the floor will last for decades. Before you start out to buy tile, place a piece of vinyl tile, or a similar sized piece of plastic, down on the floor and leave it there overnight, and, if the weather is exceptionally dry, leave it a full week. Lift the plastic and check for moisture. If moisture is present, you must lay sleepers of pressure treated wood, then lay a wood sub-floor over a vapor barrier, and come back with tile or vinyl sheet if you still want that. Personally, if this happened to my basement, I'd either paint the floor and forget it, or I'd come back with sleepers, put down a double, 10 mil vapor barrier, and use tongue-and-groove, $^5/8$" plywood as a finished floor and coated with satin polyurethane.

Sleepers in this context are nothing more than 2×4s laid with the wide side flat on the concrete and nailed in place with cut masonry nails. You must use pressure treated wood for this part of the job — it only costs about $5-$10 extra and saves repeating the work a few years down the road.

Urban settings create problems with most forms of power woodworking and my experience in woodworking in an apartment setting is limited to small buildings — a couple of brownstones many years ago, and, in both instances, the neighbors were either not home or totally undisturbed by noise of any kind.

The basic requirement is the smallest, most readily stored tools possible, along with versatile workbenches and storage. Black & Decker is still selling its WorkMate series of folding workbenches, a series that offers some help in urban settings, but unless you own a building or an immense apartment, actual urban woodworking may be one of those times when a rented shop space makes sense — because of the noise. For basement or urban use power woodworking, probably Festool's line of varied hand power tools and accessories make the greatest sense.

Their vacuums are among the quietest I have ever heard, while the tools themselves are precisely made on wonderful and innovative designs (I separate those two because excellence and innovation do not often go hand-in-hand these days).

Both Veritas planes pictured are useful in basement and apartment shops — and in any shop.

The little router plane is a particular delight, an improvement on the old, and barely available, Stanley pattern.

Greg Rambo uses his specially designed basement (actually, an extended, above ground part of the house and garage, so it qualifies in several directions) shop with great frequency.

Festool's circular saws offer plunge blades that make for easier plunge cut starts and easier storage.

Greg Rambo's shop is wonderfully airy and light, with recessed ceiling lighting powerful enough to take care of dim days and dark nights, but with enough windows and doors to allow almost light-free daytime use.

There are a number of plane makers still out there, but, in my opinion, the best of them for the average woodworker has to be Lee Valley, with its Veritas line of wood planes. This bench plane is superbly well made, but still reasonably priced. I am not knocking Lie-Nielsen here; L-N planes are also superb, but are usually copies of older Stanley planes. Veritas copies, but also improves, and is far less costly than the Lie-Nielsen planes.

CHAPTER SIX

Converting Garages to Shops

In a garage, materials access is seldom a problem, and space itself becomes less of one, so the shop may, if desired, take on a more open-handed design for those people who do not garage their vehicles. Other options for those who do garage their vehicles include the use of tilt-up workbenches and roll-away combination tools (such as the Shopsmith). Tool selection and placement has a considerable effect on ease of use of any space that is constructed for other than shop uses. In garages, a woodworker may not have the option of selecting door and window placement, ceiling height and flooring materials. Wood flooring is always better than concrete. It is more resilient under foot, thus easier on the leg muscles; it is also easier on dropped items and tools. I feel clumsy dropping a $25 chisel onto a wood floor. I feel victimized dropping that chisel onto a concrete floor.

All of this can be worked around, usually at low cost, if appropriate planning is carried out when selecting tools, workbenches and other needs. The lessons of the early chapters need careful application to the specific opportunities and problems created by converting a garage into a woodworking shop. In general, the fact that you've got an enclosed, wired and lighted space, with doors, and sometimes with windows, is a great place to start and saves 95% of the work involved in setting up a woodworking shop. The wiring and lighting are marginal for a woodshop, but those are reasonably simple to change.

GARAGES

A well built garage solves a lot of workshop space and construction problems. Most are simple frameworks with roof and siding, but there may also be a window or two, some electrical power and a light or two or more. Too, the modern garage door is close to an ideal material and equipment portal. If the garage is attached to the house, there may be enough heat bleeding off to reduce or eliminate any need for a separate heating system. Bob Grisso's shop (below left) qualifies as both freestanding and a garage, though it hasn't served as car parking space for years. There may also be circuits enough for a modest shop, but the odds are good you'll eventually need to install at least a 60-ampere subpanel. Some of the greatest shops in this book started life as car barns. Doug Johnson's shop is an example, possibly the most extreme. He had to add a second story to his garage to make space on his lot for the woodshop he wanted. His tale is more fully told in the display section, but some special arrangements were

Doug Johnson uses a winch and pulley to bring supplies up to his second floor shop. COURTESY OF DOUG JOHNSON

necessary to handle getting supplies into the shop. Brian Grella's shop is a garage in more traditional form, and is shown in the display section, as is Pete Bade's freestanding garage and shop. A large number of garages appear to end up doing duty as woodshops. Sizes are right — though I have worked my wood in a single car garage built around 1915 and found that a very tight fit. Prices are reasonable. Contracted building is a very simple matter in most localities. Bobby Weaver's shop interior is reached by the garage door shown on the top of page 100, and another about 55' away. There are also two small access doors. This end is a contracted metal garage. The other end is a steel utility building, reminiscent of World War II (and later) Quonset huts (newer versions of the Nissen hut from the War To End All Wars, World War I).

Doug's second floor shop windows offer a wonderful view while working. COURTESY OF DOUG JOHNSON

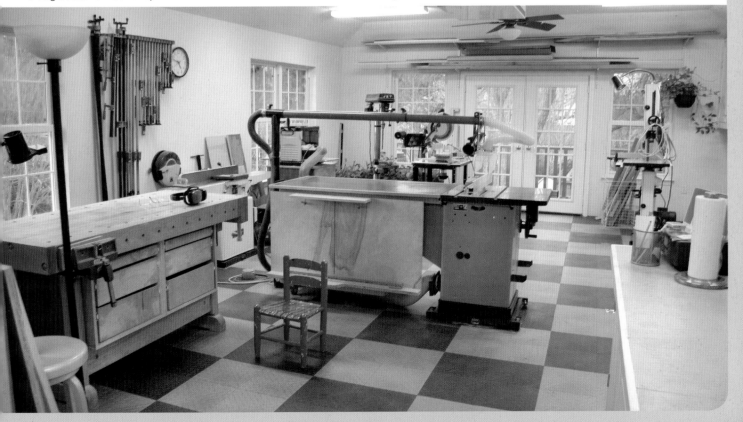

Again, drawing the outline of the building's interior is a help, locating doors and windows. Decide whether or not the garage will ever be used for vehicular storage. As far as I am concerned, our vehicles could sit in the weather, if we even had a garage. With current paints, that doesn't seem to harm anything in a mild climate, but it has also been a lot of years since my All-American car bug has bitten me. Like most kids of my generation, I was a hot rod freak, let that bleed over into motorcycles, and lost interest in anything other than transportation by the time my reflexes slowed enough to make bikes less fun. So, now, cars and trucks are to be kept available and in good running shape, but otherwise are low key, and don't come close to being family members, as was the case in the "good old days". Now that age is really setting in, I appreciate more and more the cars of the 1930s, 1940s and even up to the 1960s, but for the most part, I couldn't afford them anyway, at today's prices. As one guy I know, who has a 1972 Plymouth Road Runner 340, has said, "If I hadn't bought it new, I couldn't afford it now."

Decide what tools will fit where and what kind of outlets you need. See if there's room and power for all. Go ahead

Garage door entries to woodshops are useful.

and set up for the ones for which you're not ready. Install the electricity, pegboard and other accessories you need to complete the moderately large shop that even a single car garage provides. If you're fortunate enough to have a two car, or larger, garage, you're in woodworker's heaven — at least on a lower level. Most garages offer about 450 to 600 square feet of space, sufficient for all but the largest hobby shops. Fred Preston's shop is a garage and he says it's also

Two-car garage shops offer terrific space for woodworking. In a pinch, you can actually park a car in one, sometimes.

his first "real" shop. He turns out some good work there, too. (Fred's shop was once a double garage, but now serves a better purpose.)

Most garages, as already stated, have open studs, probably open rafters, collar beams and maybe even ceiling joists. It's up to you as to how much finishing you do. There is sometimes a benefit in leaving joists open as they become storage helpers — don't store much overhead if you have trusses, though.

The floor is almost sure to be concrete and may demand some extreme clean-up before it takes a decent coat of paint. Check with the floor-paint makers to see what they recommend for cleaning up greasy floors. Or you may go the sleeper route, which is probably preferable if the floor is really nasty. Get enough grease in concrete over enough years and it cannot be properly cleaned well enough for paint to adhere. By the same token, the adhesive for various tiles also won't work. Sleepers become the only option, outside of actually just allowing the grease to be there on the floor until sawdust gets pounded into the existing mess.

You need to make up your mind whether or not you'll place a ceiling in the garage. In one sense, a ceiling is desirable, in another, it's not. Open rafters, or lower members of trusses, make decent storage spots for light items

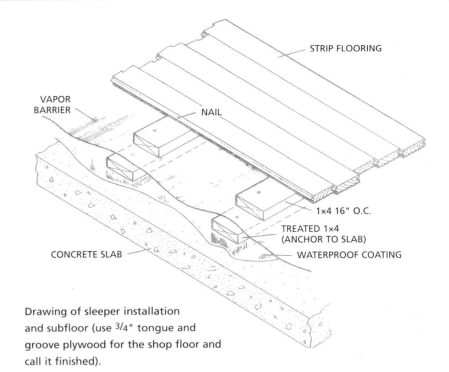

Drawing of sleeper installation and subfloor (use ³/₄" tongue and groove plywood for the shop floor and call it finished).

(very light in trusses) long enough to span at least two of the members. There are a lot of those in every woodworker's life. The ceiling is desirable because it tends to reduce heating and cooling needs while also providing a reflective surface (if light colored, which any ceiling should be) for light. Your storage needs may have to be balanced against the excessive heat loss and gain you face, plus the dust and general clutter accumulation that is always the case with open rafters over a woodworking shop.

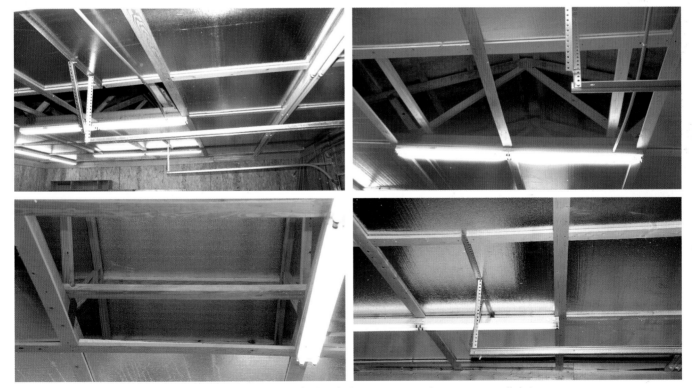

This garage shop ceiling offers a grid system that allows for insulation, storage and easy access to lighting.

You also must decide whether or not to add drywall to the studs. Certain areas are best left open, as the studs become a source of superb storage opportunities. Many woodshops end up with walls as shown at the right (jammed with storage) so covering them, rather than leaving open studs is usually the smart thing to do.

Workbenches may be built into garages, against stud walls, with only front legs for support.

The extent of the remodeling is up to you, as always, but make sure you've got sufficient circuits and as much wall space that can be taken up with pegboard and/or shelving. If you're lucky, you have expanded the vehicles right out into the driveway.

Today's garages are built with studs on 24" centers, which makes for easy installation of most kinds of drywall paneling, though I'd avoid getting involved with gypsum wallboard, which needs to be taped, have nail depressions filled and then needs priming and painting. My own shop has walls covered with OSB (oriented-strand board). That might not be legal (according to code) in some areas if you're working in an attached garage, because of the flammability. Plywood also works well, as shown in the photo below.

In most instances, attached garages with a wall next to a relaxing area of the home makes everyone happier if filled with insulation and covered with at least $1/2$" solid drywall

COURTESY OF CRAFTSMAN

(drywall in this instance means any non-plaster panel. Gypsum wallboard is too much work for the little extra sound deadening it adds in such a situation). If you want pegboard on such walls, come back and place it over the solid wall. The more substantial wall will reduce the passage of sound. None of these techniques prevent the passage of sound. That needs a second wall placed about 1" in front of the first, with no solid contact between the two, and with insulation woven in to help reduce sound travel. It is worth the expense and effort in only a very few cases.

Each garage is different, and unless built specifically as a shop (as might be the case if you pick up a garage package at a mega-lumberyard), each has a different history of use.

Evaluate the location of windows, doors and the condition of such things as overhead doors and automatic openers when getting set to do your planning. Doors may be easily added — especially standard entry doors, up to 36" wide — but you are probably better off not adding any windows. Windows give glaring light and seem to do so always at the wrong time. They're also easily broken if too low, and most residential windows, including those in a garage, are too low for workshop use. Leave those that exist in place, but don't add more unless the sills are at least 54" from the floor.

For light, install overhead fluorescent lights. You want to evaluate the electrical system and work as in Chapter Nine. Make sure you have plenty of outlets in both 120 volts and 240 volts. Also make sure you have a properly grounded electrical system. Install a ground fault circuit

COURTESY OF RYOBI

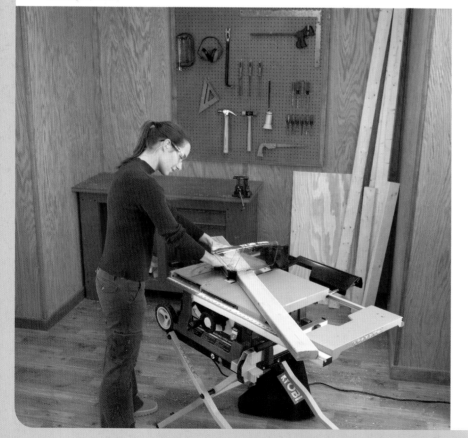

interrupter at the first outlet to protect all the outlets from problems, following it in sequence. You can also add circuit breakers of the ground fault circuit interrupter type, though they tend to be more expensive than standard breakers.

Evaluate the floor. Many garages with poured concrete floors have a central drain, and the floor is sloped towards that drain. If there is too much slope, you'll want to install a wood floor over sleepers. It's not the hardest job in the world, but does take time and cost money. Ideally, you won't have to do a thing except wash and paint the floor, or lay tile, but in many cases, bet on working out some method of leveling the floor. The only effective way to do so is to install a leveled floor on sleepers. Shim the sleepers level as you install them, starting from the sides of the room and working towards the center (or towards the drain, or multiple drain). Level all succeeding sleepers with the high ones along the walls. Install sleepers with construction adhesive and cut masonry nails, using pressure treated pine. For problem areas that are apt to stay wet, use wood treated for ground contact. Use a good vapor barrier laid directly on the concrete (vapor barriers are made from polyethylene sheeting no less than 6 mils thick —10 mils is better).

Install the sleepers so centers are either 16" (for $^5/_8$" plywood floor, no subfloor) or 24" (for $^3/_4$" floor, or $^5/_8$" over board subfloor). If it's a normal installation, using a $^3/_4$" (1" nominal) sheathing lumber for subfloor, or rough-cut 1" lumber, with $^5/_8$", tongue-and-groove, sanded B-C plywood finish floor works well. You can then either lay vinyl tile, or vinyl sheet on the plywood or you can simply coat it with a

The ability to open up an entire wall of your shop brings in wonderful sunlight, fresh air during the proper seasons and makes moving items (especially sheet goods and large equipment) significantly easier. COURTESY OF JELD-WEN

good brand of polyurethane (at least two coats, preferably three) and go about your business.

Heat installation in a garage may require the installation of a flue or wall vent, depending on the heat type selected — if any is needed at all. Connected garages typically have little need for extra heating, unless the house is under heated, but you may wish to add a couple of baseboard electric units or a small wood stove. If you do add a wood stove, you need to install a chimney with a solid fuel liner and have it and the rest of the installation inspected to make sure it conforms to regulations.

Connected garages also tend to offer easy access to any necessary circuitry upgrades by the simple process of adding a subpanel to a couple of unused circuit breaker spaces in the main service entry panel. You can, depending on the present load on the main panel, take off enough for six to ten circuits with very little problem. The six-circuit box doesn't need its own circuit breaker, but will use the breakers on the main panel. For a larger subpanel, you will need a separate breaker, either 60 or 100 amperes.

Windows in a garage will be like windows in most other buildings, too low for the most efficient shop use. The simplest solution with double-hung windows is to cover much of the bottom with a piece of plywood, raising the wall space 12" or more and reducing use of the window (opening) to the top sash unit. The plywood across the bottom should be at least $^3/_8$" thick, to eliminate broken panes from swung lumber, kickbacks and other knocks from woodworking fate. Before actually stopping up any window spaces permanently check local codes. If codes forbid such stoppage, use two small butt hinges on one side, and a slide latch on the other. In most residences, rooms are required to have a window large enough for exit of a person if on the ground floor. Do *not* make a change without checking this first, because you may end up with a disapproved installation.

Permanent closing up of the bottom of a window allows you to run benches along the wall that are higher than otherwise. Certainly, if a garage has windows at the level of some of those in residences, you are going to be badly limited in placing anything against them. If such is the case, and you can't make a change buy stopping up the lower half of the window, placing a tool such as a bandsaw or drill press in front of the window makes good use of the space. Lathes also fit, but are a bit lengthy for most windows. Drill presses and bandsaws don't create a length problems.

That big garage door is a help. If you do not have an automatic garage door opener, install one. The installation

As I mentioned earlier, some garage shops still do duty as garages. It's a good idea to protect the vehicle during woodworking activities. Saw dust is only one of the concerns. COURTESY OF PETE BADE

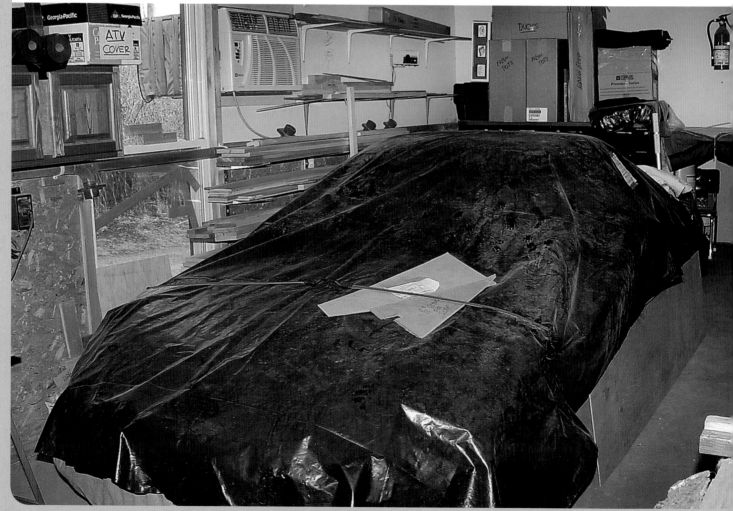

Never underestimate the value of a mouser (or two) in the shop. Keep them happy and they'll keep your shop rodent-free. COURTESY OF PETE BADE

isn't particularly difficult, and the bend-over time it saves is great, especially if there's no other exterior door in the garage. (Garage doors are fantastic materials-handling assets — and make getting larger finished projects out less of a chore.)

If the overhead door is all you have, install another exterior door, at least a 32" wide exterior model, with consideration given to a 36"- or 42"-wide unit.

In a normally-framed garage, that means removing a single stud and framing in to take the door. Build a header of 2×8 stock, with $^1/_2$" plywood used as a center spacer to get the $1^1/_2$" thick stock, doubled, to $3^1/_2$" to match the rest of the framing. If the framing is of rough-cut lumber, use double pieces of $^1/_2$" plywood as spacers. Use at least one jack stud under each side of the header and one cripple stud in its center to the top plate, if the space is large enough to allow it. Make sure the sill (floor) is level and the rough framing is plumb and insert the door unit. For a solid installation, nail through door jamb sides into the framing after shimming at the lock area and elsewhere as needed. Install moulding and the job is done.

If you decide to place a ceiling and/or use drywall construction to cover the wall studs, first insulate as local dictates make sensible. At a minimum, that's $3^1/_2$" in the walls and 6" over the ceiling (with a probable preference for at least 12" above).

Next, using either $^7/_{16}$" waferboard or oriented strand board (OSB) to cover the walls and ceiling. To decorate, you may use lath strips on the joints and maybe at 24" centers. Currently, my office is done in waferboard with lath at 4' intervals (except where I had to cut and lay a seam closer), and the whole works painted off white. It looks fine, and is

bright and cheery and cost very little. A shop will do as well. Mine does. I've used waferboard in shops before and find it an easy to use, sturdy, a low cost way to cover gaping spaces in walls and to cover old, deteriorating plaster walls without going to huge expense.

You can use another type of paneling, but I know of nothing else that works as well at low a cost (even in today's current high-priced sheet wood market, OSB in $^7/_{16}$" thickness is well under $7 per panel).

The panels go up quickly and are nailed, as is most manufactured wood paneling, at 8" intervals on internal seams and 6" intervals along the outside edges. Use a few dabs of construction adhesive to make for a surer bond, but be advised you are never going to be able to remove the panels that are glued down without taking some serious chunks out of the studs underneath.

Beyond that, setting a garage up as a workshop needs little extra work, unless you plan to leave one or more vehicles inside. Then it's more a matter of tool choice and the ability to move those tools into place easily when you have a job to do.

My old friend, Peter Bade, stores his Honda 2000 inside during the winter, as you can see from the tarp coverings. You don't drive that kind of car in upstate New York winters if you expect it to stay in good shape. He also worked out a solution for his shop cats in winter, keeping them comfy while they keep the mouse population under control.

Doug Johnson's garage shop shows a different approach: He built a second story to take the shop, because there wasn't enough room on his lot to get code approval for another building large enough to work, and his cars needed a home, so the elevated shop came into being. He then moved his tools in and has been working wood ever since, in a shop many of us would envy. He has a bathroom, and every tool he needs, all within the space of a large garage. A lift makes hauling lumber and other supplies easy, while the deck gives a great view of his neighborhood.

Thus, choose benchtop tools — assuming the garage is deep enough to allow at least a 22" deep bench against the back wall — or tools with wheels. The Shopsmith Mark V and variations make good selections, as does Ridgid's jobsite table saw. Check the items in your local tool suppliers' showrooms, in the catalogs available from most tool manufacturers and on-line.

CHAPTER SEVEN

Building the Freestanding Shop, From Tools to Foundations

Construction methods for outbuildings such as shops do not differ a great deal from those used to erect residences. You can generally get by with cheaper materials and fewer glossy finishes, but you must use the same depth and quality of footings and wall framing as for general construction. There's little reason for going with 16" on-center construction (unless archaic codes in your locale demand such construction, as they well may) when 24" on-center provides sufficient strength, and uses about a fifth less framing material.

Though not the tools you'll most frequently use in your woodworking, basic carpentry tools are the mainstay in building a freestanding woodshop.

All construction starts with layout and design, for most building inspection offices want you to present them with rough plans — and most people need those plans to work with, and from, in order to get the layout accurate. Shop structures are much simpler than residences. You don't usually add such items as bathrooms, kitchens, central air conditioning, or, for that matter, central heat. Most freestanding shop heating that I've seen (for non-commercial shops) is done with a space heater of some sort, whether kerosene, electric, coal or wood. We'll cover that in Chapter Nine, and then the choice is yours. I would suggest, for cleanliness, that your finishing area be heated with something other than wood or coal. Too, most finishes pose some problems during application and drying — and even during storage — when heat with open flame is used.

While you might have need of a good level when hanging cabinetry, keeping things plumb and level when building a woodshop make life much easier.

Water-based polyurethanes eliminate most of those problems, but are not suitable for all wood finishing needs.

TOOLS

Some of the same tools used in a woodworking shop are very handy for constructing that shop, but there are some major differences, so a look at the basics of frame construction tools may be handy. These are carpentry tools, and their selection and use is one of the factors to your success or failure in creating a woodworking shop depends.

Carpentry tools can add expense to any outdoor work, or they can be rational in cost, and add to the enjoyment, and ease, with which the work is done. Efficiency and lowest possible cost within your own range of needs are the major determining factors. If you are going to drill a total of fifty

Power tools are priced in several levels to meet many needs. The performance of a tool designed for woodworking is not the same as one designed for construction or concrete work.

holes, with none larger than about $^3/8$" inch, don't purchase a professional $^1/2$" hammer drill costing well over $300.

Of course, if your intention is to do quality work over a period of years, the smaller, inexpensive consumer drills are not the way to go.

The same price range percentages work well through the hand tool and power tool needs for carpentry. You can buy cheap, you can buy high, and, sometimes, you can buy in the middle. Your decision is going to make a difference in job costs, and in the ease with which your shop project goes together. Balance the two for best results.

One point must always be kept in mind. Truly cheap tools, the cheapest made, are never a good a savings. Panel saws can't cut a straight line, hammer faces are belled incorrectly and bend more nails than any sloppy carpenter. Cheap measuring tools are inaccurate and sloppily made, squares not square, levels don't level correctly, and screwdrivers don't fit slots, or chip and break at the tips, often both. At the same time, spending money for luxury tools is not always a good idea. Certain tools can be had in price ranges that are almost startling in variety, but the ultra special models are simply not necessary for good work, though owning them does provide a fine feeling for many people (including me).

HANDTOOLS

Basic handtools needed for any construction work include the claw hammer, the panel, or hand, saw; screwdrivers in various styles and types, planes, chisels, a miter box, nail sets, measuring tapes and rules, squares, levels, a brace

and bit set (optional in this day and age of cordless electric drills), and some small items that can be classed as accessories, such as stair stringer markers for framing squares.

HAMMERS

Claw hammers are essential. Junk hammers cost nearly as much as good ones (within a few dollars), and are a waste of money. When shopping for hammers, check for a slightly crowned face for directional control when driving nails, with a clean chamfer around the face. The entire head must be cleanly made, and the claws cleanly beveled. Nail hammer heads come in two patterns, one with curved claws, and the other with straight, or ripping, claws. Ripping hammers are used most often for heavier framing work, and are a shade less well balanced for driving nails. For heavy framing hammers there is often no other choice. Models with head weights from twenty-two ounces on up to twenty-eight ounces have ripping claws. Curved-claw hammers offer easier gripping of nails to be pulled, and a slightly better control when driving nails, so are preferred for general and lighter work.

Handle materials range from hickory through fiberglass and graphite (carbon fiber, I'd bet) to solid and tubular steel. There are slight advantages to each — wood costs a buck or so less and absorbs shock well; fiberglass (and its graphite counterparts) is easiest of all on the hand and forearm when driving nails; steel handles are the strongest, and most these days have a cushioning grip. The top consideration with any hammer handle is that it is securely attached to the head, which is a feature emphasized by all the good brands.

Head weight is a personal consideration. Standard weights range from thirteen ounces (useful for moulding, assembling birdhouses and other light duty work) to the standard sixteen-ounce head, on up to twenty-eight ounce monsters with extra handle length to provide driving power for large nails and spikes.

Faces may be plain or milled. Milled faces are only useful in hammers used for rough framing. For many years, I used a 20 ounce, curved-claw as my main hammer. With age, I've moved to a 16-ounce model. For light nailing, I now use a brad nailer, and if I have more than a dozen or two nails to drive, or am driving in harder woods, I use a pneumatic nailer.

HANDSAWS

There is still a variety of good handsaws available, but for most general purposes carpentry (of our type), only three are of use: The hand or panel saw, the keyhole (compass) saw and the backsaw. You may find some need for a hacksaw when cutting metals.

Panel saws used to be the epitome of carpentry saws used for crosscutting and ripping. Things have changed. Power tools are used far more often for those cuts, and the venerable panel saw has been relegated to clean-up chores, and to use where electrical power is not available.

For general crosscutting use, a ten point-per-inch blade is preferable (panel saws are widely available in eight, ten and a twelve point-per-inch models). Select a good model, either close to a brand's top of the line, or at the top of the line. The reasoning here is quite simple. Cheap saws do not cut straight even when new. As the saw wears, it gets worse.

Make sure handle contours are comfortable, and that the teeth are sharp. Add that to good quality, and a saw will last for decades. The newer hard-tooth and aggressive-tooth patterns from Stanley, and other makers, are quick-cutting saws that reduce effort considerably over older chisel-tooth patterns. I still use the older patterns, too, but find more and more of my work is being done with the varied aggressive tooth types — including the finish-cut, 12-tooth patterns. Most of these cannot be readily sharpened.

Keyhole saws are useful, inexpensive tools that are part of what is sometimes called a nest of saws. They're used for cutting small openings (usually in drywall), such as receptacle holes, and for notching.

Backsaws are usually a part of hand miter boxes. Instead of a top taper as in a panel saw, the backsaw will have a flat-shaped blade, with a steel or brass rib along its top to stiffen the blade. This gives a very accurate straight line cut. Again, quality tells. The better backsaws will be larger and stiffer, with better metal used in the blade so the teeth hold their set and edge longer.

SCREWDRIVERS

Screwdrivers are among the most used and most mistreated tools of all. The old slotted-head screwdriver is not gone, but it is slowing down these days as power drivers become ever more popular. Slotted screwdrivers are being replaced for most work with Phillips, square drive (Robertson) or Torx™ drivers that allow the application of more torque to the screw head without worries about the driver tip slipping and marring the work — or the worker.

Screwdrivers must have handles that fit the hand well so that constant use doesn't provide sore hands and sore forearms. One that fills the closed hand is good, and the wedge shaped models are ideal. The shanks and blades need to be of good metal and the tips must be accurately machined.

Match tip size to slot or other inset style size of the screw and apply a twisting motion. Shank length is a matter of job requirements and preferences. Use a medium length shank, 6" to 8", whenever possible, as these are the easiest to control. Move into very short lengths and very long lengths when there's no other way to do the work.

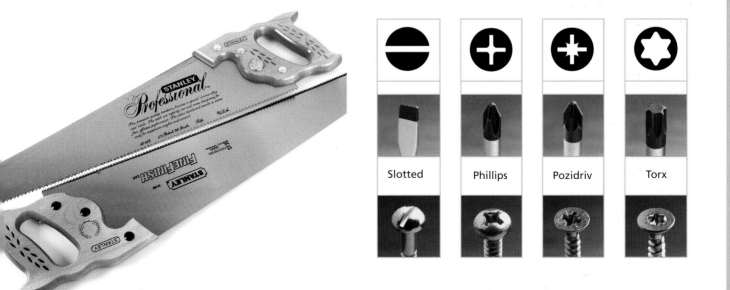

Slotted   Phillips   Pozidriv   Torx

SQUARES AND LEVELS

Squares of at least two types are essential to most carpentry, indoor or outdoor. The basic try square is a simple rigid form of metal, or wood and metal. It has a 90 ° angle and might also offer short a 45° cut across the handle base. The blade size is usually 8" or 12" long, and will be marked, as you wish, in inch or metric measurements.

A slightly different form of the standard try square is the combination square. Combination squares have blades that slide in the handles, and offer both 90° and 45° markings with ease, though generally with slightly less accuracy than does a good try square — the loss of accuracy is of little importance in most carpentry work.

Framing, carpenters' and roofing squares are versions of the same tool, a stamped L of metal with a 2"-wide blade and a 1¹/₂"-wide tongue. The square may be of aluminum or steel — stainless steel is the best, though the heaviest and most expensive and hard to find these days — and may have ink-filled or unfilled numbers and tables. The long member makes for a good straightedge on much work, and the square is essential to many kinds of framing work, from checking square on corners to laying out rafters and stair stringers.

Woodworkers' Supply carries a large, folding carpenter's square that is claimed to be accurate to within ¹/₃₂". This tool makes layout of your cabinets a lot easier and is handy for checking square in window and door framing.

Stanley has a carpenter's line of T-squares, at a minimum a 2' version is a good idea. These are available in 4'-long, heavy duty versions as well.

Not too long ago, I got my hands on a Starrett miter gauge, the ProSite™, and used it a few times. It is a direct-

Squares are an essential part of carpentry (and shop building), just as with woodworking.

reading miter calculator that reduces or eliminates mistakes in figuring miter cuts, showing two different cuts for each joint, and generally making itself useful. It's not exactly cheap (probably in the $70 range most places, and possibly a bit less), but it can be worthwhile if you do much angle cutting — and it's useful later if you plan to build large cabinetry that might need crown or similarly complex (to us who do such moulding once every few years) work.

Levels are essential. Three types of bubble levels cover every job likely to be required by woodshop carpentry work. The standard spirit level, at least 2' long, is needed for leveling window sills, plumbing door frames, and for plumbing posts and other uprights. For doors, a 72" or 78" level is a good idea, but a 4' level is minimum. The 9" torpedo level does the same jobs in spots where the longer level won't fit. Line levels clip on to mason's cord and serve to provide a level over a long distance, as with the original layout of the building.

This trio of levels does it all.

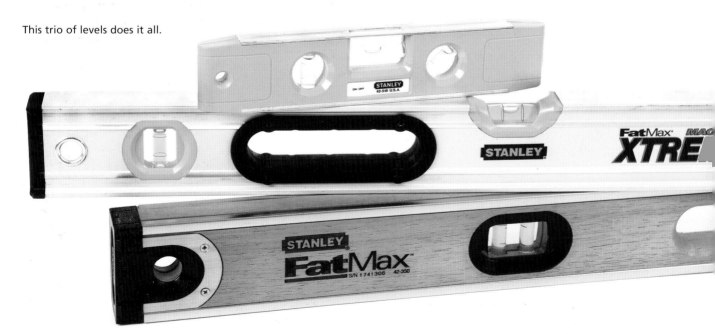

A friend of mine was siting a metal building a few weeks ago, one of the low-cost buildings that get advertised as carports, and complained to me that he could no longer find a water level. I checked. I not only can't find one locally, I can't find one, period. If you want to cover the distance he had to cover — a 40'-long rectangle about 16' wide — your options are fewer now, though it's simple enough to find a laser leveling device for those distances. All you need to do is fork over $500, probably closer to $900, and hope the day isn't too sunny.

Instead, Bobby took a 75' garden hose, located a 10' long piece of clear hose (not easy), cut the 10' length in two, placed one end at each elevation, and leveled the place (mark each piece of clear hose an equal distance up from the regular hose — no less than a foot up, no more than three; the accuracy of the level then depends on your accurate markings). Accuracy isn't within $1/32$", but it is more than enough for siting a building. Overall cost was about $8 because he had the garden hose on hand.

I'm not covering all the hand tools you'll need for all the jobs in this book, but this is an overview of the most important. Items such as nail sets, specialized screwdrivers, mason's hammers and so on will make themselves known to you as you work.

The standard circular saw. This tool will get you through almost any construction project.

POWER TOOLS

For the basics of carpentry, you can squeeze by with only two power tools: A power drill and a circular saw. Note that braces and bits, hand drills and other hand powered drills were not mentioned earlier. The reason is simply the assumption that everyone has at least a lightweight electric drill. I've got several braces, plenty of bits for them, a hand drill or two, and an old Stanley push drill (which gets five times the use of all the other hand drills put together). Hand drills, though, are seldom used where there is any

An angled framing nailer gets into tight spots and can cut hours (even days) off a framing project.

My Bosch cordless drill is a clutched, hammer drill.

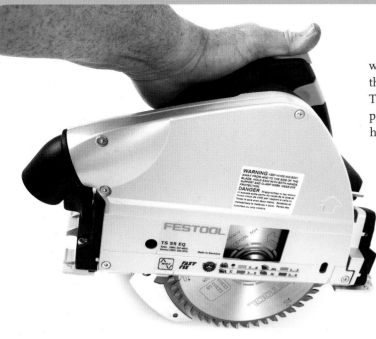

The best circular saw I've ever used. This Festool saw cuts right to the edge of any work.

power available, and often not then, with today's wide range of cordless tools.

At one time, plug-in power was needed at a job site if work was to be done quickly. These days, cordless drills have reached such an extreme of power that there is little reason for buying a generator for on-site use. Even circular saws are available in decent cordless models, with enough power these days to do most jobs.

One note of personal bias here that may need explanation. I prefer to buy tools from what might be called old-line manufacturers, such as Black & Decker, Bosch, Craftsman, DeWalt, Festool, Freud, Grizzly, Hitachi, Milwaukee, Triton, Woodtek and similar companies. I know that a number of those companies are not old line, of course. I also know that just about all the tools are made in Taiwan or mainland China these days. Even with those considerations, I've found over the years that tool companies that are based in the U.S., Japan, Australia and most of Europe tend to have stricter standards for quality control, regardless of the actual country of manufacture. My point is that the tools that show up in slick boxes near the check-out counters, or in bins at the back of the store, with no name, or someone's idea of a cool Anglo-Saxon name, are more often a waste of money than any real help in doing quality work.

Recently, I've swung over and tried Festool tools. I've got a circular saw system, a jig saw, a random-orbit sander and a vacuum. These are still made in Germany and carry the premium that German engineering and production bring. Festool also offers some remarkable innovations to go with the top quality. Some innovations are nothing more than stackable tool boxes, built to fit one atop the other. Simple. Handy. We'll see more as we go along.

Circular saws are nearly essential for carpentry, and are wonderful for rough-cutting to length most kinds of wood that are too large to fit into a shop or a shop's machines. The Festool version has a guide that makes it much more precise for rips and wide crosscuts than most, without having any need to buy aftermarket guides (the Festool guide is marketed as an accessory). While no power tool is an absolute necessity, estimates show that carpentry work done with specific portable power tools is on the order of five- to seven-times faster than using hand tools alone. It is also at least five- to seven-times easier. Not long ago, I watched a neighbor construct a moderated-sized shed. He did all the nailing by hand. Recently, I've been using air powered framing and finishing nailers, and sheathing staplers, and hope to never again do the sort of work being done on that shed. With an air nailer, he'd have finished a week earlier — at least.

Electric drills offer the widest tool range of all. Points of interest are chuck size, power and comfort in the hand. The pistol-grip electric drill, on drills up through a $1/2$" chuck, is nearly a standard in the industry. The primary differences in construction are in feel and what might be classed as balance point. There are many quality differences as well.

Top-quality drills have more ball bearings, better fitted casings, longer and heavier power cords that are more easily replaced, a better quality chuck, and a more powerful and better made motor.

You pay for all these features, but if that drill is expected to be used for heavy work, or over a long term, it is worth the extra cost. For general carpentry and construction work, a $3/8$" chuck is basic, as is variable speed and reversing. Variable speed drills let you start drilling without center-punching holes (most of the time) to prevent the drill bit's walking off line. Add at least a five ampere motor — heavier is better — and you'll do fine. If you wish to do much drilling in masonry, get a drill that offers a hammer-drill feature (and use the appropriate masonry hammer drill bits). Cost rises, but the time and energy savings is considerable.

For driving screws, get a clutched drill. Any variable speed drill does a fair job of driving screws, but a clutched variable-speed drill will stop driving the screw before it torques the head off, or before it slides off and mars the work. My Bosch $3/8$" corded drill sports about a seven amp motor, is clutched and a hammer drill and never misses a beat, no matter how it's treated.

Specific power drivers for screws and small nuts and bolts are also made. The newest models are impact drivers, usually cordless, and may be small, like Bosch's PS-10 or larger like Milwaukee's 12-volt 2401 — which is still small, just not very small like the little Bosch. Porter-Cable is in the fray, as are DeWalt, Ryobi, Ridgid and others.

Cordless electric drills have reached the point where they are almost good enough to replace corded drills in many construction uses. A couple of mine are actually pretty decent hammer drills. A few years ago, I used one of Bosch's early cordless rotary hammers for an article. It was 24 volts, then the top of the mark, and went through concrete with more ease than I anticipated.

For general drill selection, avoid consumer's models, and go for the lower-end professional models. These drills offer the same features as corded drills, with slightly lower capacities in wood, steel and masonry. If you decide to go cordless, get a drill that has a battery pack that charges quickly, preferably in about an hour, and buy a second battery pack. The variety is wide, but for easy use in moderate duty, select a lightweight model in 12 volts, and for heavier use, jump on a 14.4 or 18 volt version. The price differences aren't too bad, but there's no point in slinging around the extra weight of the 18-volt battery if you don't have to. My heavy duty cordless work is handled by Bosch and DeWalt 14.4-volt cordless drills, while the lighter duties are taken care of by two DeWalt 12-volt drills.

Batteries: NiCad is the standard and still popular; lithium ion is becoming the new standard and seems to me to hold up exceptionally well; NiMH (or nickel metal hydride) was touted as the coming thing some years ago. It isn't, at least for tools or anything else I've tried. NiMH batteries have an annoying tendency to speedily self-discharge (let it sit for 30 days and you're wise to recharge it before use). Too, NiMH batteries, in my experience, have a very limited lifetime: I've got a Makita 12 volt with NiMH batteries that is about six or seven years old. The batteries have been shot for at least four of those years. They'll charge. If you use them instantly, you get six or ten screws driven, or eighteen or so holes drilled — small holes and small screws.

If memory serves, NiMH was first put forth as a less polluting battery, one with fewer nasty chemical bits. That may be so, but, unfortunately, like many so-called "green" products, it costs more and does less than the products it replaces. So I recommend that you avoid any cordless tool with NiMH batteries. They work fine powering my flash units in the field, but at $8 for four, I can dispose of them

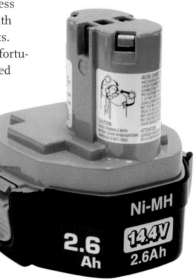

Nickel-metal-hydride batteries are a good balance between performance and price.

after a couple hundred charges without too many qualms — except to wonder just how they're reducing pollution when more head to the dump more quickly. NiCads may be more poisonous — maybe — but they last longer, hold a charge better and are second only to lithium ion batteries (Li-Ion) for overall use, I believe.

Circular saws offer far greater cutting speed than handsaws. They are also more accurate in most hands, especially on longer cuts. There is a wide variety on the market, with blade sizes ranging from 4" upwards to 16". Industry standard is $7^1/4$"; there is little need for most of us to vary from that, except possibly with Porter-Cable's 6" blade saw, the Saw Boss, that is lighter and easier to use for many people. It's 1 to $1^1/2$ pounds lighter than similar $7^1/4$" saws.

When circular saw shopping, look for a thick base plate, with some thought given to a drop foot base plate (easier to adjust for depth than tilting plates), an 8'- to 10'-long cord, a top handle (easier control for most people), a $7^1/4$" blade size and at least a 10 ampere motor. Again, the lower levels of professional lines are the best place to begin looking.

Festool also offers an accessory guide that is used for their router, jigsaw and circular saw, available in several lengths. It is worth considering as an added feature. The Festool circular saw looks a bit odd, compared to many standard pattern saws, but it works very well, makes safer plunge cuts, and will certainly endure as well as my old Porter-Cable circular saw (old enough to have been out of production for half a decade or more, but still going strong) or any of the others that have made faster trips through here.

For the person who wants the ultimate in circular saws, Bosch and Skil offer worm drive saws that can go all day, every day, without a deep breath, never mind a gasp. Skil's SHD77M makes extensive use of magnesium to reduce its weight to 14 pounds, a weight matched by the Bosch — the Bosch, though, is available in both a top handle, at 15 pounds and the slightly lighter, classic rear handle.

If you've just got to have a cordless circular saw, Bosch's 24 volt $6^1/2$" 1660K is my recommendation, but don't faint when you see the price, almost three times what you'd pay for Milwaukee's excellent $7^1/4$", corded circular saw.

Many other power and hand tools are available, and you'll form your own list of preferences as you go along. It is possible to write an entire book about selection, use and care of carpentry and woodworking related tools.

Give thought to getting either a power miter saw, or a radial arm saw from Ryobi or Sears as a supplement to your circular saw, and as a means to ease repetitious compound cutting chores — as well as an aid to accuracy in mitering and similar cuts. With the radial arm saw, a lot of fuss is needed for accurate set-up, while a good power miter saw, even a sliding compound miter saw, does most of the same work (no ripping, no dadoing) with greater ease and easier to sustain accuracy.

TOOL CARE

Tool care is mostly common sense. Make sure electrical tools have good cords and do not get their plugs mangled. Keep all tools as clean as possible, and lightly oil or otherwise lubricate or protect those that need it. Use tools for the jobs for which they're intended: The screwdriver is a prime example. Screwdrivers are to drive screws, and in a pinch do well at opening paint cans. They are not pry bars, chisels, or levers and should not be used as such, though virtually everyone has used one or more in those ways, often wondering, afterwards, why the tool no longer drives screws well. In special cases, follow the tool manufacturer's instructions for tool care.

In most cases of tool care, keeping the tool clean and dry after use is the main factor in keeping a tool sharp and working for as long as its built-in quality allows.

Use a round-bristled brush to get off sawdust and other debris, making sure, with electric tools, to get into the vents around the motor.

Wipe the tool down with a dry, soft rag — old worn-out tee shirts are great for this job, as they are for many others — after use.

Those tools that tend to collect resin, pitch and gum often need another step or two. For saw blades, a fast wipe with mineral spirits removes slight traces of gum build-up. This can be followed with a coat of light machine oil, or a substance such as WD-40 can be sprayed on.

For blades that get heavy use and thus build up heavy coatings of gums, more severe measures are needed. There are commercial gum dissolvers that work well with circular saw and other blades, but probably the best, and cheapest, gum remover is Simple Green (above). Soak in warm water and Simple Green at a very strong solution; a wipe with a damp sponge gets rid of the residue. Keep the sponge well rinsed in warm (tepid) water. Rinse well.

Once the last bits of gum and cleaner are off, use a good coating of WD-40 to protect the blade from rust, again locating an old tee shirt to dry the blade thoroughly. Water does not harm metal, unless it is left to stand and start a rust cycle that ruins any tool.

Any tool can be cleaned with water and Simple Green when grease and other dirt builds up beyond the point where it can be easily removed by wiping

with a dry cloth. Use soft cloths, rinse well, and make sure that no electric motor windings get wet, then dry thoroughly. Liberally coat any exposed steel or iron parts with WD-40 or light machine oil.

The primary objection to oiling any saw blade, plane iron or similar wood cutting device is the effect the lubricant has on wood finishes. Wood finishes don't stick to oily surfaces. This doesn't matter if you are cutting framing stock, but on siding, and in other areas where finishes are applied, make 2' or longer cleaning cuts with any blade before applying the blade to good wood.

TOOL SAFETY

Tool safety is also a matter of common sense, but needs some knowledge, with power tools particularly, of reactions to force.

Make sure you have a clear cutting line, and that tool cords will not snag as you cut. Snags usually just pull the cut off line, wasting material. At other times, a snag can cause a tool to be yanked loose from the cut — and the hand. That's dangerous.

Wear eye protection, whether safety glasses, goggles or a face shield. If goggles and glasses steam up on you often, try a face shield. If steaming is still a problem, cut three or four $3/16$" slots, about $1^1/2$" long, in front of the mouth and nose areas of the shield. A lot of years ago, we'd rub raw potatoes on the inside of SCUBA masks. I've never tried that with woodworking goggles, but it might work. Others spit in the mask and rub it around. I didn't find that worked as well as the spud wipe.

Keep the area around your feet clear: Make sure extra tools, lumber and cut-offs, plus general scraps and junk, cannot trip you, or otherwise interfere with your free movement and work.

Follow the manufacturer's specific safety instructions for any tool. Check for the direction of force with all tools. Be sure to check for the direction of kickback that can

occur with some power tools. Circular saws and table saws both kick back strongly. A jammed circular saw will kick itself back, towards the worker, so make sure the lower blade guard drops into place freely. It also helps to stand slightly to one side when working with circular saws. Table saws kick back the material because the tool is too heavy to move. Make sure guards are in place and correctly adjusted and keep your body out of line of possible kickback. Also, make sure no one walks through the kickback path.

Always think before you work and as you're working. Keep safe tool usage foremost in your mind.

FOUNDATIONS

Choosing the type of foundation for any freestanding woodworking shop depends on a number of things, including the site, the size of the shop to be built, your desires and skills and the thickness of your wallet. If you can afford anything you want, the shop layout and tool selection planning sections of this book are probably all you need to read. If, like most of us, you're going to do most or all of the work, then you need more detail on techniques of construction. There are a slew of construction methods that are suitable for shop construction, ranging from the least costly, usually pole building, to standard platform framing.

Pole building works as its own foundation, but, unfortunately, doesn't have a widely accepted method of planting the poles. Most published information is on methods used in hard freeze areas of what might well be classed as the far North. In those sites, pole selection and hole digging and backfilling methods are exceptionally complex, as they are in areas with sandy soils. I recommend avoiding pole building in such areas, except for the simplest sheds, because by the time you get a backhoe in to dig the holes, and then backfill with cement, the cost nears that of pouring a 4" thick concrete pad (unless the ground is exceptionally uneven, at which point even complex pole construction begins to look more reasonable).

For more reasonable areas, where depth of freeze is generally under 36", and the soil compacts well (thus needing nothing but a dirt backfill on a 48" or shallower hole depth for above-ground pole lengths to about 12' maximum), pole construction is cheap and fast. Rent or borrow a tractor with a power takeoff and a 12" or larger auger posthole digger. Pop in your holes and clean the bottoms. Insert poles and plumb — round poles are plumbed on only one side, but square poles are plumbed on all sides. I suggest you plumb the exterior side of round poles, as it speeds getting things under cover. The photos you see here are of a neighbor, Puddin' Updike, drilling the holes for my shop. Puddin' (also known by his real first name, Holmes) was my first landlord in this area a great many years ago. He's a semi-retired farmer who is also a retired quality control person for a local manufacturer. He wouldn't even take gas money for the time he spent doing my work. I'd known for nearly two decades that he was a great person; that was definitive proof. May you have the same good fortune.

Setting the foundation for a pole building may require heavy equipment, depending on your soil. Puddin' had the equipment!

A posthole digger attached to a power takeoff on a tractor makes this work easy.

Up close and personal. If you need to dig a 12"-round hole 2' into the ground, an auger like this is the only way!

SETTING UP FOR THE FLOOR

Brace and backfill. If you're on reasonably level ground and pouring a concrete floor, it's simplest to use two 2×6 base braces on the exterior of the poles as general guides and forms for the floor. Use bolts or lag screws to attach the top 2×6 to the posts (a minimum of $^3/_8$" × 4" lag screws, one per post, plus at least two $3^1/_2$" [16d] nails). Attach the bottom board to the posts with three, 16d nails per post. A $^5/_{16}$" × $3^1/_2$" lag screw, plus two nails is even better. If you are covering the boards with siding, the lag screw heads should be set into a hole to allow the siding to lie flat. Drill holes — counterbores — in a large enough diameter to accept a flat washer under the bolt or screw head. Poles and these lower boards must all be of pressure treated or creosoted wood. My poles are all pressure treated, Wolmanized™ to marine standards.

Use a level on the top edge of the bottom board to set your line and drive the nails first. Come back, drill and bolt or screw the boards in place.

Once the boards are in place, lay in 6" of clean gravel, and cover that with 10 mil polyethylene sheeting, overlapped at least 18". Using care not to penetrate the sheeting (you can use Tyvek sheeting, which is less prone to ripping, but is more costly), lay in reinforcement netting (4' × 4') for the concrete and have the floor poured and smoothed. It is not my object here to explain the dynamics of pouring and smoothing a concrete floor, as that's been done well by others. Unless you've got considerable experience with concrete, I strongly suggest you quit at the purchase stage and have someone else direct the pour and finish the floor. Finish takes special tools and a lot of skill, and is something you can usually get done for a specified price per square foot — settle that in advance!

I've already written that I'm not a lover of concrete floors in shops for several reasons. Their lack of give can make your legs awfully tired when you work a lot of hours on a project. Too, the first time you drop a new $35 or $40 chisel point first onto concrete, you'll understand my other objection. Concrete can be painted, and should be, to prevent it dusting. It may also be covered with sheet or tile vinyl. Neither replaces a good wood floor, but both are better than bare concrete.

POLE CONSTRUCTION FRAMING

Pole construction requires a different type of framing. Instead of vertical studs, you place horizontal nailers on

A framed floor will require piers spaced appropriately throughout the construction.

A look at the side framing, headers are not needed in pole framing if doors and windows are set inside poles.

the exterior of the poles. The nailers can be almost junk wood, as long as they provide a solid surface for nailing — the stock must be nominal, or actual, 2" thick for this. I used nailers of green or almost green, rough sawn Southern yellow pine direct from the sawmill. These are nailed on the outside of the poles, and the siding is nailed to them. The work goes fast — poles are normally placed on 8' centers. You can overlap with boards, using 16'-long boards to form a unit of three posts. It's easy to keep from breaking joints on the same post, too, though the nailers are not really needed as structural members — such methods do tend to stiffen the nailers, which is handy. Or, the posts can be placed on 12' centers, depending on pole thickness, depth of planting and so on — because boards are nailed only at wide intervals. Use a minimum 3$^{1}/_{2}$" nail here, three per post. A dab of waterproof construction adhesive might not go amiss, though I didn't and my shop is now a teenager. Set nailers on 24" vertical centers.

Otherwise, roof framing is the same as for any kind of structure: the poles being topped with 2×6 lumber and the rafters set onto the top edges of that lumber. You may use shed roof styles, too, if the span isn't too great (about a 14' maximum without taking all fancy precautions).

Platform framing is the method of choice for many buildings. Most residences in this country are built this way, and so are many middle-sized outbuildings. Platform framing is relatively easy for one person to carry out (until you reach roof framing, which is never easy for one person, no matter the roof style or size). The method allows great flexibility and is fairly low in cost. A wide variety of foundation types may be used.

Poured concrete floors work well, but are built differently for platform framed structures than for pole buildings. Here, you lay out the building size, and then set forms for the floor. The procedure in laying gravel, sheeting, reinforcement wire and pouring cement is the same, but you set anchor bolts around the perimeter — spaced no more than 8' apart — and tilt your walls onto those bolts, after which you run down a nut over a washer to keep the walls from blowing off in storms. Walls are constructed on the poured floor, and tilted into place, where they are plumbed and braced until joining walls are attached.

Crawl spaces work well with platform framing (my shop has a semi-crawl space, which lets me store some odd things underneath). A footing, set to the depth needed locally to prevent frost heave, as is the footing for the

Headers are needed over doors and windows in standard frame construction.

After framing, a vapor/water barrier wrap makes it feel more finished.

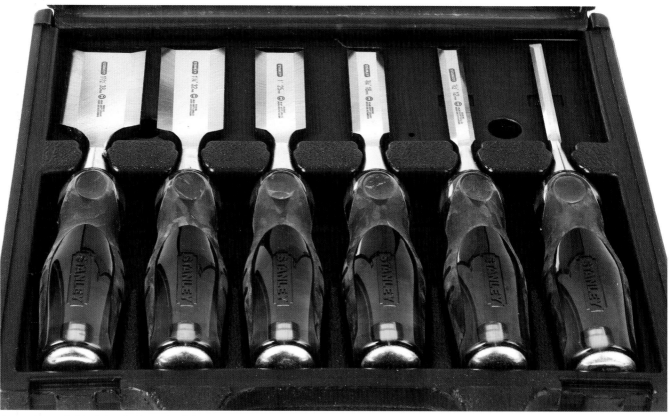

A good set of chisels is a help with all framing.

poured floor, is dug and poured, and then concrete block is laid on the footing. Usually, codes require a minimum two-block height above grade. Insert at least two screened ventilators in the crawl space walls so that moisture doesn't build too high and cause rot.

Forget full basements, but give some thought to piers. Piers are placed on footings, again at the proper depth for your weather, and can be erected in a little less time than crawl space foundations. My central piers are built this way and serve as support for the center beam. Layout tends to be slightly more complex for a whole building, because you need a row up each outside edge of the structure, and a central row as well. Once laid out, the holes are more quickly dug than are footing trenches, and laying four blocks per pier is faster than laying a two-block high foundation around the full perimeter. In some areas, you may also elect to use posts as piers, with a pre-cast concrete collar, and soil cement as a backfill.

118

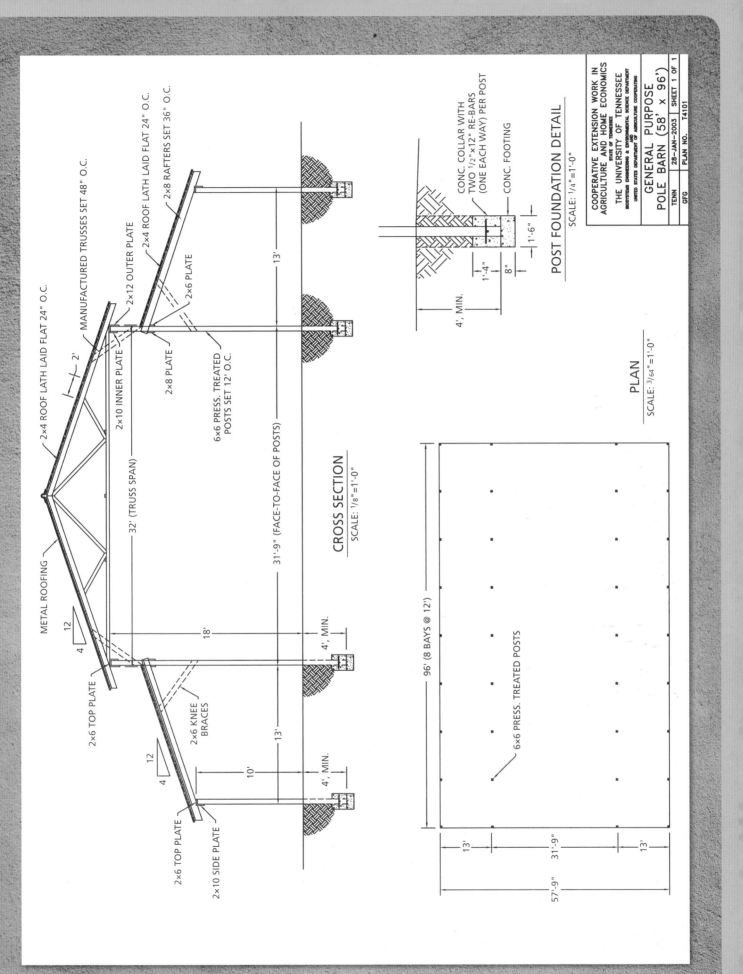

CROSS SECTION
SCALE: 1/8"=1'-0"

2×4 ROOF LATH LAID FLAT 24" O.C.

MANUFACTURED TRUSSES SET 48" O.C.

2×4 ROOF LATH LAID FLAT 24" O.C.

2×8 RAFTERS SET 36" O.C.

2×12 OUTER PLATE

2×6 PLATE

2×10 INNER PLATE

2×8 PLATE

6×6 PRESS. TREATED POSTS SET 12' O.C.

METAL ROOFING

2'

32' (TRUSS SPAN)

31'-9" (FACE-TO-FACE OF POSTS)

13'

13'

12 / 4

18'

4', MIN.

2×6 TOP PLATE

2×6 KNEE BRACES

2×6 TOP PLATE

2×10 SIDE PLATE

12 / 4

10'

4', MIN.

13'

4', MIN.

POST FOUNDATION DETAIL
SCALE: 1/4"=1'-0"

CONC. COLLAR WITH TWO 1/2"×12" RE-BARS (ONE EACH WAY) PER POST

CONC. FOOTING

4', MIN.

1'-4"

8"

1'-6"

PLAN
SCALE: 3/64"=1'-0"

6×6 PRESS. TREATED POSTS

96' (8 BAYS @ 12')

13'

31'-9"

13'

57'-9"

COOPERATIVE EXTENSION WORK IN AGRICULTURE AND HOME ECONOMICS

STATE OF TENNESSEE

THE UNIVERSITY OF TENNESSEE

BIOSYSTEMS ENGINEERING & ENVIRONMENTAL SCIENCE DEPARTMENT
AND
UNITED STATES DEPARTMENT OF AGRICULTURE COOPERATING

GENERAL PURPOSE POLE BARN (58' x 96')

| TENN | 28-JAN-2003 | SHEET 1 OF 1 |
| GFG | PLAN NO. | T4101 |

My finished pole barn shop looks like it's been part of the landscape for years.

This description covers the construction of a platform-framed building, 24' × 40', on a crawl space foundation, with some notes to cover other situations. The idea is to keep things as low cost as possible, so we're looking at several options for roofing, and siding, several of which are more economical in installation than in actual cost — some forms of metal roof, for example, are almost as costly as shingles, but go on so quickly they save labor time. If you're doing your own labor, the savings are small to nil, but, as sometimes happens, if you can find a person who has overbought some form of roofing material, whether metal or asphalt/fiberglass shingle, you save lots of money. Don't check only dealers for this kind of savings. Talk to local builders and see who might have misjudged a job, or lost a job for whatever reason in some stage after buying materials. You can sometimes save a lot of money this way, as you can checking window factories and distributors for factory seconds.

SITE SELECTION AND BUILDING LAYOUT

You want to build a shop. You've got some space in your yard. Sticking the shop in that space makes sense, so you locate a corner and go.

If you do it that way, I hope you're a lucky type, because there are a number of considerations that need a bit of earlier thought. First, possibly foremost, is the location of the new structure in relation to existing structures, walkways, power lines, septic fields and tanks, sewage lines, water

lines, wells, driveways, trees, bushes, flowers, herb and vegetable garden spaces, springs, power company access lines and the general lie of the ground. You'd also best pay some attention to local codes relating to setbacks. Some are 10' and some are 15'. Always and forever check local codes before starting any structure larger than a tool shed.

On my property — almost two acres that seems to provide plenty of space behind the house and excluding a storage barn/shed already in place on one edge — there are severe limits. We've got fruit trees spaced along one area and those must be allowed to retain access to the sun. We've got young shade trees in other areas, a patio in another and a deck off the back of the house. We also have a septic field that takes almost one entire side of the lot near the house. The back corner of the lot is too steep, and faces forward onto a spring that flows year round in an area that my wife is has turned into a large rock garden.

Then the power pole was on the opposite corner of the lot from where I wanted to place the shop, so I had to think of costs of adding poles — the local power company doesn't like to use consumer-installed poles, and I need a separate service to the shop, as most of you will if you elect to go with a large enough shop to require a freestanding building. See Chapter Nine on electrical service for details of those needs.

My first thought was to run a long line off the house service entrance panel and use a 60-amp subpanel at the shop. My second, and much better, thought was to call the

Not all shops use framing. This is the side of Bobby's new quonset hut style shop.

My final site was not level, which was a factor that saved a great deal of money when it comes time to pour a foundation or floor — especially a floor, because forming up and filling to pour a concrete floor is expensive. That's the reason I went with poles. My lot drops off about forty inches from the left front corner of the shop to the left rear corner.

There is sufficient space for a building of at least 32' × 52', and my planned structure was 24' × 40', though I would have preferred 48' if finances had permitted. I backed off the second story office I had originally planned. The shop also ended up 25' wide because I missed a measurement.

Site your shop with reference to all the variables above and any others that fit your locale and situation.

Determine where one corner of the building will lie and drive a peg at that spot. Now, make up some batter boards. These are eight pieces of 1×4 wood, each nailed to 2×4s: The first batter board is notched in the center to accept a cord, and the 2×4s have points cut on their ends. Your 2×4 length needs vary depending on the site. Level sites require 2×4s only 18" or so long. You may run into a need for some as long as 6' in hilly terrain. The usual type of batter board uses three, 2×4s and two boards, nailed with the boards near the tops of the 2×4s. Each batter board is saw kerfed (slotted) when the spot for the mason's cord is determined. Drive the first batter board assembly in place about 4' behind and outside the peg marking one corner, but roughly aligned so the cord notch lets you carry mason's cord directly over the peg and on to the next corner. Drive a second set of batter boards about 4' past the spot for the next corner, parallel to and facing the first set, if you're using the two piece units.

When all four corners are in place, and batter boards are set level, run the mason's cord, and settle it around until you've got square corners. At some point, there may be a need to actually move a batter board set-up to allow for squaring all four corners. There are two ways to make sure your corners are square: The 3-4-5 (or 9' × 12' × 15') triangle method to determine square, or measure the diagonals and make sure they are exactly equal. I suggest you use both methods, one as a check on the other. Unless you erect moderate size structures often, you'll find your waste allowance is much smaller if you get finicky over measurements. It takes only a simple goof to waste materials and cost good money, plus time wasted making corrections.

Once the cords are set, kerf the batter boards that aren't already notched, and set the cords in, pulling them tight.

power company to check the cost of a buried line to the shop location, some 185 feet from the pole. This is something that varies immensely from area to area, but I was astonished at how low the cost really was. It was only a few days after the shop was up and wired that a power company employee with a huge Ditch Witch was bumping his way along, with the digger also pushing cable into the slit trench he was digging.

For my shop, plumbing is a port-a-potty and a garden hose for any water needs, but some of you may wish to go further. I may someday go as far as running a frost-free standing tap to within about ten feet of the new building. Clean-up is simpler with at least some access to water. I'd like to put in hot and cold and drains, but the price goes up accordingly, so that's out of the question.

All this and more needs to be taken into consideration.

Using a very light plumb bob, drop your measurement to the ground, centering it on a stake with a nail in it.

There are some major variations in construction methods from this point on: For pole construction, drive a small (1" × 1") stake dead in the center of each pole location; for poured concrete floors, and crawl spaces, the excavation line is about a foot outside the line formed by the mason's cord. For pier foundations, you work a half-and-half set up, with exterior lines of pier footings set 1' to the outside of the line, plus about double whatever extra width you need to match your blocks. With standard 8" blocks, which are 16" (nominally) long, you need a 32"-wide footing. If you can locate them readily, go with 6" blocks, and you get a 2'-wide footer (footings are always at least twice as wide as the wall or other object being placed on them). For a 32" wide footing, go 24" outside the mason's cord. For a 24" footing, go 16". These are minimal settings, as a standard crawl space wall footing is 16" wide (the block that rests on that footing is nominally 8" wide).

Once the foundation is in, floor framing starts.

GATHERING MATERIALS

Laying up materials to build a shop, whether the construction means remodeling a basement or garage or other area, or the construction of a separate building, is an art form that can be used to save many thousands of dollars. It's a craft, for the practice of the way of thinking, plus the practice of attending auctions, sales and the side rooms of manufacturers of housing products. This tends to sharpen the skills needed to save money anywhere.

In my planning for shop construction, I've been able to save a great deal of money simply by listening to a friend or two — and allowing one of my good friends to go ahead and buy things for me when I'm not around.

Starting with the need to trust one's friends, that latter procedure also means keeping friends up-to-date on needs. I'd have been in moderately rough shape if Bobby Weaver, while attending an auction, had bought me enough fluorescent fixtures to light my shop a week after someone else had done the same. I might have lost very little, because the price I paid for those fixtures was ridiculously low, but

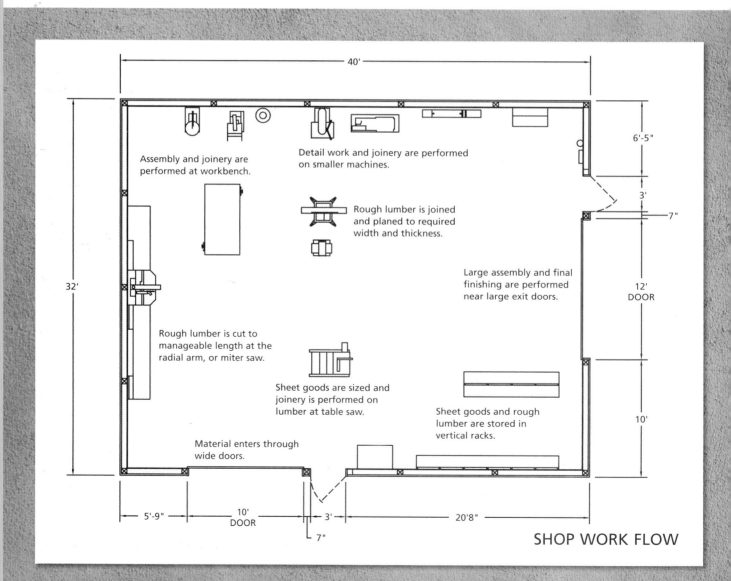

Assembly and joinery are performed at workbench.

Detail work and joinery are performed on smaller machines.

Rough lumber is joined and planed to required width and thickness.

Large assembly and final finishing are performed near large exit doors.

Rough lumber is cut to manageable length at the radial arm, or miter saw.

Sheet goods are sized and joinery is performed on lumber at table saw.

Sheet goods and rough lumber are stored in vertical racks.

Material enters through wide doors.

40'

6'-5"

3'

7"

12' DOOR

32'

10'

5'-9"

10' DOOR

3'

7"

20'8"

SHOP WORK FLOW

The majority of stand-alone shop construction is done with standard framing.

For good strength and reduced material costs, a site-built box beam (shown partially assembled) works very well.

the idea holds true. I'm not in the business of selling used lighting fixtures, for one thing, and the same thing might have applied to other items from flue block to cement block to insulating sheathing, roofing and on.

Bobby found the light fixtures at a school surplus/used equipment auction, where he also bought a lot of the shop benches and laboratory benches, used in his first shop. The latter shows a need for imagination. The drawers in the floor cabinets from school labs were in good shape, but the doors weren't. Bobby didn't want the doors for most, so faced no problem there. He simply removed the doors that didn't work, installed the cabinets along the walls, and topped them with fresh, $3/4$", A-C sanded plywood.

He used several workbenches, removed after decades of pounding, from high school workshops. Some reconditioning of the tops, and the vises, was needed, and some vises were replacements, ones he'd picked up over the years at various auctions and yard sales. None were even close to new, but all operate and operate well.

Another point: Don't get fixated on having all new equipment. Bobby had three table saws, all Craftsman models ranging back to 1929 in patent, and all were bought used. One has a Delta Unisaw Jetlock fence (bought very cheaply from an owner who replaced the fence with an aftermarket type), a definite improvement, and the others had all been retuned by Bobby for his uses.

An accurate miter saw at the job site makes the framing move smoothly and efficiently.

Not all work can be done on a convenient work surface. Cordless tools simplifiy the process. Watch your step, though!

I've got two interior doors, sitting and waiting for use, for which almost no money changed hands. Those were the results of a change in plans for an industrial building, so are good interior fire resistant oak-faced doors that retail for way over $100 each.

Cheap, but good windows may present some problems, but all areas now have re-installers — companies that replace old windows. Some do a neat job of removing old windows, and are willing to part with those for very little money. Some let you have them for the hauling. The same may hold true for doors.

As far as doors in the design go, you want the largest doors possible, without losing too much wall space. If you plan to build a boat — and I can remember a truly huge number of boat builders from my youth, many of whom had major problems with getting the thing into the water after construction, because parts of the project were too large to leave the shop without dismantling walls — or a similar project, see about doing the large assembly of the project outdoors. That saves shop space, and allows you to build a project of phenomenal size without increases in shop size.

Check the "Items for Sale" columns in any local newspapers. There are usually several such lists, some of which even cover contractors' leftovers. Craigslist.org may also help.

Drive around and check new home construction. Talk to supervisors on job sites and see if they're holding on to any extras that the supplier won't accept as returns — most contractors today work out a return policy with suppliers, and most are returned, but there are often exceptions, and it's possible to save a considerable amount of money on insulating sheathing board, shingles and similar products.

Check yard sales. Some are worth fooling with, most aren't, but considering some of the things I've sold out of my front yard, and bought out of others, it's worthwhile to make a quick stop at the larger sales. Don't figure everything is right up front and on show. Ask. Often, especially in country areas, there's an outbuilding crammed with goodies that are too heavy (like floor joists, doors or windows) to tote out to the yard every time a sale is held. Too, remember that neither flea market nor yard sale prices are set in stone. If you find an item late in the day, you can almost bet on getting a break from any tagged price. The reason is simple. Everything that doesn't sell has to be returned to storage.

Check for local manufacturers of building products. Here, we have a large window and door manufacturer barely 45 miles away. They often have over-runs and returns of special orders, and non-pick-ups of special orders and similar stock. And the prices are substantially reduced over similar quality products at a dealer. We also have a huge number of small sawmills producing all kinds of rough lumber from poplar and yellow pine. The number of mills helps keep prices down, and makes for fast delivery, even though most don't cater to individual buyers.

Look around for school sales, and any municipal building sales: As much as I hate to say it, a great deal of tax money is lost in early recycling of materials such as lights, tools and similar items. School sales may be the most prolific and popular for tools, shop and lab items. Keep in mind that items from one area, such as lab countertops and cabinets, work well in other areas — benchtops, cabinets and such in the wood shop.

For those using rough, green lumber from local sawmills, I suggest buying from a mill that bands its stock, after which you cover the top of the lumber with a tarp or old metal roofing, and allow it to sit for a minimum of three months (six months to a year is preferable). The lumber won't be truly dry, but is more amenable to suggestion in the form of cutting and nailing than when truly green. Cutting and nailing green, yellow pine is a working education in itself.

Trimming nailer ends at the back of the shop.

Consider constructing some items (some only) of used lumber. I had planned to purchase used telephone poles to build my pole building shop. The price is about 10% of the price of new. Again, you have to ask around to find out who has, or can have, such materials. Call the phone company's maintenance division as a start. Most pole work around here is done on contract and the contractor is supposed to get rid of the poles. Other areas may work it in a slightly different way.

Do not buy used lumber in any other form. It simply isn't worth the hassle of pulling nails before cutting. And if you're checking to see if there are nails while you're cutting, be sure you're going to ruin a number of saw blades. If you can locate an old barn, with posts, joists and other materials of chestnut, forget the above. I gave some thought to tearing down two log tobacco barns this past winter. I was told they were built with chestnut logs and that appears to be true. The rest is junk, but easily hauled to the dump. The owners want the area cleared. Winter is the best time to work on this kind of thing, as both insects and snakes are dormant.

Sit back and think. Think of what you need. Think of who carries the things you need. Think of who uses the products you need. Think of who used the items you need. Think of all the angles of buying cheaply and then start looking. The amount of money you can save ranges from little to a lot, depending no how hard you think and how hard you look.

Too, it's fun. You'll meet people you'd otherwise not meet. From them, you may get leads to other places and ways to save on constructing a freestanding shop or remodeling a basement or garage shop.

CHAPTER EIGHT

Framing and Sheathing the Freestanding Shop

Framing and covering a shop building gets you to the point where you itch to begin work on projects of smaller size. This chapter gets you to the point of moving in and setting up your tools.

Looking west across my shop "floor" with the joists down and the briding nailed in place.

FRAMING FLOORS

Floor framing is a simple matter for shop structures, because most are done without stairwells, interior partition plans and similar fancy stuff. Depending on the width of the shop, you need joists of a particular size, as indicated by the charts on the following pages. In most cases, 2×10 joists suffice, with maximum spans for each on 24" centers (from the center of one member [in this case, a joist] to the center of another) of about 10' and 14'. If you're using Southern yellow pine, those figures can be stretched a bit, but they should be fudged in the short direction when you use white pine.

Sills are the base for the entire floor frame and come in several different types, all of 2" dimensional lumber. A flat 2×6 or 2×8 sill board, bolted to the foundation, is used for crawl space walls and the sill in a concrete floored place is nothing more

Strategically placed piers support the floor span.

TABLE 11
APA Rated Sturd-I-Floor[a]

Span Rating (Maximum Joist Spacing) (in.)	Panel Thickness[c] (in.)	Fastening: Glue-Nailed[b]			Fastening: Nailed-Only		
		Nail Size and Type[e]	Maximum Spacing (in.)[d]		Nail Size and Type[e]	Maximum Spacing (in.)[d]	
			Supported Panel Edges[f]	Intermediate Supports		Supported Panel Edges[f]	Intermediate Supports
16	19/32, 5/8	6d ring- or screw-shank[g]	12	12	6d ring- or screw-shank	6	12
20[h]	19/32, 5/8	6d ring- or screw-shank[g]	12	12	6d ring- or screw-shank	6	12
24	23/32, 3/4	6d ring- or screw-shank[g]	12	12	6d ring- or screw-shank	6	12
	7/8	8d ring- or screw-shank[g]	6	12	8d ring- or screw-shank	6	12
32	7/8	8d ring- or screw-shank[g]	6	12	8d ring- or screw-shank	6	12
48	1-3/32, 1-1/8	8d ring- or screw-shank[i]	6	[i]	8d ring- or screw-shank[i]	6	[j]

(a) Special conditions may impose heavy traffic and concentrated loads that require construction in excess of the minimums shown. See page 40 for heavy-duty floor recommendations.
(b) Use only adhesives conforming to APA Specification AFG-01 or ASTM D3498, applied in accordance with the adhesive manufacturer's recommendations. If OSB panels with sealed surfaces and edges are to be used, use only solvent-based glues; check with panel manufacturer.
(c) Panels in a given thickness may be manufactured in more than one Span Rating. Panels with a Span Rating greater than the actual joist spacing may be substituted for panels of the same thickness with a Span Rating matching the actual joist spacing. For example, 19/32-inch-thick Sturd-I-Floor 20 oc may be substituted for 19/32-inch-thick Sturd-I-Floor 16 oc over joists at 16 inches on center.
(d) Increased nailed-only 6/12 or closer schedules may be required where floor is engineered as a diaphragm.
(e) See Table 5 for nail dimensions.
(f) Supported panel joints shall occur approximately along the centerline of framing with a minimum bearing of 1/2 inch. Fasten panels 3/8 inch from panel edges.
(g) 8d common nails may be substituted if ring- or screw-shank nails are not available.
(h) Maximum joist spacing for 20 oc Span Rating is 19.2 inches.
(i) 10d common nails may be substituted with 1-1/8-inch panels if supports are well seasoned.
(j) Space nails maximum 6 inches for 48-inch spans and 12 inches for 32-inch spans.

Table 12
Recommended Uniform Floor Live Loads for APA RATED STURD-I-FLOOR and APA RATED SHEATHING with Strength Axis Perpendicular to Supports[a]

Sturd-I-Floor Span Rating	Sheathing Span Rating	Minimum Panel Thickness (in.)	Maximum Span (in.)	Allowable Live Loads (psf)[b] Joist Spacing (in.)						
				12	16	19.2	24	32	40	48
16 oc	24/16, 32/16	7/16[c]	16	185	100					
20 oc[e]	40/20	19/32, 5/8	19.2	270	150	100				
24 oc	48/24	23/32, 3/4	24	430	240	160	100			
32 oc	60/32[d]	7/8	32		430	295	185	100		
48 oc	1-3/32, 1-1/8		48			460	290	160	100	55

(a) Two-span, dry, normal load duration assumed.
(b) 10 psf dead load assumed. Live load deflection limit is l/360.
(c) 19/32 inch is minimum thickness of Rated Sturd-I-Floor.
(d) Check with supplier for availability.
(e) While Span Rating is shown as 20 oc, the actual joint spacing is 19.2 inches.

APA Panel Subflooring (APA RATED SHEATHING)[a][b]				Maximum Nail Spacing (in.)	
Panel Span Rating	Panel Thickness (in.)	Maximum Span (in.)	Nail Size & Type[e][g]	Supported Panel Edges[h]	Intermediate Supports
24/16	7/16	16	6d common	6	12
32/16	15/32, 1/2	16	8d common[c]	6	12
40/20	19/32, 5/8	19.2[d]	8d common	6	12
48/24	23/32, 3/4	24	8d common	6	12
60/32[f]	7/8	32	8d common	6	12

(a) For subfloor recommendations under ceramic tile, refer to Table 15. For subfloor recommendations under gypsum concrete, contact manufacturer of floor topping.
(b) APA Rated Sturd-I-Floor may be substituted when the Span Rating is equal to or greater than tabulated maximum span.
(c) 6d common nail permitted if panel is 1/2 inch or thinner.
(d) Span may be 24 inches if a minimum 1-1/2 inches of lightweight concrete is applied over panels.
(e) Other code-approved fasteners may be used.
(f) Check with supplier for availability.
(g) See Table 5 for nail dimensions.
(h) Supported panel joints shall occur approximately along the centerline of framing with a minimum bearing of 1/2 inch. Fasteners shall be located 3/8 inch from panel edges.

than the sole plate of the stud wall unit, again bolted to the foundation — the poured concrete floor — at 4', 6' or 8' intervals (check local codes both for intervals and anchor bolt sizes and types). Sills on pier foundations are simply the outsides of boards set horizontally at right angles to the floor joists. There can be, as size requires, one, two or three sill boards to make up the unit, but most are just doubled when piers are 8' on one center, and a center beam of three boards is used to double the span using a center row of piers (these may be 12' on center).

Joists are either set upon, or (in pier or platform post construction) hung from, the sills. Sills need to be pro-

tected from termites, so are made of pressure-treated wood, though they'll be protected from weather and won't contact the ground. A .40 pounds-per-cubic-foot protection is enough. A termite shield is also helpful. Termite shields are of metal, usually aluminum since that's a place-once-and-forget material, formed at least 3" wider than the sill, with 1 1/2" of the outside edge (and the 1 1/2" inside edge also if it is on a pier or crawl space) turned about 10° downward. This is what I used on my center piers. Termites can't tunnel over this. Any that somehow manage to reach the sill are defeated by the PT lumber. Frame the floor using a three-member center beam, if needed (spans

Engineered I-joists are set in place resting on sills attached to the top of the foundations wall. COURTESY OF APA

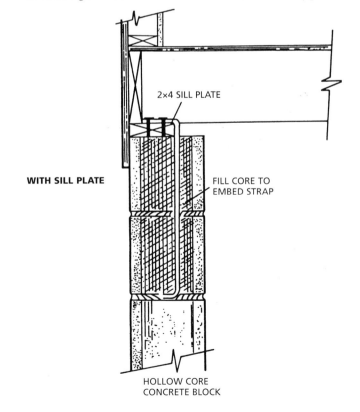

WITH SILL PLATE

2×4 SILL PLATE

FILL CORE TO EMBED STRAP

HOLLOW CORE CONCRETE BLOCK

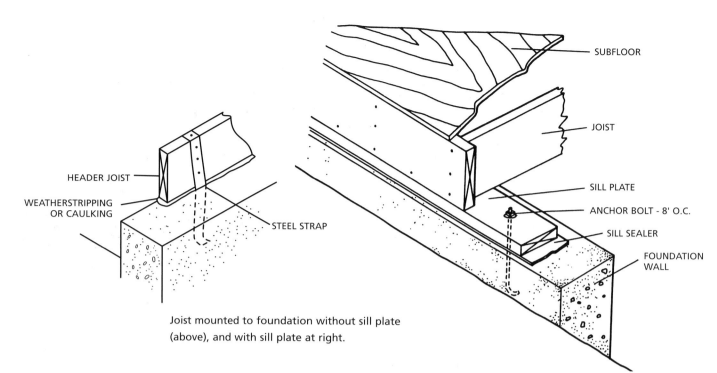

SUBFLOOR

JOIST

HEADER JOIST

WEATHERSTRIPPING
OR CAULKING

STEEL STRAP

SILL PLATE

ANCHOR BOLT - 8' O.C.

SILL SEALER

FOUNDATION
WALL

Joist mounted to foundation without sill plate
(above), and with sill plate at right.

Beam is leveled at pier with cedar shim stock. Note aluminum
termite shield, an absolute essential in this area.

Joist hangers are stronger than toenailing.

over 14' require a center beam). Set the sills and center beam and use joist hangers.

To place joists, start from the center of both the beam and the outside sill and measure out the OC (on center) distances. Check the width of actual joists — nominal 2" lumberyard materials will be a standard 1½" thick, but sawmill lumber may vary from 2" to 2½" thick. Use half that distance to mark one edge of each joist position, and use a square to drop the line down the face of both beams and joists.

Use joist hangers, or toe nail joists in place at 16" or 24" intervals. Bobby Weaver did his shop on 16" centers using rough-cut yellow pine lumber (full size, unplaned), with 2×8 joists for a 24'-wide (actual span is half that minus the width of outer foundation walls and half that of the center piers in Bobby's crawl space foundation, or about 11'). In most cases, and certainly with more standard strength and size lumber, go with 2×10s on that span. Use 16d or 20d nails, three per joint. A dab of construction adhesive is a good thing, too, but don't make mistakes: Once this stuff sets up, it doesn't let go.

Bobby used the smartest method I've seen of reducing flooring costs and getting a sturdy, two-layer floor similar

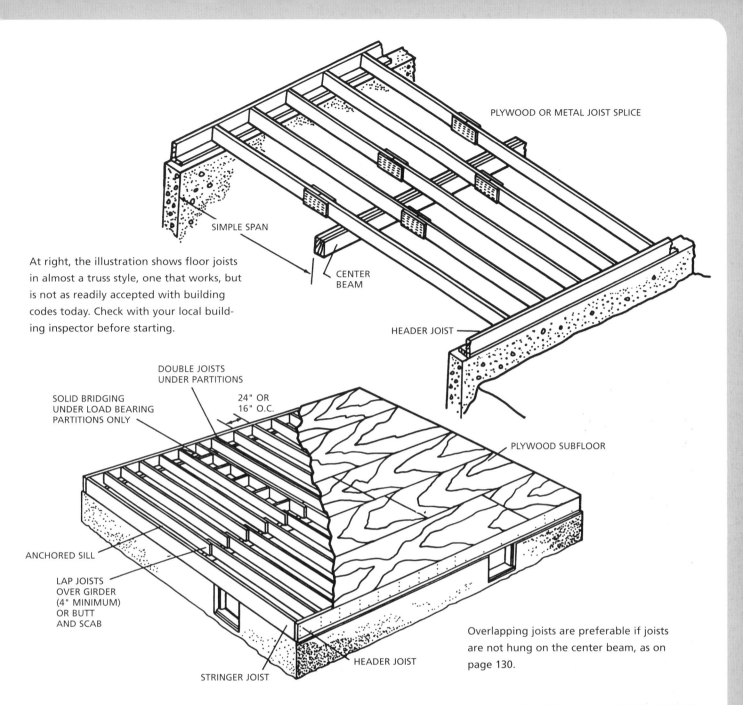

PLYWOOD OR METAL JOIST SPLICE

SIMPLE SPAN

At right, the illustration shows floor joists in almost a truss style, one that works, but is not as readily accepted with building codes today. Check with your local building inspector before starting.

CENTER BEAM

HEADER JOIST

DOUBLE JOISTS UNDER PARTITIONS

SOLID BRIDGING UNDER LOAD BEARING PARTITIONS ONLY

24" OR 16" O.C.

PLYWOOD SUBFLOOR

ANCHORED SILL

LAP JOISTS OVER GIRDER (4" MINIMUM) OR BUTT AND SCAB

Overlapping joists are preferable if joists are not hung on the center beam, as on page 130.

HEADER JOIST

STRINGER JOIST

to those used in wood floored residences. He used rough-cut, 1" sawmill yellow pine for a subfloor — placed at a 45° angle to the joists and nailed with $2^3/4$" (8d) nails. This is not unusual, though plywood has become the subfloor of choice in residences. Use a dab or two of construction cement on each joist as the subfloor passes over. I did my shop the same way, two or three years later, using rough poplar for subfloor and a present from my wife, Frances, for the floor: $3/4$" tongue and groove sanded plywood. Frances and I nailed the entire mess with pneumatic nailers. Bobby came back and placed a final floor of $5/8$", tongue-and-groove, sand-

The floor sheeting is nailed in place. COURTESY OF APA

ed plywood, using 2¹/₄" (6d) nails, 6" apart on the edges and 8" apart on inner nailing lines. This was then coated with four layers of polyurethane (you may not want to go this far, but Bobby had gotten his poly at an incredibly low price at an auction). The resulting floor was sturdy, squeak free, and easy to clean and maintain. It was also as easy as possible on the legs and feet. I've built many projects in Bobby's shop, and enjoy the working conditions, except for the slight crowding that is a product of two guys who are basically lone workers spreading out on large projects in one shop, no matter how large or well-equipped. Bobby's shop was well-equipped, as you'll already have gathered. His new shop, built on the foundation, and floor, of the old shop are gaining ground on the old shop for number of tools. Once the floor is in place, the remaining framing is done on the subfloor in standard construction — frame out the walls and tilt them into place. A helper is necessary.

Standard 24" on center (OC) framing is best for walls in shops. You may, if you wish, use the slightly more sturdy 16" OC spacing, but for all practical purposes, the 24" OC is a good standard. Again, check local codes. The wider distance is almost universally accepted now, but a check is wise.

Make note of any details of framing for windows and doors in the drawings. These details are easily taken care of in planning stages, and in framing the units on the floor. Careful layout and cutting is essential to easy final assembly. Door and window rough openings are made to within about ¹/₂" to 1" the actual size of the door frame to be set into the opening. For headers, use 2×6s (span to about 4': For larger spans, use 2×8s), doubled, with ¹/₂" plywood separators to get it out to size with the rest of the framing. If you're using rough-cut lumber for framing, change the spacer thickness as needed. You need separators only at about 1¹/₂" around the perimeters of the headers. Window

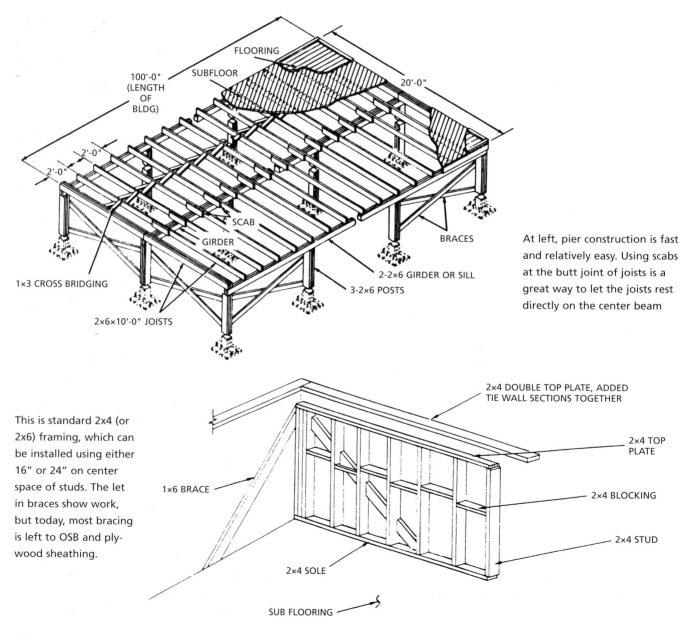

At left, pier construction is fast and relatively easy. Using scabs at the butt joint of joists is a great way to let the joists rest directly on the center beam

This is standard 2x4 (or 2x6) framing, which can be installed using either 16" or 24" on center space of studs. The let in braces show work, but today, most bracing is left to OSB and plywood sheathing.

Post and beam framing is open and easy to erect, but posts are hard to plumb when you're working alone.

Bracing is a major benefit (and need) in holding the posts plumb.

A large square is a great help in plumbing and squaring a frame for a large window or door. COURTESY OF WOODWORKER'S SUPPLY

sills are placed and supported with cripple studs (cripple studs are short studs, cut to fit a particular need such as this) at ends and center. Walls are framed with a doubled top plate that is left an appropriate distance from each end, where an added piece ties the adjoining wall in tightly.

Tilt the completed, braced wall into place and secure with braces. You need helpers here, unless the wall is exceptionally light and short. I've done (and observed) large walls with one person doing all the work. It is no fun and can be dangerous. The wall is either nailed to the

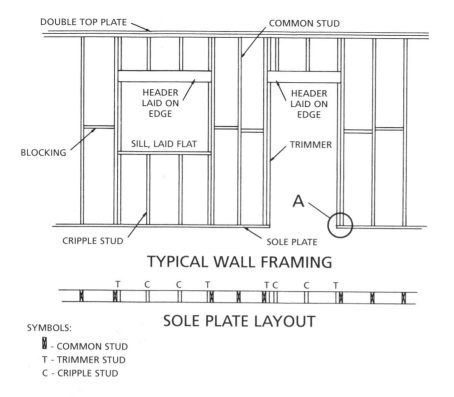

DOUBLE TOP PLATE COMMON STUD

HEADER LAID ON EDGE HEADER LAID ON EDGE

SILL, LAID FLAT TRIMMER

BLOCKING

A

CRIPPLE STUD SOLE PLATE

TYPICAL WALL FRAMING

T   C   C   T   T   C   C   T

SOLE PLATE LAYOUT

SYMBOLS:

⊠ - COMMON STUD

T - TRIMMER STUD

C - CRIPPLE STUD

Typical framing in a stud wall that has both a window and a door. The headers are made of 2x stock, sized to fit the space, with a ½", or thicker, plywood spacer between the two 2x boards.

Careful plumb and level work speeds the actual window installation (above). Caulking prevents later wind and water leaks with the attendant problems (above right). The window slips right into the properly plumbed and caulked opening (right). COURTESY OF SIMONTON WINDOWS

subfloor or bolted to the anchor bolts in the concrete floor, through the holes in the sole plate. The wall must be accurately plumbed before being finally fastened down tightly. It must be well braced before you go on to framing and placing adjoining walls. Bracing is done with 2×4 material to the ground or to the foundation wall, depending on site needs.

With the framed walls in place, you frame the roof. In most manuals, you'll find wall sheathing covered at this point. That's fine unless you live in an area where it rains with some frequency. It's best to tie in the roof system (which also strengthens the overall structure) and get it covered before sheathing the place. I live in such a place.

ROOF FRAMING

The easiest, most sensible way to frame a roof is to use trusses. Period. I don't care whether you're framing a cement block structure, a platform-framed building or a pole structure. You save time and energy by using trusses, though you do lose some storage space in the rafter area, and the

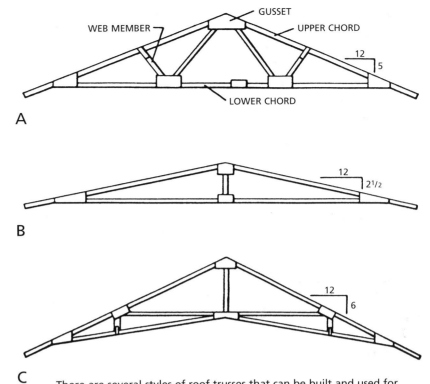

There are several styles of roof trusses that can be built and used for shops. Usually, it's cheaper and more efficient to order them to the size you need, but it is possible to build your own, using preformed metal connectors or plywood gussets cut to fit as needed.

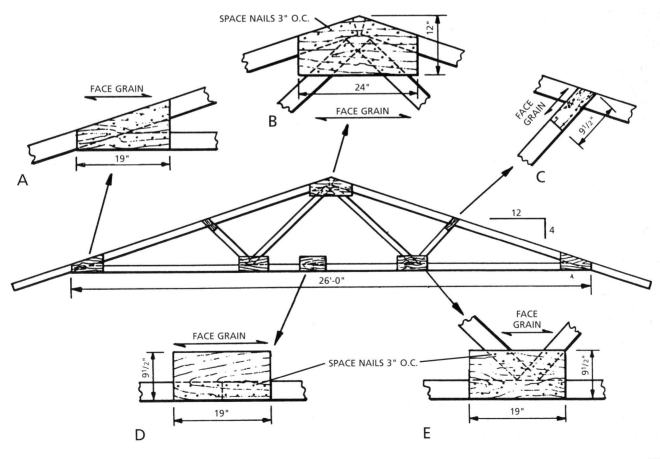

Manufactured trusses on a manufactured beam are great for open spaces in a shop, leaving no posts to bump into when swinging long boards or sheets of plywood. CREDIT APA

cost is about double that of stick-built rafters and ceiling joists. It is faster, cleaner and usually stronger to go with trusses, and unless you've put up an immense building, the cost isn't that rough. It doesn't matter what kind of roof you're going to install, for the trusses are, like rafters, adaptable to most all you're apt to use. There's another advantage to using trusses, too. The entire span distance is free span. Otherwise known as wide open, free span means you're going to have 24' of open width for 24' of span (minus the distances of the framing for walls, and wallboard).

If you're using a short run shed roof, as you see in our pole building example, then forget trusses. That span is only about a dozen feet, and is done with 2×6s. Otherwise, rafters are too much work.

Trusses require at least two people on site. A crane is a help with larger spans, but for trusses spanning up to 28', three people to help are usually enough — if they're strong and willing to work.

All roofing work demands great care. You're off the ground, as is at least one of your helpers, so you must

Cordless saws truly ease nailer trimming on roof rafters. There are no cords to trip on in a job that can be dangerous in its own right. Many people now wear safety harnesses in such work. CREDIT APA

My center beam, being made. Large, sturdy picnic tables make wonderful emergency workbenches.

The center beam is up and the ceiling joists are being placed.

Roofing nailers like this one save even more time than do framing nailers, holding about 250 nails per load. COURTESY OF CRAFTSMAN

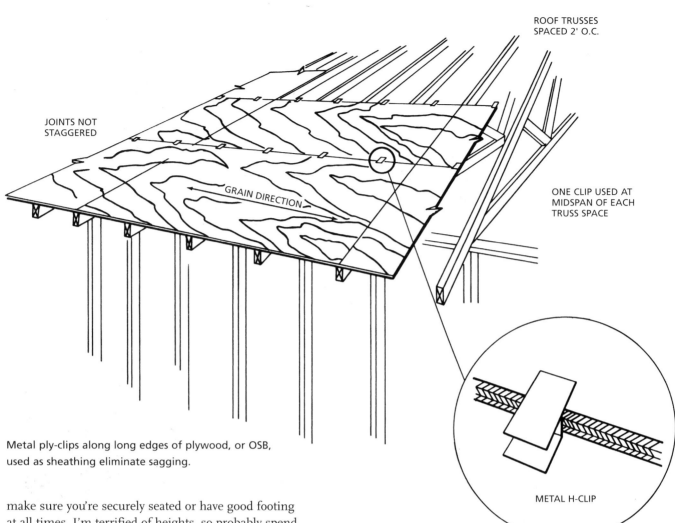

JOINTS NOT STAGGERED

GRAIN DIRECTION

ROOF TRUSSES
SPACED 2' O.C.

ONE CLIP USED AT
MIDSPAN OF EACH
TRUSS SPACE

METAL H-CLIP

Metal ply-clips along long edges of plywood, or OSB, used as sheathing eliminate sagging.

make sure you're securely seated or have good footing at all times. I'm terrified of heights, so probably spend more time clinging than is really needed, but so far it has worked. Most locals don't use safety gear, but it is available and needs to be used.

Trusses are spaced 24" OC and are nailed, with or without nailing anchors, into the top plate. Toe nail with 16d nails if no anchors are used. Otherwise, use the correct nails for the type of anchors used. Other forms of work can be a hassle, as we can attest. I built box beams for my shop (three, 16'-long beams), and it took three strong people to hoist them into place on the center poles.

ROOFING

Roofing is a far more complex subject than this treatment will consider. We're looking at only two methods, and doing those quickly.

Roof sheathing comes first, and is done (on 24" OC material) with $7/16$" oriented strand board, waferboard or CDX plywood if you're placing shingles. Use recommended nailing patterns, usually with 6d nails at 6" intervals on the outside edges of the sheets and at 8" intervals up the inside nailing lines of the sheets. Do not ever break two butting sheets of plywood on the same joist. To achieve this, simply start the first row with a full sheet of plywood, and the second with a half sheet, and on up the roof (or vice versa).

If you're placing metal roofing, place nailers at 24" intervals, making those nailers cross the rafters at right angles. Do not break nailers on the same joist if they're directly in line on the roof. That is, break on a joist, then no break, then a break is fine, but do not break, and break again. The nails used here vary in length depending on the thickness of the nailers. My shop roof used rough 1×4 stock, for which a $3^{1}/4$" (12d) nail is fine. Most work of this type is done with 1" stock that takes a 3" (10d) nail.

For shingled roofs, you first measure the roof to see how much material you need. Shingles are sold in bundles, usually three bundles to the square, which is a unit that gives you 100 square feet of exposed shingle roofing. Prices vary depending on durability, style, color and other factors. Look for a moderately priced 25-year fiberglass/asphalt shingle in a simple pattern. In most areas of the United States, a light color to reflect heat away during summer months makes good sense. In the north, and in Canada, a darker color absorbs heat during the longer cold months. You also need tar paper underlayment.

The manufacturers call this stuff asphalt felt saturated underlayment, which is OK by me. It's tar paper. Add

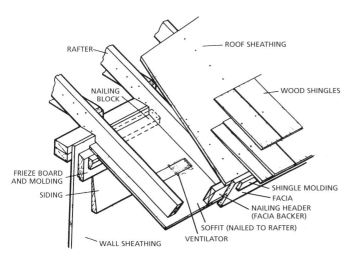

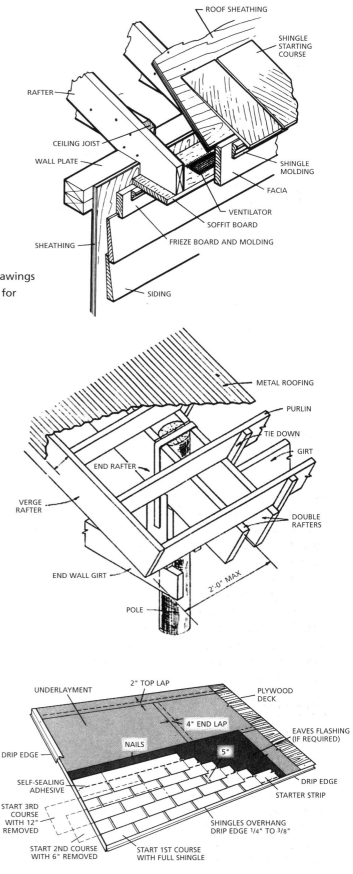

There are several different ways to box a roof edge. The top two drawings show a couple. The lower roof framing drawing shows one method for tying rafters to poles in pole building construction

enough drip edging to cover the eaves and the gable ends. Start the entire job by applying the drip edging along the eaves, nailing, with flat head galvanized roofing nails, every 10". Then lay the tar paper, overlapping at least 2" over each preceding course. If you run out of a roll and start another in mid-course, overlap at least 6"; make certain the lap is 6' from any end or obstruction. If you've added a chimney for a wood stove or other heat, carry the underlayment 4" up the vertical side of that chimney.

Underlayment is used to protect the roof deck until shingles are down. It also protects the roof deck if shingles are later damaged. Do not, ever, use impermeable materials such as polyethylene sheeting for this job, as water must be able to slowly percolate out of under-roof areas.

SLOPE, RISE AND RUN OF ROOF

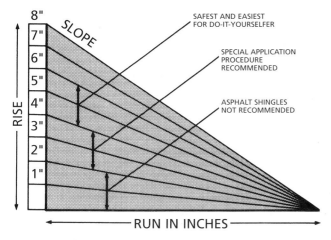

The chart shows the slope where asphalt shingles are best - and the easiest for do-it-yourselfers to work. Tool low a slope means the roof will leak, and too great a slope needs to be left to professionals. COURTESY GEORGIA-PACIFIC CORPORATION

This pattern for laying shingles is for plywood decking. It's called the 6' method. COURTESY GEORGIA-PACIFIC CORPORATION

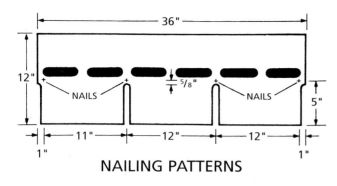

NAILING PATTERNS

The nailing pattern for a three-tab asphalt shingle.

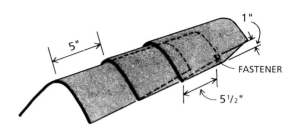

Fastener location for ridge shingles.

UNDERLAYMENT

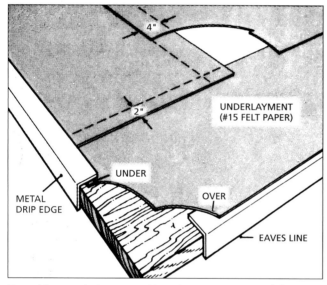

Eave drip guard placement. Note the arrangement of the underlayment over the drip guards, too.

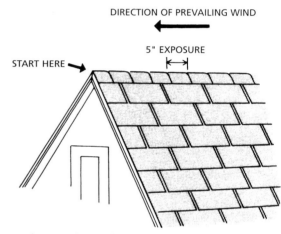

Layout of Boston butt ridge.

FLASHING

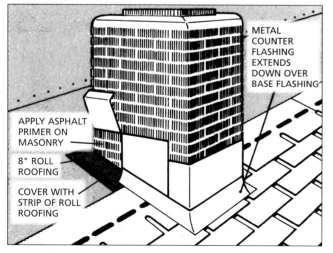

The last of the drip edging goes on the gable ends, over the tar paper.

We're not looking at valley flashing in this book because the roof isn't supposed to cover a complex enough building to require valleys. For flashing around chimneys, apron flashing extends across the front and rear of the chimney, and step flashing is used on the sides. All is bent to a right angle, with half running up the vertical and half on the horizontal, but with the step flashing designed to allow steps up the roof. The top of the flashing should be placed in mortar joints, or cut lines, and given a medium coat of top quality asphalt coating. The bottom of the apron flashing goes over the shingle below it, but the step flashing goes under the shingles — each succeeding (vertically) step flashing piece goes over the one below it, and feeds onto the apron, finally.

With flashing on, or ready, lay out chalk lines on the tar papered roof. Do not depend on the lines printed on the paper. The paper may not be on exactly straight; the lines are not close enough together anyway. Lay out chalk lines the depth of the shingles, minus $3/8$", up the roof for the

Two people are essential for aligning 16'-long steel roofing sections.

first one, and then the depth of the shingles from the top edge of the first course, and each succeeding course, on up the roof. Usually, shingles are 12" deep, but that varies, so check and lay your lines accordingly.

Shingles are laid in a specific manner, but often manufacturers include nailing patterns and layout patterns that differ somewhat. Always begin by reversing a first course of shingles, laying them with tabs towards the ridge line, and nailing through the tabs. Allow about $^3/_8$" overhang. The first real course goes over this reversed line, and gets the same amount of overhang. Start the course with a full shingle. Start the second course with two-thirds of a shingle, and the third course with a third of a shingle, after which you repeat the full shingle, and go on up until you reach the ridge line.

Repeat the process on the second side. At the ridge line, you can use a commercial ridge vent (which I recommend), or you can cut shingles between tabs and use them to form the ridge. This is called a Boston ridge, it works well and is quick.

METAL ROOFING

Metal roofs are a whole 'nother story. Metal roofing goes on over nailers spaced 2' apart up the rafters. The roofing is available in varying widths, but usually it's got a 2' or 3' exposure for width, and lengths may range from 6' to 16'. It is not essential to have edges meet at rafters, but a good

nailing pattern must be established. I'm more comfortable if metal roofing is screwed down, instead of nailed. Clutched cordless drills and impact drivers make this a simple job these days. Use the length, and style of screw recommended by the roof manufacturer, placed where the manufacturer recommends. Usually, these screws will be $1^1/_2$" or 2" long. They may have little rubber washers to serve as gaskets.

Aluminum roofing is easier to deal with than galvanized, but galvanized tends to be considerably cheaper. At this moment, somebody locally has galvanized overstock that is ridiculously cheap even for this area: 36 square feet sells for $23.40, about 65¢ a square foot. It's only available in 12' lengths 3' wide, but worth looking at. Assume a 20' × 36' shop, and your costs for roofing include just 24 of these sheets, under $600 for roofing, including nails (screws are higher). Add trusses in 20' width, nailers of rough pine, and various fasteners, and come up with a total roofing cost of way under $1,500. That's roofing economy these days. It pays to consider different materials, methods and timing. Check the miscellany and other sources for sale ads. My galvanized sheet roofing has been up since 1994 or 1995 and shows no problems or rust.

Sheet roofing goes on fast, though handling 12' × 3' sheets only makes sense with two people on the job. It also helps if one of those workers has some experience installing metal roofing.

Two guys nailing make quick work of putting ridge cap on my shop roof.

There are other disadvantages to sheet metal roofing and they must be considered. Steel or aluminum provide no R value at all. Both heat and cold are immediately passed on through. Thus, you roast in summer and shiver in winter; a wood stove or other heater doesn't help a lot unless it's kept well-stoked. Air conditioning for a hobby wood shop may not be really practical, but big fans are. You'll need huge fans with a tin roof.

Or you insulate. I recommend that solution, and use a minimum of 6" of fiberglass insulation. If you place a ceiling on the trusses, then you might want to lay in 8" to 12" of insulation — this works well with any style of roof, but is more close to an essential with metal roofing. Insulation, unfortunately, is often on sale but seldom overbought and sold as overstock so wild price reductions aren't frequent, though it pays to check around. I've found as much as five bucks a bundle (about 50 square feet) difference in price locally for the same materials.

One thought on attic or ceiling insulation does come to mind. Many builders erect metal-framed shells for various companies. Today, those shells are well insulated. The roof insulation is top notch, and ends are cut off and dropped rather than carted around to start a new row, at least in most installations I've seen. A quick question to the person in charge can sometimes get you enough left over insulation to do your shop twice over for the trouble of hauling it away. You may have to haul away all the extra to get the bit you need, but it's not that hard to get rid of, if *you* end up over-stocked.

You may also want some natural light in the shop, light that doesn't glare through windows. Skylights are the way to go, and today's options are wider than ever. Skylights should be installed before the shingles go on. Remember

Skylights, both round and rectangular, are useful, but need to be screwed down to the roof to prevent problems in high winds.

COURTESY OF VELUX

142

Large windows *must* be installed with at least two people for accuracy and safety. COURTESY OF SIMONTON

that there are tube-style skylights that are easier to install (no rafter cutting, a simple tube leading down to the interior piece).

WALL SHEATHING AND FINISH

Once the roof is under cover — sheathed and covered with tar paper, or fully covered with a tin roof — consider enclosing the sides of the shop. We've covered all the planning needs for doors and windows, and you know my view on standard windows in the shop (great for ventilation, but lousy for light) so let's go from there, assuming all framing has been properly done.

Side wall sheathing is carried out to the window and door frame edges and right to the corners. You use either plywood, Homasote board (sheathing insulation board that is reasonably cheap), waferboard, oriented strand board, 1×6 pine or poplar, or rough or planed sheathing board. The latter two are probably the cheapest, but take the longest to install and are the most difficult to install, as they must be installed at a diagonal (45°) to the studs. It's necessary in other cases to let in bracing for flat (90° to the stud) installations. Let-in bracing is cut into the studs at a 45° angle and is a time-consuming pain to do. Either run the board sheathing at an angle, buy commercial metal bracing, or use plywood or engineered board.

Bracing is not normally needed in pole buildings.

For plywood and similar materials, use the plywood, or OSB (oriented strand board) on the corners, covering three studs (in 24" OC framing: Cover four studs in 16" OC work). The material is applied vertically, and is nailed at 6"

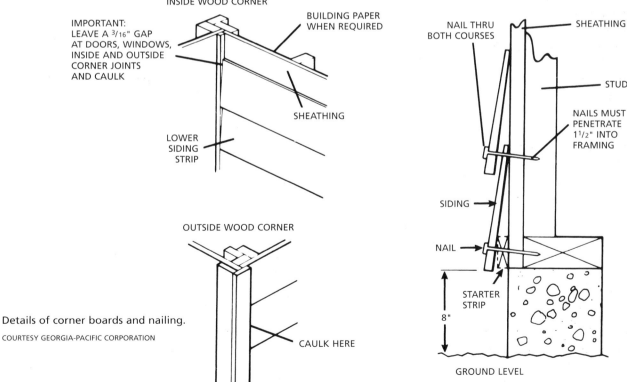

Details of corner boards and nailing.

COURTESY GEORGIA-PACIFIC CORPORATION

LAP SIDING

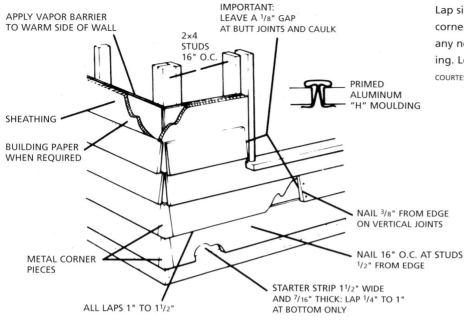

APPLY VAPOR BARRIER
TO WARM SIDE OF WALL

IMPORTANT:
LEAVE A ¹/₈" GAP
AT BUTT JOINTS AND CAULK

2×4
STUDS
16" O.C.

PRIMED
ALUMINUM
"H" MOULDING

SHEATHING

BUILDING PAPER
WHEN REQUIRED

NAIL ³/₈" FROM EDGE
ON VERTICAL JOINTS

NAIL 16" O.C. AT STUDS
¹/₂" FROM EDGE

METAL CORNER
PIECES

STARTER STRIP 1¹/₂" WIDE
AND ⁷/₁₆" THICK: LAP ¹/₄" TO 1"
AT BOTTOM ONLY

ALL LAPS 1" TO 1¹/₂"

Lap siding starts with installation of the corners, both inside and outside, and any needed door and window moulding. Leave ¹/₈" gaps for caulking.

COURTESY GEORGIA-PACIFIC CORPORATION

intervals along the outsides and 8" intervals on the inside nailing line or lines. Again, construction adhesive helps add structural rigidity.

With the corners braced with the plywood, use homasote or other insulating board to finish out the sheathing. It's cheaper and more effective in the long run.

If you are using metal siding, or vertical board siding, you may elect to pass on the sheathing. During stud framing, add bracing and 1×4 or wider nailers. For pole-building methods, use 2×4 or wider nailers. I used board and batten siding, with vertical boards of 1"× 6" and 1"× 8" poplar and southern pine, with battens of varied materials, mostly southern pine, some walnut and some poplar. My board-and-batten siding is placed over Tyvek® and Typar®.

Metal as a siding material is fast and cheap during erection and lends itself well to shop use, but offers no insulation at all.

In pole construction, wall framing is done inside the poles, and there is no need for headers over doors and windows (simply use cripple studs from a horizontal member to the top plate) because the framing doesn't support any of the building's weight. I suggest doing the framing on the inside (the outside pole edges are already plumb) edge of the poles, setting a plumb line there for any later interior finish walls.

Siding goes on over the sheathing.

Start by placing moulding boards on building corners, and around doors and windows. Siding, whether vertical or horizontal, butts on these boards and the resulting small cracks are sealed with caulking compound.

Use plywood siding, board siding or any of the other available materials. One company, Georgia-Pacific, empha-

sizes vinyl, hardboard, and a new type of plywood that looks like beaded tongue and groove material. Cementitious board siding is very popular these days, costs close to what vinyl does, cuts and installs much like wood (given lots of consideration to protecting yourself and the area from the cement dust when cutting), is rot and insect proof. It comes primed and you should paint it, though you don't have to.

You may also, as Bobby Weaver originally did, choose to use rough cut lumber direct from the saw mill set horizontally as clapboards. True clapboards are cut in a taper

My shop window framed out and the structure wrapped in Tyvek.

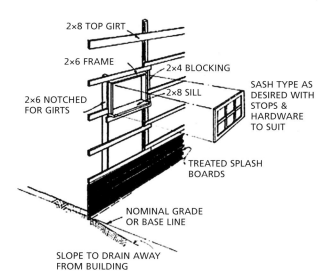

2×8 TOP GIRT

2×6 FRAME

2×4 BLOCKING

2×6 NOTCHED FOR GIRTS

2×8 SILL

SASH TYPE AS DESIRED WITH STOPS & HARDWARE TO SUIT

TREATED SPLASH BOARDS

NOMINAL GRADE OR BASE LINE

SLOPE TO DRAIN AWAY FROM BUILDING

Typical window installation. COURTESY GEORGIA-PACIFIC CORPORATION

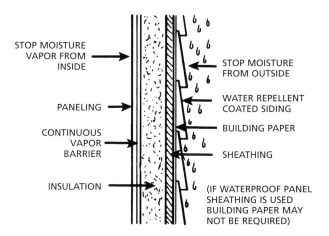

STOP MOISTURE VAPOR FROM INSIDE

PANELING

CONTINUOUS VAPOR BARRIER

INSULATION

STOP MOISTURE FROM OUTSIDE

WATER REPELLENT COATED SIDING

BUILDING PAPER

SHEATHING

(IF WATERPROOF PANEL SHEATHING IS USED BUILDING PAPER MAY NOT BE REQUIRED)

Wall design for residential construction. You may, or may not insulate your shop walls, but vapor barriers are essential if the wall is closed. Use building paper for sheathing.

COURTESY GEORGIA-PACIFIC CORPORATION

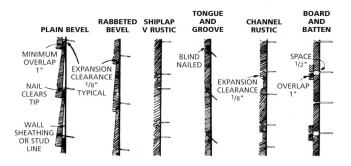

PLAIN BEVEL · **RABBETED BEVEL** · **SHIPLAP V RUSTIC** · **TONGUE AND GROOVE** · **CHANNEL RUSTIC** · **BOARD AND BATTEN**

MINIMUM OVERLAP 1"

NAIL CLEARS TIP

WALL SHEATHING OR STUD LINE

EXPANSION CLEARANCE 1/8" TYPICAL

BLIND NAILED

EXPANSION CLEARANCE 1/8"

SPACE 1/2"

OVERLAP 1"

Nailing patterns for siding of different types. You will probably use plain beveled, flat tap or board and batten siding. Board on board is like board and batten, but it uses wider stock.

COURTESY GEORGIA-PACIFIC CORPORATION

across the width, but rough cut material goes up nicely as clapboard without the fanciness. Bobby built a cheat, a small chunk of wood that could be hooked over the already in-place course to position the next course.

I went with vertical siding. I used a pneumatic nailer and $2^1/_2$" nails. Originally, I planned to let the siding remain for about a year before coming back with any kind of finish coat. I realized just about that time that the rough look was a help. The slightly ragged look kept the tax valuation down, while also (I hope) discouraging most thieves.

If I ever do coat the exterior, I'll use a dense stain, instead of paint. There is less pigment, and thus a more permeable final coat, with opaque exterior stains such as ZAR RainStain or Thompson's Exterior Stain. Cuprinol is also a good brand. The greater permeability of the final coat means there's less chance of blistering later on.

Application of vertical siding depends on the style selected: Plywood siding, whether classic T1-11 or GP's Ply-Bead, comes in 8', 9' and 10' tall panels to suit different wall heights. They're available in $^{11}/_{32}$" (fine over sheathing) and $^{19}/_{32}$" thick panels. If you choose to use no sheathing, use the $^{19}/_{32}$" for siding.

Vertical board and horizontal board siding must have sheathing underneath for stability—plywood adds a large amount of rigidity that 6" boards cannot.

For either type of siding, snap a level line around the base of the woodshop sheathing, so that you have a starting point. This is after nailing all corner moulding and window

Typar housewrap isn't as famous as Tyvek, but works the same: Use solid sheets to cover whenever possible and then pierce for openings for windows and doors.

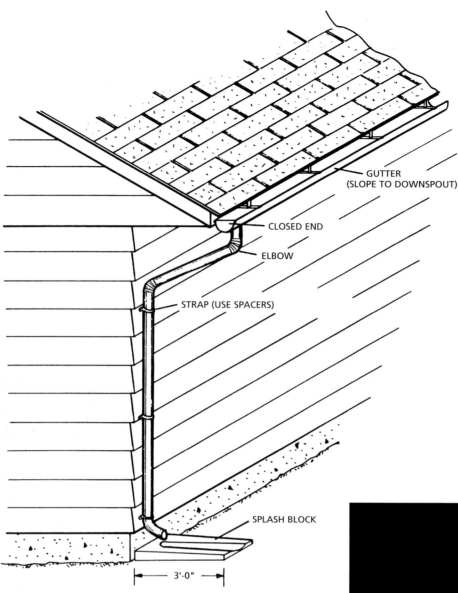

GUTTER
(SLOPE TO DOWNSPOUT)

CLOSED END

ELBOW

STRAP (USE SPACERS)

SPLASH BLOCK

3'-0"

Gutters, gutters, whose got the gutters. Guttering can be bought in easy-to-carry lengths (well, 10 feet), or you can have someone come in and make seamless gutters for probably not much more than it costs to buy the bits and pieces and install the whole works yourself.

and door moulding in place. Corner moulding is usually made 1" to 4", depending on style and desire, longer than the siding is low.

Start horizontal board siding in one corner, at the bottom, and nail at the top and halfway down the middle of the course. I use a Campbell-Hausfeld sheathing stapler, with 2" staples and find it works wonderfully — and saves a lot of hassle trying to hold a strip of siding in place while I drive that first nail. Wham, and the first staple is in with just a squeeze of the trigger.

Siding is easier with two people, but can be done with one and a few slights: For slights, or cheats, you use a few 1×4 boards, pointed on one side of one end and notched

Careful caulking where siding ends assures a tight seal.
COURTESY OF DAP

146

on the other, to help support long siding pieces. An additional help is a little notched board about twice as long as the siding is wide. The notch is cut into the board exactly the height of the part of the siding that is to be exposed to the weather (the exposure). Place the notched board on the already-in-place siding course, and use the top of the board to set the next piece, leaving the first piece perfect. This saves a lot of measuring.

Vertical board siding is also started in one corner, against a corner moulding piece (if such moulding is used; it need not be with most kinds of vertical siding). The board edge must be plumb and you nail as indicated in the drawings. Board and batten is the most common kind of vertical siding, but there are also board and board, batten on board, and a couple of fancier ones (shiplap is great, but more costly).

Bring the siding on up to the eave line, cover the gable ends and you're getting very close to occupying your shop.

Trim work includes cornices — fascia and undereave soffit, along with the needed moulding. You may also choose to leave your eave ends open. Around here, that's too much of an invitation to starlings and a variety of stinging insects such as hornets and wasps. Finish work includes proper caulking of all exterior seams that are normally caulked (do not caulk under windows, or at the base of siding or trim pieces).

For a true exterior finishing touch, you may want to add gutters, though they can be added later. The easiest gutters for the do-it-yourselfer to add are the snap-together vinyl types. Those all come with adequate instructions for installation — and most provide brochures that make selection of parts a simple matter. Without gutters, you need to spread gravel at least 4" thick and 18" wide as a splash area under each eave.

When the shop is all done, regardless of size, start producing projects for your own and your family's enjoyment — or for sale.

Metal semi-prefabs (each arch in Bobby's had three pieces to be bolted together before it was tilted up and bolted to the next arch) go up fairly quickly. The buildings need no framing, but are expensive to insulate and they require scaffolding during erection. You may also need a scaffold to change light bulbs.

CHAPTER NINE

Electrical, Power, Lighting and Heat

Electrical current needs for a woodworking shop are obviously very important today. We'll start by examining what I believe is important for hobby shops, and from that point, you can go on and read or not read the rest of the chapter. I do not recommend you do your own electrical wiring unless you have considerable experience in the field. In many areas of the country, it is illegal, even when done to code, for a homeowner to do wiring. You must check, and, I strongly suggest, even if you plan to do your own, you get a local electrician to at least give advice.

It is wisest for all DIY electricians to have a journeyman electrician inspect the completed job before having the building inspector in. That inspection prevents many problems, not the least of which is conditioning the building inspector to expect low grade work on your site if you fail the first formal inspection. Goof it up once, and you can believe the next inspection will be even more thorough. Building inspectors aren't in it to keep you from getting things done, but their job involves public safety, and they work to make sure you are going to be safe in the building being erected. Hire it done, or make sure you do it right. Wiring is a job where neatness counts, but where design is also of great importance, which means you need correct sizes of all boxes for the numbers of conductors passing through, and terminating, in the boxes, the correct size wire or cable, and neat, tight connections.

All information presented in this chapter fits my understanding of the National Electrical Code's most current revision but I suggest you get your own copy of the code, or a translation of it, and check any wiring design work you do to make sure all switch, junction and other boxes are rated for the number of wires passing through, all cable and wire is at least of the size recommended, all circuits are of correct design (no more than eight outlets, for example, on any 120 volt 20 ampere circuit, though with tool circuits where a tool may require more than 15 amperes on starting surge [the reason 15 ampere circuits are not suitable in general], six outlets is probably better), and so on. One of my basic prejudices, in some cases, aluminum wire is allowed, especially in heavier cabling applications. Do not use aluminum wire if you can find a substitute, even with today's insane prices for copper. Period. Copper may cost three or four times as much, but aluminum "creeps" and even specifically engineered connectors for aluminum do not seem to me to be sufficient protection against such movement. You can, over time, end up with high resistance areas. Think of the high resistance items around your house, and you'll know why that's undesirable in circuitry. The area of high resistance gets very hot, sometimes red hot. The result can be fire. Avoid aluminum wire as much as possible. You will almost certainly have to use aluminum cable in the larger sizes, though.

Plan and install wiring to suit your needs, not mine, and not those of your pal down the road. Certain commonalities exist, but there are often major differences. If you have all 240-volt stationary tools, you'll need more 240 volt circuits than I installed (seven), and if you do not have, and plan never to use 240 volt tools, then you can probably squeak by with just one such circuit — sooner or later, you'll find a need for such a circuit, so it doesn't pay to wait until installation costs more.

My descriptions here will necessarily be brief, with less detailed installation instructions than I am sure many of you will like, but electrical wiring is a complex subject and one that deserves (and needs) more detailed treatment than can be supplied in a single chapter. I suggest you work with a local electrician, (or with a good instruction manual or code book) if you have some experience and training, but lack knowledge of details and specific device wiring needs. As a reminder, the wiring set-ups covered in this chapter are not suitable for industrial, three-phase applications. For home and hobby (and most small production) shops, three-phase electricity provides no benefits whatsoever. There are design difficulties, as well as differing opinions on what kind of set-up works best with starters, wiring, etc. It isn't worth the cost of hiring a journeyman industrial electrician to lay out and install a system that offers no benefits.

You may be wiring a garage, or part of a basement, and need only two or three new circuits, or you may wish to wire in a subpanel off your main service entry panel. All are possible and practical, assuming an up-to-date service entry panel.

SERVICE ENTRY

Because it's the beginning of the circuits in your house, the service entry, and the related service entry panel, provide the best starting place. Service to most residences (and

Drip loops are essential elements of many overhead service entries. This one is showing signs of passing time (it was put up in 1962).

A fully installed meter for underground service. Note the PVC pipe at the base of the unit. At right, the meter box before it is wired in, with just the pipe back extending into the interior of the shop wall.

small shops with independent service panels and meters) begins at the service entry head or meter.

SERVICE ENTRY HEADS

This is where it all really begins. The service entry head is the device by which electricity is transferred to the house from the pole or other power company terminal. You find a minimum ground clearance for the service drop as it goes to the service entry head, usually 10' (this varies, and there may be a range, with the entrance head being listed as having to be between 10' and 30' from the ground: 16' is usually a safe point to attach your service head for the line drop). As always, check local codes before applying any of my figures. Local and national code information always supersedes mine. You supply enough wire of the appropriate size to allow a drip loop (about 12" extra, minimum). A 100 ampere (the minimum) service demands #3 THW copper conductors (with fewer than six branch circuits, you can get by with a 60 amp service: My recommendation is that you don't try). The service head must be within 24" of the point of attachment for the incoming service cable (a cable is an assembly of

wires), and must have a crooked neck (with the openings downward: Each wire will be run through an individual opening in the service head seal). Ground wires may be bare or insulated. For a 200 ampere service, you'll need to use #1 THW copper conductors. Local codes may be more generous with the 200-amp service.

Always caulk the top of such fittings, leaving the bottom clear of caulk so that any water that does penetrate can run out.

Don Pittman is installing the cabling to my meter head box.

than is necessary, and trim it off neatly. Most indoor cable has brown paper separator inside, and that may be left hanging by sloppy electricians. Bend cable to fit around corners, and at right angles going in to the buss bars, instead of just slopping it across the interior spaces of the panel, and trim off all excess insulation and separator paper. Use cable ties whenever you can to maintain neatness.

Most service entrance panels come with a fitted and proper main circuit breaker installed. Mine is a Square D, with a 200 ampere main breaker. The brand name of the panel is of importance for a couple of reasons, not the least of which is the quality of the product. Pick a name noted in the field. You also need to know the brand name, and occasionally the model number, of your service entrance panel in order to buy the correct circuit breakers for that panel. Different brand breakers attach to the panel in slightly different ways, though the technique is similar for most.

When you attach circuit wires to the circuit breakers, you attach the black wire to the circuit breaker, and the white and green (or bare) wires to the neutral buss or bar. That's for a 120 volt circuit. For a 240 volt circuit, you attach either two black wires, or a black and a red wire, to the circuit breaker and the white wire to the neutral bar. You only have a black and a red wire in the same cable if it is a three-wire cable. Most of the cable we use is classed as 2-wire with ground, with black, white and bare wires. The breaker then tilts and snaps into its place on the panel, you punch out the insert on the panel's face, and you can apply power to the circuit.

Now, we've done the end job. That is, while the service drop, head and entrance panel are where the power first comes into the house, the circuit breaker is the last item hooked up when you install a new circuit. It is

The service entry head is installed on the structure, usually at a gable end (if gables are used), and a rigid conduit is dropped to the meter. The final line drop into the house is behind or below the meter head, and enters the service entry panel from an appropriate spot. Unless, of course, and like mine, the entry line from the pole is below ground, in which case, you'll have an entry similar to the one shown.

SERVICE ENTRY PANEL

This is where your circuitry array starts. The service entry panel holds all the circuit breakers for the entire shop. Sub panels, in basement shop and add-on shop wiring installations, do a similar job. Keep the service panels about chest high, and leave a minimum of 30" of access around the panel. More is better, and the access must be maintained so that later needs can be safely met (the 30" working distance allows you to work around and on the panel without making contact with possible conductors).

The wires enter the panel with the black wire attached to the power buss, and the white wire to the neutral buss. The grounding wire (bare or green or green stripes on white) also attaches to the neutral buss. Do the job neatly, as already noted. Strip no more insulation

Bobby Weaver's service entry panel installation.

151

Bobby made sure every breaker was identified with the correct circuit.

the first item cut off, or removed, when you work on an old circuit. NEVER work on a powered circuit.

You will work near power in the service entrance panel, and it is partly for this reason I recommend you gain some experience, or have an experienced electrician at least advising you, when wiring a shop. Or wiring anything else.

CIRCUITS

There are two primary types of circuit needed for the hobby woodworking shop, of the types classed for residential use. The lighting circuit is obvious, but the small appliance circuit is mainly a kitchen circuit name.

Lighting circuits are just what the name states, circuits that carry electricity to your lights. I recommend always splitting lighting circuits, so that any room has two, or more, such circuits. My shop has two circuits with fluorescent lights, one on each side of the shop, plus a third circuit of incandescent lights up the center, so any lighting failure is unlikely to ever be total. This may be even more important in a shop than in a home, for if you blow a light circuit breaker, and the machinery keeps running, you can be in considerable trouble. Thus, if you have two rows of fluorescent lights in the shop, one on each side, have one row on one circuit, and the other on another. It takes a lot of fluorescent bulbs to pull down a lighting circuit, so you can add, if you have one, a second story to each side of lights and still have plenty of

power to spare. Lighting circuits are wired with #14 cable, and use 15 ampere circuit breakers. There is no real reason to place either ground fault circuit interrupters or surge protectors on such circuits. For those who don't often use the formula, a 15 ampere, 120 volt circuit lets you use up to 1650 watts of power (power [watts]=volts × amperage). That's a lot of any kind of light bulbs, which is why a single circuit is all that's usually recommended for lighting.

Small appliance circuits provide a different service. In a home, they provide 20 ampere service to non-dedicated circuits. They offer circuits for microwave ovens, toaster ovens, refrigerators and appliances. These are wired with #12 cable, and should have both surge protection and ground fault circuit interrupters (for shops). You will be

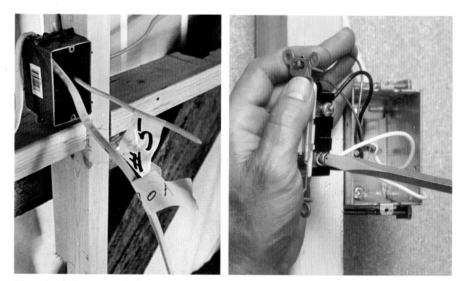

Blue plastic boxes are inexpensive, but replacing boxes with stripped holes after the wall is closed up is a pain. At right, always set the loop for the wires on the terminal so that the opening is closed further as you tighten the screw.

152

Bobby Weaver's 115 volt circuits pass through four receptacle boxes. He used 1" plastic conduit because wire pulling is easier in that than it is in ¾".

using lightweight stationary, and heavyweight portable, tools on these circuits, so you want as many as you can get. According to code, you can wire in as many as eight receptacles per circuit. Try it with six per circuit, first. While you'll seldom run two tools at a time in such circuits, you may find you're running an air compressor and a router, or another pair of tools, on the same circuit from time to time. That's no real difficulty, unless you get double starting surges from the motors, at which point the breaker pops. Thus, it's nice to have extra circuits, with fewer outlets on each.

My suggestion here is that you leapfrog the receptacles, running two circuits along each wall (at least), with alternating receptacles from each circuit. To really add some versatility, run a third circuit above the other two. For residences, NEC requires an outlet every 12' It is expressed differently, stating that no point along a horizontal line on a wall shall be more than 6' from an outlet, but that's how it works out. Any receptacles or outlets 5¹/₂' above the floor level are additional. You should have no problem with such a requirement, since any sensible shop construction, using my leapfrog method, should have an accessible outlet (receptacle) every 3' along the top of any bench, or along any wall, at least 18" above floor level (24-36" is a better minimum to avoid bending, while 54" gets it above the bench level and above any plywood that may be tilted against the wall where there is no bench — it's frustrating to have to dig behind a half dozen sheets of plywood to plug a tool in). Space it out to 6', if you wish, but no further. With receptacles spaced any more than 6' apart, the tangle

of heavy duty extension cords gets nearly obscene. In my own shop, I leapfrogged, but did it at 4' intervals, a minor mistake. Three feet is preferable, 2' good.

An important note here: regardless of what kind of wiring you do, you'll need extension cords in a modern shop. Do not ever use any extension cord with under a #14 wire (up to 25' and 12 amperes), and aim for #12. If the extension cord is over 50' long, use a #10 (you used to have to make your own, but they are now readily available).

In areas where wall benches are used, all circuits must be placed so as to be accessible above or alongside the benches. It's much easier on the back, the nerves and your general level of irritation to place all circuits a minimum of 24" up the wall from the floor. I'd rather have outlets at eye level than floor level!

Special outlets are available for (and must be used for) 20 ampere circuits only. These have a T-tab on one side of the receptacles and are not used for 15-ampere circuits.

You may, if you choose, run one or two 15 ampere general circuits around and above the benches. If you do,

the above receptacles become essential for the 20 ampere circuits so you know what kind of circuit you're plugging lamps or tools into.

Most shops will have supporting poles up the center, or in other areas.

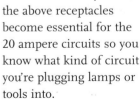

Bobby placed his 230-volt circuits on a line above the 115-volt circuit.

153

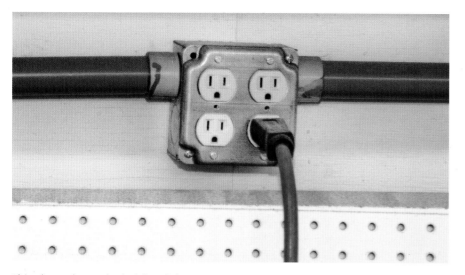

This photo shows the height of the wall circuits. The 115-volt circuit boxes are the lowest in the shop, and are placed so the bottom of the box clears a 48″ tall sheet of plywood or other material, meaning there's no need to hold the sheet out, set the plug, and then hope the sheet doesn't make a mess when tilted back.

Place receptacles on such poles or posts, using conduit to protect the cables.

For most shops, whether connected, freestanding, or part of a basement or other area, keep in mind you'll want at least two receptacles outdoors, on separate circuits. If codes allows, they might be on separate indoor small appliance circuits, which are unlikely to be in use if you're outdoors working. I placed eight around my shop. Almost all of us have the experience of needing to work on something outdoors, whether part of a project, an oversized project, or simply one that has too much mess (fumes, paint, paint remover, etc.) to be handled inside. And it's annoying to have to run heavy duty extensions all over the place. Make the need for extensions an unusual one in your shop.

For the bigger tools you want 240 volts, usually on a 30 ampere circuit breaker. No big deal, but you need to plan correctly, or you won't have a big enough panel to accept the number of 240 volt circuits finally needed. Your woodworking shop can become quite a 240-volt site if you wish. In general, tools that usually use 240 volt electricity include the following: Table saws, radial arm saws, planers, jointers, shapers and air compressors. Specialty tools may also use 240 volts, as may some routers and similar tools based on European patterns (always make sure, though, the tool is based on European patterns not made for use with European circuitry, which is usually 50 cycle, versus

the 60 cycle we use in this country and Canada).

Generally, any tool that demands much more than 15 amperes at 120 volts changes over to 240 volts, reducing amperage load by 50%. That is, a table saw that has a motor that runs on 20 amperes at 120 volts (2200 watts) requires only 10 amperes at 240 volts to produce the same power. Thus, a 30 ampere, 240 volt circuit (the most common size for residential and small shop use, though 50 ampere breakers, such as those used for ranges, are also readily available) allows 6600 watts of power (the 50 amp unit allows a whopping 11,000 watts). In practical terms, that means larger, lower-rpm motors (under 10,000 rpm) in saws, planers and similar tools can be run, up to about 5 hp, versus a limit of $1\frac{1}{2}$ to 2 hp with high torque units (routers and corded drills) on 120 volts.

Most circuit breakers for 240 volts are also physically twice the size of single pole, 120 volt breakers, and take two spaces in service entrance panels. Plan for such space eaters. In a 40 space panel, five such breakers take 10 spaces, leaving 30 for other uses.

A 240 volt outlet.

Your shop needs at least twice as many 20 ampere 120 volt breakers as it needs 240 breakers, so you can figure on another 10 spaces going there. For 15 ampere breakers, figure another 3-4-5 spaces, depending on your lighting and light duty needs.

A minimum service entrance panel size for a moderately large hobby shop needs to have 30 spaces. Forty is better because it allows for possible future needs.

Individual and immovable tools — table saws, radial arm saws, and planers are the three most common, with air compressors close behind — may require separate disconnects. In most cases, a heavy-duty receptacle is used, and the disconnect (switch box) isn't needed. Again, check with your local building inspector.

All of this seems to leave a 200 ampere panel breathing hard. There are, already, 10 of the 20 ampere and five of the 30 ampere, plus at least three of the 15 ampere breakers to be settled in. There's a complex formula for all of this, involving the percent of use each circuit is expected to have, with much of the factoring dependent on things that don't truly affect a woodworking shop—the demand factor for a kitchen range, for instance, 8000 watts on any 12,000 watt or under combination of surface burners and ovens. For each kilowatt above 8000, you add 400 watts.

For small appliance and laundry circuits, allow 1500 watts per circuit. It's an overly generous allowance for the 2400 watt rating possibility of such 20 ampere circuits (actual wattage is only 2200 on 120 volts, but is 2400 on 120 volts. The voltage depends on your locality, and is variable from minute-to-minute anyway. Up north, I always used 120 and 240 volts, while in Virginia I always use 115 and 230, primarily because that's how my local electrician friends describe it in each place).

LIGHTING DEMAND

Lighting takes a demand factor of three watts per square foot, which is fairly modest. As noted earlier, I like to allow two full circuits for nothing else but fluorescent ceiling lights, plus another couple of 15 ampere circuits for general lighting. Most 15 ampere circuits allow three watt lighting over 550 square feet, so three circuits for a total of 1200 square feet is about right for shop use. It is what I have. My difference is the recommendation that you split the circuits so that any one room of the shop, if it's a multi-room shop, has at least two lighting circuits. If you have a single room shop, make sure the lights are on two separate circuits. The circuits then can go on and provide lights elsewhere, as well.

In residences, you can apply a load rating system that is a bit simpler than trying to figure totals as above, and then add in load factors. In fact, with shops, you may find you absolutely have to go with this kind of figuring, because anything else finds you searching out 400 ampere service entrance panel sources when all your heavy tools are added up. That is, figure the lighting at 3 watts per square foot, and small appliance circuits at 1500 watts. Figure one large tool circuit at 1500 watts. Then list all your tools at full load ratings — if the tools aren't rated in watts, simply multiply volts in your system (120 or 120) times the ampere rating listed on the tool. Add all this up, and apply a 100% load rating to the first 10,000 watts, and a 40% rating to the remaining load.

Talk to your local building inspector about the types of loads you expect from various tools; see what is acceptable locally. You may be allowed to take lighter loadings on your small appliance circuits. Obviously, a one-person shop with two table saws, two radial arm saws, spray equipment, a

Bobby's shop is a metal building. He installed lighting down boards bolted through the ceiling. The insulation is a yellowish color, sort of sickly looking, but it works very well, and lightens the shop.

planer, a jointer, and similar tools isn't going to have everything operating at once. In fact, seldom will more than two tools even be idling together. It does make good sense to allow for friends who may want to work with you — and you may need their help on occasion — so there could actually be three larger tools in operation at the same time, with an air compressor in the background, its motor kicking in only when enough air is bled off to require the tank be refilled.

In almost every case, a 100 ampere service entrance panel is enough for current uses, but please check. Local codes may force you to a 200 ampere unit. Actually, a 60 ampere unit will do in almost every instance, though there's not much room for expansion with the 100 ampere panel, and none at all with the 60 ampere type.

This newer breed of cable staples is less likely to cut cables when you drive them down. The plastic coating is a help.

SUB PANELS

Sub panels may require their own circuit breaker (corresponding to the main breaker on your service entrance panel) if they hold more than six devices (circuit breakers). Six devices and fewer may be fused off the main service panel: Sub panels are protected with breakers at the main panel buss bar.

For small shops, a 60 ampere, six-circuit array may be plenty. Lighting may already be in place, as in a basement or garage, so those circuits don't need to be added, and all you need do is wire in the tool circuits, as required.

WIRE

For most all hobby shop wiring jobs, you're going to use #14 two-wire-with-ground indoor cable, or #12 two wire with ground. Both have a black power wire, a white for neutral and usually a bare ground. The first size, the smaller, is used on 15 ampere circuits, and the latter is used on 120 volt 20 ampere circuits, or circuits up to 30 amperes in 240. You may also use #12, three wire for the 240, which will have a white neutral, and two power leads, one black and one brown. New wire uses different colors for different wire thicknesses.

Cable insulation is fine for protected wiring, where it's not likely to be slammed with board ends, or hit with tools. In areas where wiring runs down walls or posts or along joists and is otherwise unprotected, it needs to be enclosed in either plastic or metal conduit. Either is easy to find, and the plastic is exceptionally easy to work (the metal requires a tubing bender, a tool that's not expensive if you're using it often, but is expensive for a single use: Borrow or rent one).

There are a number of different junction, switch and utility boxes that are apt to prove useful in wiring any shop. Junction boxes are made in a wide array of sizes and shapes, but most often we use round, octagonal or square boxes, and, as the name implies, they are used where you must make junctions in wires. At no time do you ever make joins in wires outside a junction box, or add a switch or fixture without its own box. Joins are made using wire nuts. These are sized to the wire in the cable, and are screwed on to the stripped wire ends, making a sturdy, insulated connection.

While there should be no problem with pass-throughs, check current NEC regulations to make sure the size box you are using is sufficient for the number of wires in it. The cubic inch capacity of the box determines the number of wires that may be joined in that box. Usually, it's far more than you or I are ever going to care about, but in cases where a very shallow switch or junction box is used because of wall depth, you could find a problem.

Both unprotected cable, and conduit, must be supported at points during runs. Conduit is usually required to be supported within 3' of every box, fitting or cabinet, and at intervals not over 10' in runs. Cable is *not* properly installed with steel staples, though for one reason or another most of the building inspectors I know will pass it. There are non-metallic (usually nylon or another plastic) straps between two nails that are properly used to support cable, at the correct intervals of not more than $4^1/2'$, and within 12" of entrance to boxes, fixtures, etc. (These things are a pain in the tail to install, but are safer.) Cable going into boxes and fixtures must also be held by cable clamps. Bend cable gradually. Give it a radius of at least 6" and you're far less likely to damage the wires than if you give it a hard 90° bend over 1" or so. Copper wire is very flexible, but it does break if flexed too hard.

Wiring a shop, or any building, is a fairly complex job. I'd suggest that you decide what you want in the way of receptacles and lights, and have an electrician do the actual work. It will then look easy. If you decide to do it yourself, be careful, talk to your building inspector, and make sure you follow the most recent NEC (National Electrical Code). As I noted before, if you lack wiring experience, locate a friend who has some, and who can at least inspect the finished job for you. If no friend can do that for you, spend a few bucks to hire a journeyman electrician to look the installations over.

LIGHTING THE SHOP

Shops have different lighting needs for different areas. There's nothing like making a job easy, but proper shop lighting isn't always easy.

Whatever kind of shop you have, the first need is for a soft, non-glaring light, generally from the ceiling. I find this works best when fluorescent lights are used, with either 4' or 8' long tubes. I dislike the color of the light that those give, but the actual light is soft, and nearly glare free, something that cannot be said for most inexpensive forms of overhead incandescent lighting.

From there, you need to think about the lighting needs of individual tools. Some work fine with general light — the planer fits in here, as does the shaper (we're assuming a good level of light). Detail work

Dale's shop shows a different application of both wiring and lighting. He ran his light fixtures in two directions, as shown. He also popped some circuits up through the floor to save using as many extension cords. This is much easier if you have a full basement under the floor.

needs more light, as close to shadow free as possible. That means working lights so that they're either directly overhead the tool and work being lighted, or come in from two or more sides to eliminate the shadows formed by one light with a second (and a third, if needed) light. Workbenches, radial arm saws, lathes and table saws are prime examples here.

Other tools need specific lights, right at the work, almost on the work surface, allowing you to pay very close attention. Drill presses, scroll saws and band saws are particular tools here, and are often supplied with table mounted lights as standard equipment or options. Drill presses sometimes even have the light built into the underside of the drill, as do some band saws. Where such lights aren't supplied, you might consider picking up a sturdy gooseneck model or two. Get those with either magnetic or clamp bases.

The general idea is to work with the lighting until it is nearly shadow free, while keeping it soft enough to remain glare free. Harsh light — such as that supplied by uncoat-

ed 200-watt incandescent bulbs — can be really rough on the eyes over a period of time, often a short period of time. My erstwhile basement shop was lighted with incandescent fixtures, except over two workbenches. The 200-watt coated bulbs gave me some severe eyestrain problems after a few weeks, and reduced my time in the shop by at least 40%. At the time, fluorescent replacements were out of the question. It was a rented space, after all, and I'd already spent a lot of money wiring the place, among other things. One point: Hobby shops as rentals aren't a good idea.

The change in lighting comes in the finishing areas, oddly enough. To get a smooth, scratch-free finish, you need to get an angle on the surface and check for smoothness. The same holds true when applying layers of clear finish. You need to be able to make sure all areas are covered, and glare-free, soft, shadow-free lighting just doesn't do the job.

For best results in finish areas, I'd suggest two stand-mounted halogen flood lights, set at right angles outward from your eyes, and at about a 15° to 30° angle to the sur-

157

This dual heat/air conditioning unit does almost all the work for the arched end of Bobby Weaver's shop, most days.

face of the work. That gives just the right kind of light to let you see whether or not there are scratches. The lights are easily portable, for ready movement around the work, and from the sanding area to the finish coating area.

There are a slew of specialty lights out there. You may find some at reasonable prices that allow you to use, as is or adapted, for woodworking, and some may do better on specific jobs than anything I know of, or have mentioned.

HEATING THE SHOP

Heating a woodworking shop is a nuisance. The best deal I ever had was the rental shop, which, in one corner, contained the oil furnace for retail stores overhead. It cost me nothing, and supplied more than sufficient heat in clean form. I couldn't use volatile finishes during much of the winter, but most of my finishing work in the past was done with brushes, so using water-based finishes as soon as they became available was an easy step.

Like all heat sources that are actually fired — which means using open flame — the furnace limited my winter finishing chores. The same holds true of wood heat and gas furnaces; leaving only heat pumps, electric baseboard and electric furnaces, as safe methods of heating a shop during those times when you'll be applying finishes with volatile solvent bases. Basically, that's another argument for

changing over to one or more of the various water-based finishes (though the two brands of stains I prefer to all others are mineral-spirits-solvent based, I've mostly switched to water-based poly finishes, reducing smell, danger, clean-up time and cost — I now buy mineral-based solvents about once every couple of years).

Heating is more of a problem for freestanding and garage shops, and less so for basement shops. The basement shop is usually sufficiently heated from the furnace for the house, so your only need is care in applying finishes, or other substances that are likely to prove volatile (I recently used Behlen's pore filler on an oak project, and love the stuff, but must note it uses naphtha, probably the worst solvent available outside of lacquer thinner [liquid gunpowder in my opinion] for volatility). It sounds a bit odd, but the major concern in heating a woodworking shop is more apt to be the type of finishing you do than anything else, though filtering dust out of the air is another. Cost is always a factor, and one you work to lower in many ways. Wood heat is a superb way to defeat higher costs, though both wood and new wood stoves have gone out of sight for pricing in recent years. Even in my rural area, the insurance companies now insist on inspecting wood heat installations to see that they're safe, and the local building inspection office charges a fee for a building permit for such installations.

Here's a look at Bobby's unit from the inside.

I do *not* object to an expert overseeing my work, but for a major part of my life I lived with only wood heat. I've installed flues, cleaned chimneys, had chimney fires, and generally done all there is to do from cutting firewood and splitting it to getting burned out (that occurred on an August 8, though, and had nothing to do with anything other than 50+ year old wiring and hungry mice). I've written two books on wood heat, and innumerable magazine articles, as well as living with it as a total heat source and a partial heat source for, well, a long time. So I've got a pretty good idea of what's safe and what isn't. It still costs me $25.00 to have someone else verify that.

The cheapest heat source you can install is electric base-board. It is simple to install, relatively low cost, and old units in good condition are readily available. It is also the most costly heat to feed, though that may not be a major problem in a workshop that is only heated part of the time — when you're actually in the place. This may not work in some far northern areas where it gets super cold, versus my current locale where 10° Fahrenheit is cold, and people tend to exaggerate coldness for drama and local color.

Forget new electric furnaces, as they're costly, both to install, feed, and may be hard to find. It's possible you'll find a used one or two around, as mobile home owners discard theirs and install oil heat to reduce costs. I got

mine that way, along with the realization that an immense circuit breaker (90 amperes) is a high ticket item at around $120, at least for me. That and the cable added up to a significant cost, and three years later, the furnace quit. No "new" used ones showed up, so I'm currently using two propane heaters. They work fine, if the door is opened a crack, but I'm giving thought to a wood stove for next winter, even though chimney costs are rough.

Oil stoves and furnaces provide excellent heat sources, and are relatively low cost, compared to Btu-per-hour output. Large oil stoves serve as well as furnaces in shops that are primarily open space. The same holds true of gas heaters and furnaces, though gas furnaces tend to be a bit more costly around here. In both cases, we're talking hot-air heat. Any fuel you use today is going to be expensive. The switch in the past five years has been from seeing propane/natural gas as cheaper than oil, to finding oil is, for now, marginally cheaper than gas.

Forget boilers and other forms of water heat. They are much too expensive to install.

Construction-style space heaters (often called torpedo style) are very handy, but cannot be used in an unventilated space; they gulp huge amounts of air for combustion. Most of these run on kerosene, are moderate in price, and can be wheeled to other cold areas if needed, but a window or

Bobby placed these two small fans to move heated, or cooled, air from the front shop area, to the back, which was originally set as a garage, but is now serving as a kennel for his English bulldogs.

door has to be left open when they're in use. Propane models are often easier to start, and stink much less, but cost a bit more.

Do not use unvented kerosene heaters of other types (those with a wick). They tend to turn out too little heat for you to leave a door or window open, which creates problems when you collapse from lack of oxygen just as you get warm. Such heaters seldom turn out more than 17,500 Btus, so aren't suitable for a structure, or room of any size. You'll find sanding or saw dust building up on the wick when the heater isn't used. That's a mess to clean and dangerous to light.

My two Coleman propane heaters, combined, turn out about 90,000 Btus when going full blast, but at that pace, each uses most of a four gallon tank of propane in seven or eight hours. That's a lot of money to heat a hobby shop, but usually the high setting is only needed for an hour or so. After that, I can switch to a single heater on its mid-range. That procedure still burns about four gallons of propane a day, which adds up too fast. That's the reason for my thinking about wood.

Use the cheapest heat you can afford to install. As noted, baseboard electric heaters are cheap, but costly to run, though that does depend on the cost of electricity in your particular area. Wood stoves are next, but must have a good and efficient flue, while cord wood costs have gone out of sight in some areas, making running costs almost as high as an oil furnace in some locales. Possibly the best set-up is an oil stove or a gas heater. In country areas, the

gas (propane) heater needs a tank or two, and the oil heater requires a tank, with most being supplied from a 275 gallon unit.

Figure on cutting heat either off, or way back when shutting the shop down. Most hobby shops are in use for fewer than four hours a day, so heating costs shouldn't be too bad, no matter the source of heat, if you keep solid control of the thermostat or firewood stack, at times when the shop isn't in use.

You might worry about what will happen to your stains, paints, varnishes and similar perishable (by freezing) items when the shop gets really cold, after you've shut down the baseboard electric or let the wood fire go out.

Prevent those worries by finding an old, non-running refrigerator (or two, or three if more space is needed) and removing the condenser and other weight and useless gear. Oddly enough, a big, old chest freezer is not as efficient in storing things as is an upright freezer or refrigerator. Simply store all stains and similar stuff in the heavily insulated box, close the door and go about your business. It takes some long term cold with no shop heat over quite a long period to freeze materials inside such a box. I am using an old refrigerator now, and have it placed outside my shop. Save yourself some problems and don't do as I did. When I first set the box, with my stepson's help, that was what we did — ploped it on the ground, shimed it so the door opened easily and went on to do other things. It rained for about three days running. I went to get some stain, and lo, and behold, almost all the cans had lost their labels and were starting to rust. When we placed the refrigerator, I didn't bother to look up. It was under the eaves, except for the door, which meant draining rain water hit the rubber gasket directly. This is not a new refrigerator, so it is somewhat leaky.

COOLING THE SHOP

Air conditioning has become a fact of life for most of us, especially in the South, and a bearable shop gets more use than one that has you dripping from the instant you open the door until after you leave.

Floor fans can take care of a lot of the cooling needs on moderately warm, or even moderately hot, days, but on the days when temperature and humidity are nearly squared — 90° and 90% — some form of air conditioning can make a shop usable.

At the moment, I'm running two small window units. I expect by year's end, or this time next year, to have replaced both with much larger units. Window units built to today's standards are fairly economical to operate, especially in a wide open space like my shop. They are neither as cheap nor as efficient as central air in a properly ducted system, but most of us won't have that in our shops, unless we're working in an attached garage or a basement, where the question is moot anyway, since neither heat nor air should be needed.

Dale Toms has the only detached shop that I have seen around here with central air. He installed it at the same time he installed his oil furnace.

Bobby Weaver heats with wood most of the time, but he cools with a standard air conditioning unit. On this one, poked through the front wall of his shop, he also included a heating element for those mild days when cranking up his immense wood stove is less practical — or for when he just feels lazy.

The fans he has placed over the door to the back room in his shop can move air as needed, whether cooled or heated. His back room is reached through a garage door and is about the size of a $1\frac{1}{2}$-car garage, in addition to the basic 24' × 40' of his shop.

SYSTEMS PLANNING

As you plan shop construction and layout, sit down and think about how much you'll be using your shop. Then figure out what kind of heat you'd like to pay for. Wood can be economically banked to last through the night, if you have a good, nearly air-tight stove. Other heat may cost too much to leave working overnight. Check local costs. With oil prices fluctuating wildly, no fuel is going to remain unaffected. Don't expect any permanent drops in the prices of oil-related items, whether plastic grocery bags or heating fuel (or any other fuel). Be realistic, too. If you're only going to be in the shop two or three times a week, you don't want to pay for heating the place when it's empty and unused. Or I sure don't. Setback thermostats work well for those with fancier heating systems. Simply drop it back to 45° or so to prevent freezing. Most such thermostats have timers, too, so you can set it at the low temp and have it rise when you know you'll have shop time. Or just set it low and run it up when you come in.

And that should about take care of the mechanical systems in any shop. We're not covering water here, because, desirable as it is, most hobby woodworking shops are going to be created near homes, or in homes, making water a reasonably accessible item without adding plumbing (supply and drain-waste-vent) materials and installation to the cost of the shop. My shop water is going to make the trip in five gallon jugs. Yours may, too.

As far as bathrooms go, there are many solutions that don't require expensive pipes. Doug Johnson is about the only one I know with a complete bathroom in his "garage" shop. Doug's garage got extended onto a second floor, which then became the shop (heavy tools were moved into the shop with a fork lift). In the process of laying out the shop, which had to be placed on a relatively small lot with no room for another building, Doug decided that he would need more than running water, thus installed a nearly full bath. It lacks a tub, but does have a luxurious-looking shower stall.

CHAPTER TEN

Shop Displays

The shops you see in this section belong to real people. They vary from a tiny shed in West Sussex, England, to a large freestanding single story, brick-front shop in central Virginia, with most stops along the line. Some come close to elegance, but all serve the purpose of turning out work the shop owners wish to create, at a pace and for a price, each of them can manage.

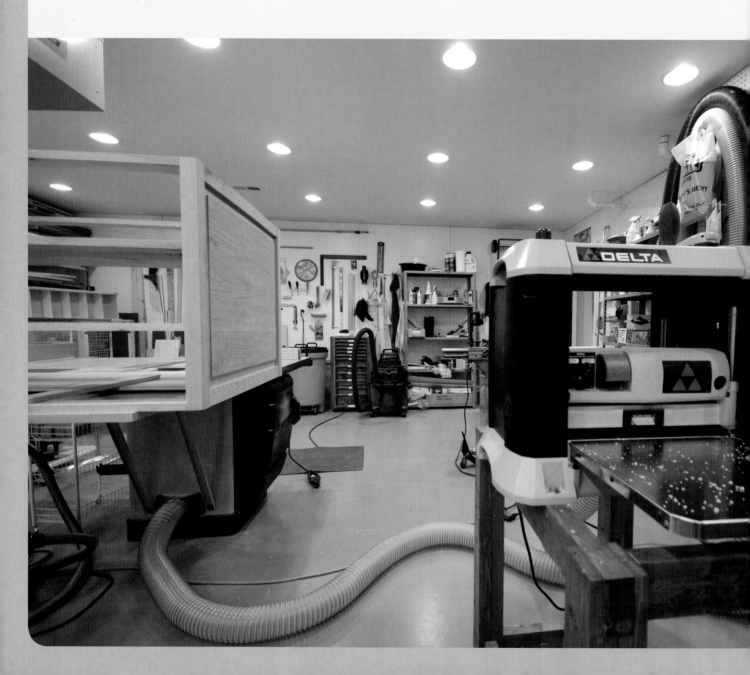

Mike Girouard's Shop

Mike Girouard's shop is located in West Sussex, England and is one of the smallest you're likely to see. According to Mike, "An advantage of the small shop is that everything is less than two steps away. Everything else is disadvantage. You are limited in scale to what you can build. You are limited to the numbers and kinds of tools you can house. (I don't even have room for a dust collector!)"

If the exterior of Mike's shop looks like a garden shed, that's evidently the way it started life. To see what he builds in this shop, check www.foggytown.com.

ABOVE Mike Girouard's shop shows what can be accommodated in a very small area, where the owner turns out excellent work.

TOP Mike Girouard uses an unusual exterior building, a small garden shed. He is limited by available building space in his yard, among what we can be sure are other neighborhood considerations.

Joe Zeh's Shop

Joe Zeh's shop is located in Massachusetts, in the town of Worthington. That's in the Berkshires, close to my old stomping grounds, and one of the most beautiful areas in the United States. Joe turns out some absolutely incredible work there, with much of it showcased on his web site at www.srww.com (that's Swamp Road Woodworking, as super a site name as you're likely to see, in my opinion).

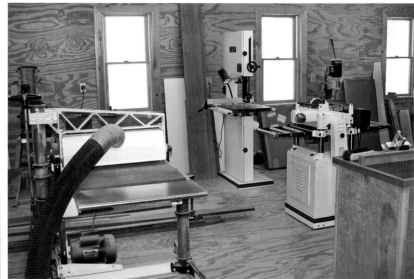

ABOVE Joe Zeh has an excellent shop layout, aided by his overall neatness.

LEFT Joe's table saw becomes the mainstay of a workbench area that also serves as an outfeed station, and, at times, an assembly station.

LOWER LEFT Joe's mitersaw table is about as good as I've seen. Adjustability of the table in both directions is assured, there's an extended fence, and several feet of support on each side.

ABOVE His tools are laid out nicely, set far enough apart to be easy to get between with a load of half-assembled whatever or a sheet or two of plywood. At the same time, he hasn't made things so large he gets worn out moving from tool to tool.

RIGHT His router table is also nicely made, and hides some excellent storage features.

Greg Rambo's Shop

Greg Rambo's shop is located in the Smith Mountain Lake area of Virginia, country that is just as lovely as that in which Joe Zeh lives. When I asked Greg how his superb shop evolved, he noted: "Like most people, my evolution into woodworking was initially prompted by need and later evolved into a hobby. The initial needs were storage motivated, such as shelves and closet organizers, and later it became Shaker inspired furniture.

The shops evolved also, from a router and circular saw on saw horses in the garage to a cramped space in the basement to a dedicated room. My current 22' × 33' space was designed using the article from the book about designing shops for small spaces. The best hint was cutting out scale outlines of equipment and shoving them around a scale plan of the space available. It was important to include notations on electrical outlets and lighting design.

The initial layout, and I say initial because a shop is never done, was driven by imaginary work-flow diagrams for various projects. We started with the table saw and included enough space to manipulate both 4×8 and 5×5 pieces of plywood as well as 8' to 10' boards from the forest I cut down to build the house. The next pieces of equipment were the jointer and the planer. These were made mobile because of the wide variety of wood sizes the machines would have to process. The next area is a work center for cutting joints of various types. The work bench is a part of this area as is the band saw, compound miter box, router table, drill press and mortising machine.

The lathe and an old work table, mainly used to sharpen tools, were added in the best place available at the time.

Storage walls were constructed using a box approach based on the design of the brick. These units are stackable and interlockable and movable and modifiable to fit the storage needs of about anything you want to put in them. There are not enough boxes to fill the space presently and this remains another project when enough 2"-inch wide stock has accumulated to build another box or so.

The dust collection system is adequate but could use improvement. The problem centers on the conflict between machines away from the wall and being able to move mate-

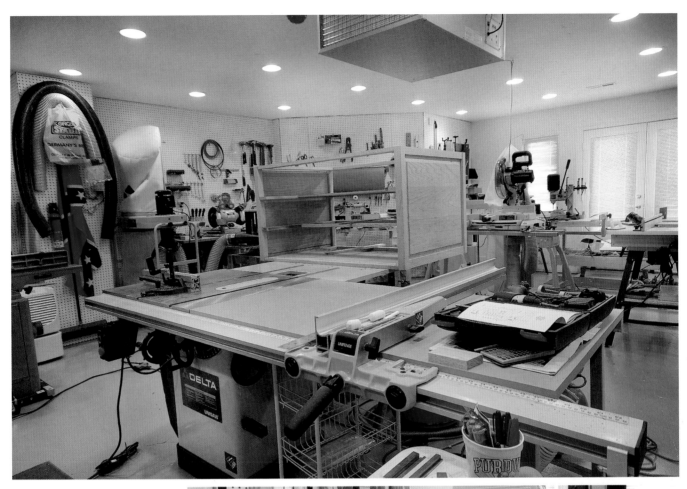

OPPOSITE Greg Rambo may lack some tools, but the lack is not evident. He has all the useful ones, and has made some excellent storage shelves for his shop, too.

ABOVE Greg was worried about the partially built entertainment center interfering with photographs. I felt it adds something to his shop, showing at least a part of the kind of woodworking he does.

RIGHT He has built one very good clamp stand, mobile and holding a lot of clamps in different styles and sizes. When you look at it, you realize it is made without waste — no waste materials, no wasted space on the stand.

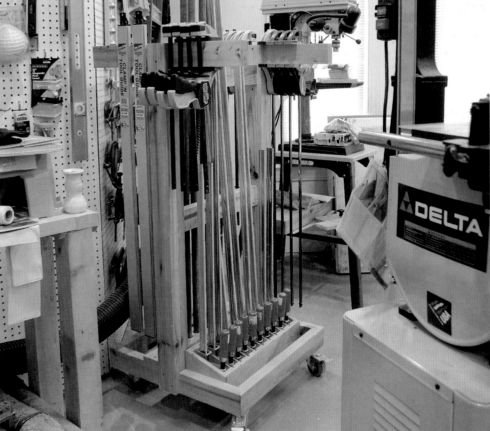

rial across their tops. It would be nice to have ceiling-mounted ducts but the material movement problem is intensified.

The wood storage system is primarily for the current project. An oak tree that died in the front yard resides in the garage. A barn in Montgomery County contains red and white oak, poplar and hickory.

The current entertainment enclosure is creeping up on completion and then a period of shop improvements begins, starting with the storage boxes, a dust enclosure for the router table, a woodworking oriented top for the drill press and a wall storage system behind the table saw which will also receive the compound miter saw."

What can I add, after photographing Greg's shop? Not a whole lot, as he's thorough, descriptive and accurate, but as the photos show, my camera saw some fantastic light in the shop. The use of glass, much greater than I would usually like, works extremely well here.

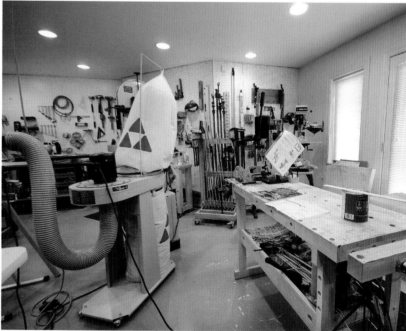

Fred Preston's Shop

With some minor editing, here's Fred's shop, in his own words:

"This was my first real shop. Before this one I had a 9×12 shed with dirt floors that I shared with all my other junk. Then I had a 10×12 room in the house that I shared with more junk. Then we bought a house [but no shop] so I had a room in the house — you guessed it — I shared it with my other junk. Over several years I acquired many tools and much more junk. You see the pattern here? Finally I was able to build a shop but it was too large a project for me alone so I had it built by a local garage builder. I helped.

Then I looked into having it powered it up. Electrical contractors are high-end guys! For what they quoted for running a service wire to a subpanel and hooking me up with a couple of lights and [yes you read this correctly] an outlet, I bought a book and wired the whole thing with 110/220 and lights.

Mind you I knew nothing about electricity — couldn't even spell it! My woodshop now has its own meter and a 200-amp panel with more breakers than I will ever need. Then I started collecting and upgrading tools. I now have

TOP Fred Preston's shop is filled, but not messy.

ABOVE Fred has worked out a way to get a well-used lathe, a grinder and a refrigerator in a very tight space.

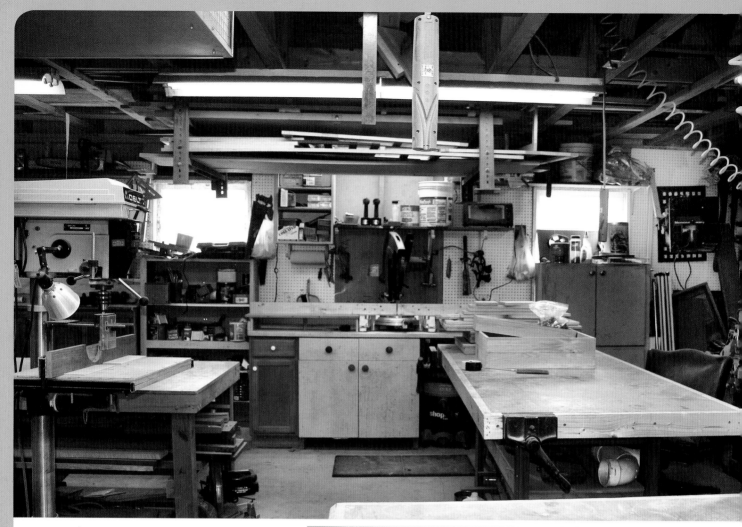

all I really need. It's getting to be a real letdown to go to the local Klingspor and other stores and be able to leave with the wallet intact!

My tools were purchased with the thought of retiring some day and being able to supplement my income through the shop. But for now I just build stuff for the house family and friends. After all, it's a hobby isn't it?

ABOVE As we all must, Fred has planned for his own work style and work flow. Wood storage under work, assembly or other benches, as on the left, is a good idea.

RIGHT Access stairs to Fred's basement shop provide plenty of surface for clamp storage.

TOP This is the heart of Fred's shop, showing the shop-built outfeed table on his table saw, as well as the shop-built table on his drill press. Fred didn't fool around when he bought his planer, either.

ABOVE Another shot of the heart of Fred's shop shows the jointer, a worktable, a workbench, plus a wall cabinet and radial arm saw that weren't visible in the other shot.

Brian Grella's Shop

Brian Grella's garage woodshop is what one might call a classic garage shop, with the centerpiece being his Powermatic 66. Regardless of what else you have in your woodshop, a PM 66 marks you as a serious woodworker, just as having a Delta Unisaw or a General 360.

Garage shops tend to be almost as tightly packed as shed shops, and Brian's Tarheel State shop is no exception, yet he doesn't allow clutter (hey, at least in the photos he sent). Those plastic barrels are handy for holding scrap wood, trash and other things. Around here, you can sometimes find them for sale at soft drink bottling companies.

TOP Top Brian Grella's garage shop has easy access for large tools, as well as a good amount of workspace. He has plenty of tools, but hasn't really overcrowded things.

ABOVE Brian's storage and workbench area also provides a hiding space for clamps, toolboxes, and other items.

OPPOSITE TOP This photograph shows a miter saw, drill press, router and the ever-present pegboard, well loaded with a variety of tools.

OPPOSITE RIGHT This view shows wood storage, and a jointer, placed so that the wood moves easily through the jointer. A variety of old barrels and boxes gives room for cut-offs that are still useful length (when aren't they?).

Doug Johnson's Shop

Doug Johnson's garage woodshop is a special case. As the photos show, he originally had no room for anything but the family cars. There was no room on the lot, either, for another building if he wanted to stay within codes (always an excellent idea). So he had to either park the cars elsewhere, or try something else. The something else he tried was building a second story strong enough to support a lot of woodworking machinery.

Doug's Texas shop has just about every piece of necessary woodworking gear you can think of, all well placed. There's a reasonable amount of dust free storage in closed cabinets and drawers, good protection with an overarm guard on the table saw, and a reasonable amount of materials storage. For a cramped city lot, Doug has worked out an excellent solution. If you look at Doug's photos carefully, you'll see that almost all his larger pieces of gear are mobile, too, which means it's easy to change the layout almost instantly.

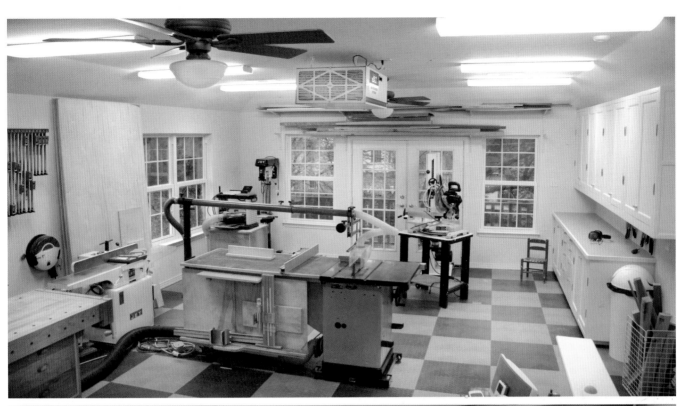

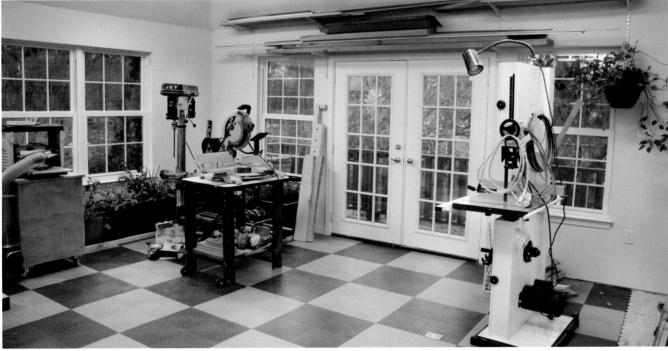

OPPOSITE ABOVE This shot shows why Doug Johnson's lot was too tight for another building and why he couldn't use the garage.

OPPOSITE LEFT So, he went up. I'm sure this isn't a first, but it's unusual, adding a floor above a garage in order to construct and outfit a woodshop.

TOP In the process, Doug made sure his shop is light and airy. There are plenty of storage cabinets and the tile floor is easy on the eyes.

ABOVE Wood storage over doors to the deck is useful, while Doug's band saw is nearby, and the planer across the room. I didn't think to ask him if the plants were real, but considering the light, I'd bet on it.

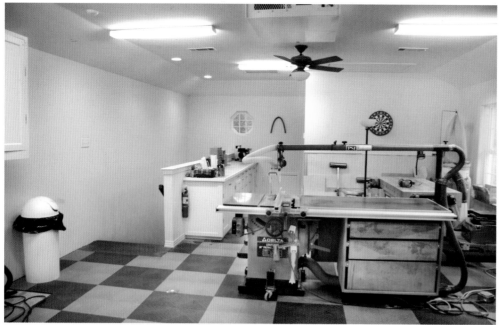

LEFT Stairs to Doug's shop are wide, but the overall lifting of heavy loads is done on the deck and then into the shop. Larger projects also go out that way.

BELOW Wall-hung clamps show a neater nature than I have: I cannot find that much wall space in my shop, nor would I remember to hang them up.

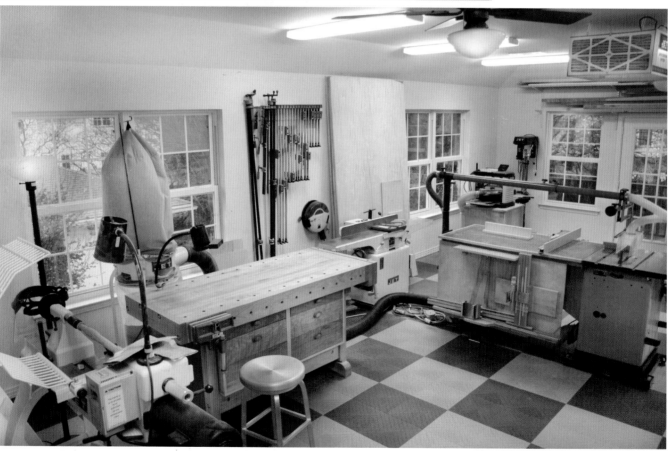

Another point in this garage woodshop's favor is the full bath. With a shower stall built in, Doug won't be tracking sawdust into the house.

At this moment, it is the only woodshop I know of that requires you to mount a flight of stairs to start working. The last one I knew of was mine, with hand tools on the second floor of an Albany, NY brownstone, so long ago I have trouble recalling the address — not really, 438 Clinton Avenue (after DeWitt Clinton).

Peter Bade's Shop

Pete and I first met at Isaac Emmet Young Junior High School in New Rochelle, NY, back when dinosaurs still roamed the earth, the world was youthful, he passed math handily and I barely scraped by. That led to his becoming an engineer for IBM, who is now enjoying a relaxing retirement by helping one of his sons build a reasonably large home in upstate New York, close by Pete and Caroline's retirement home.

These shots are from Pete, because I won't get up there until after this book's deadline.

He semi-shares the workshop building with his Honda 2000 during the winter, which is why you see the well covered vehicle in the pictures. He won't drive on upstate New York roads in winter with that car, which makes a great deal of sense to me (I lived in nearby Albany for nearly a decade). The cats stay comfortable in the shop through the same cold and snow, as you can see.

Pete is a meticulous craftsman, born in Germany. He has a wonderful understanding of a wide variety of mechanical and non-mechanical things, assisted, of course, by education, but also by natural bent. Last year, he bought his wife a great looking

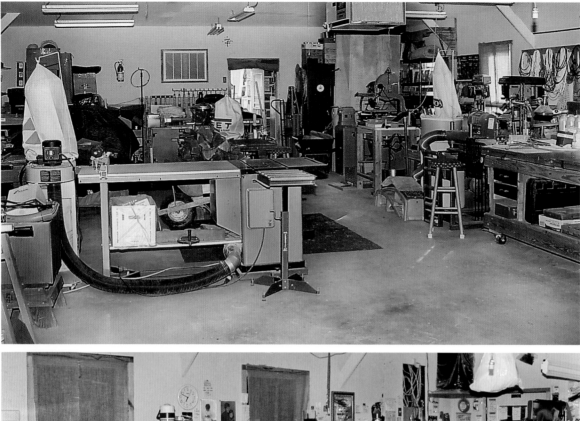

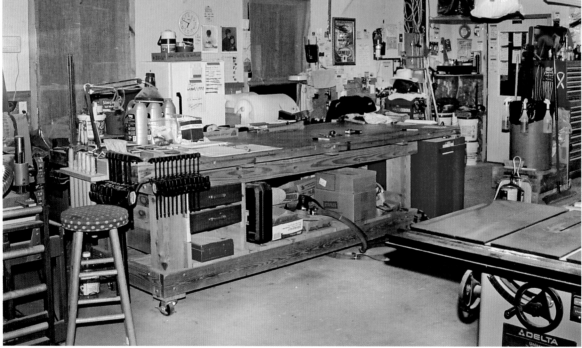

vintage Mercedes convertible. He then proceeded to just about totally disassemble the vehicle, reassemble it with all new parts where needed (tires, brakes, some engine parts), then drive from upstate NY to Texas to visit a son, coming back by my house in Virginia, and, if my memory is correct, by another son's place near Washington, DC, before rolling on home, without a problem, except that Caroline was tired of sitting in a small car. Not a bad test drive or birthday present.

His shop is home-built, of course.

TOP A mobile dust collector currently serves as the main protection on this side—there are a couple more around the shop, plus an air cleaner.

ABOVE Pete's workbench is sure not European in style, but is utilitarian, providing plenty of workspace as well as storage under the top and clamp storage at one end.

ABOVE Turning is another Bade enthusiasm, and he's well equipped to carry out a major project or two.

RIGHT Clean-up tools stand ready, as does a toolbox for working on the Honda.

BELOW RIGHT This Honda 2000 is well protected from upstate New York winters. It simply doesn't see them at all. It is also well protected from any sawdust and other shop borne messes.

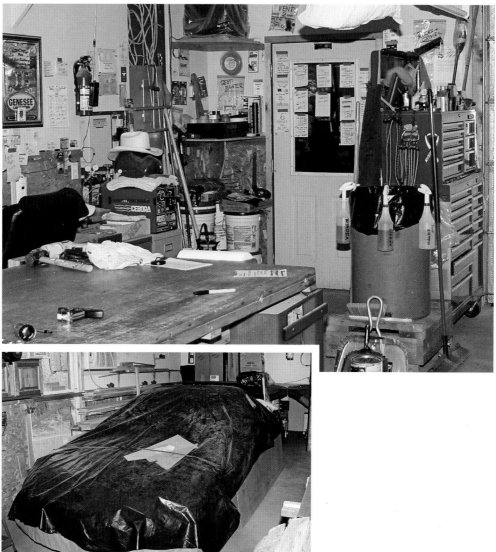

Dale Tom's Shop

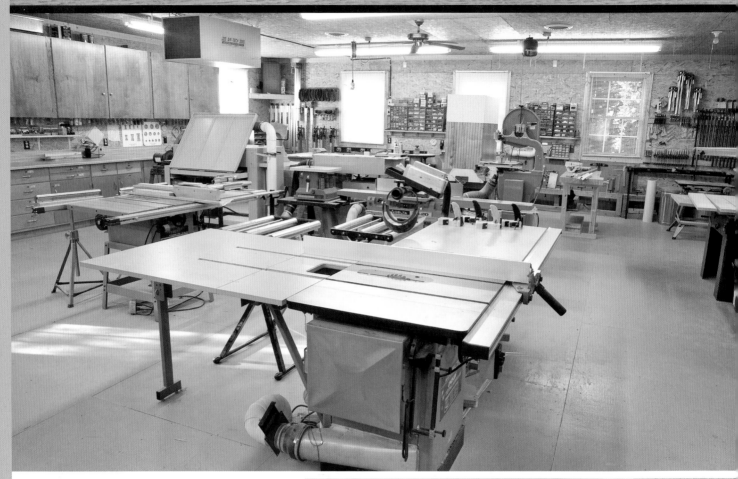

Dale was a friend before I started building my shop. At that time, he had a fairly extensive basement shop, that suffered from the major failings of all basement shops, a low ceiling, difficulty with noise penetrating to the living quarters and similar difficulty with dust getting tracked into the living quarters. If all goes well, you'll have seen Dale at his DJ-20 on the cover of this book.

He went past the building of sliding doors (you should, too), and installed a good garage door. He also saw how quickly my shop became undersized. That's where he got that 24" Grizzly band saw; when I was doing an article on such saws, he bought it from Grizzly. So, instead of the 25' × 48' that my shop takes up, Dale's woodshop is 32' × 48', from which he loses only the space of a set of stairs to a full basement. He puts the horrifically noisy tools there, his air compressor and his dust collector.

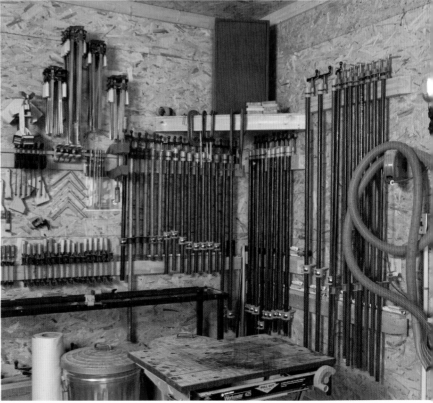

Dale graduated from Berea as a wood technology major, tried a year or so with a building-supply dealer, and quickly shifted into computer work at a time when such work paid well. That job presented him with tension that needed release. Add to his education and preferences, that led to woodworking as a hobby. As years passed, he got further into it, and now turns out some ambitious projects that work.

As amateurs go, Dale is almost over-equipped, with a huge belt sander, a 20" planer, a Unisaw and a Delta contractor saw (with an Incra jig mounted on the contractor's saw), a 14" Delta band saw, a 14" Delta radial arm saw, the aforementioned Grizzly band saw, a DJ 20 8" jointer and a host of smaller tools, including a stock feeder. The shop floor is plywood, painted gray. Joists are 2×12 on 12" centers. Walls are OSB, ceilings are a full 10' tall (I misfigured and came up just shy of 9', which means bumping some boards into the ceiling, and making tipping 4×8 sheets of plywood less easy than it might be).

Well, you can see for yourself. It's a woodshop for an advanced woodworker, who spans a good breadth of skills, including lathe work for his latest twist to the hobby, turning pens.

OPPOSITE ABOVE Dale Toms and I have been friends for something like a decade. I built my shop. He watched. He built his without making the mistakes I made. Note the seam along the top of the wall: his walls are about 16" taller than mine, a big help.

OPPOSITE Dale uses lots of clamps, so made sure he had plenty of storage for them.

TOP Dale also likes large tools, as this 14" Delta radial arm show indicates. He's also neat, though not persnickety about it.

MIDDLE The view from the other end shows Dale's main garage door to the left, while a standard entry door is to right in the end wall.

BOTTOM Again, Dale Toms' penchant for large tools is evident with the Powermatic planer (20"). His wood storage is seen a bit in front of that, right next to the entry door. His Unisaw is in front of that door, then his Delta contractor's saw is behind that.

Mark Lange's Arizona Shop

Mark's shop is 24' × 30'. He feels the primary considerations when doing the layout were:

"Adequate light. The four existing fluorescent fixtures were supplemented with nine additional fixtures and the single-bay garage door was replaced with a French door to provide both natural light and a wide entry/exit for materials and projects. The walls are white ¼" melamine that provide reflected light and permit ready access to anything behind the walls. In addition, I painted some of the cabinets white in order to maintain the light level. All cabinets are mounted to the walls with french cleats, permitting easy re-positioning;

Plenty of storage. The workbench drawers and tool cabinet serve as the primary tool storage locations. The workbench drawers were offset to allow clearance under the benchtop to permit use of clamps on the benchtop. Clamp storage near the benchtop makes for efficient

TOP Mark Lange has a shop with no excess space, but plenty of room. Actually, at 24' × 30', Mark's shop is bigger than most, but he has a good array of tools, and keeps wood on hand. That view isn't bad, is it?

ABOVE The interior of Mark's shop shows that neatness counts.

access — a very important consideration when doing glue-ups and one finds out during the glue-up that not enough clamps were pulled from the rack. An inexpensive parts storage system provides organized storage for fasteners, screws and other small parts. Finishes and table saw accessories are stored in the tall cabinet near the table saw. The other cabinets are used for various items that only see occasional use. Wood storage is provided in a rack along one of the shop walls; sheet goods are stored on a storage base next to the table saw. The foam insulation board on the sheet good storage base is used to break down sheet goods on the floor using a circular saw. A rolling cutoff rack is next to the sheet good base for short sheet good cutoffs. Other cutoffs are kept in the compartments on the wood rack and in buckets; scrap is purged approximately every two years. The center portion of the ceiling joists were left exposed in order to provide storage for longer items or those things that are seldom used. Insulation and melamine were applied to the top of the trusses.

The large table saw outfeed table allows cutting sheet goods; the rolling assembly bench was built so that it can serve as an infeed table for sheet goods. The jointer, band saw, planer and drill press are clustered around a utility pole that makes for efficient use of space and easy access to those tools. Two floor sweeps help keep the shop clean; a trash-can cyclone protects the dust collector impellers. I obtained the metal ductwork from a local fabricator and have found that it increased the dust collector performance tremendously compared to using plastic spiral pipe for all runs.

TOP Mark has a good dust collection layout, and has arranged his tools to suit his working patterns in the available space. You can see that's he's not likely to runout of wood for a few days.

ABOVE Another shot of a shop center post shows Mark's dust collection tubing, a good, high-end set up.

TOP LEFT & RIGHT Most of us would be quite happy to have Mark's workbench, with its large drawer storage area. His clamp storage is neatly kept on the wall.

ABOVE The workbench supports many kinds of projects.

This shop layout has allowed me to construct large and small projects. The rolling assembly table is used for some assembly. For very large projects, I can use the assembly table and half of the workbench for assembled elements while the remaining workbench half is used as a work surface for remaining sub-assemblies.

The benchtop mortiser is used occasionally, so it is mounted on a plywood base and attached to the workbench when it is needed. In a similar manner, a metal vise is attached to a plywood and 2×4 base and mounts in the wood vise on the workbench when metal work is performed. Retractable extension cords at both ends of the shop are used for hand-held power tools. A retractable shop light is handy when trying to measure or perform operations inside of a cabinet carcase.

RIGHT Mark has two tools that fit nicely against a post, a drill press and a band saw. I've got mine located in a similar manner, but one at each post.

BELOW LEFT Mark's mortiser rests on the floor, on a plywood base, from which it is lifted and clamped down when needed. His hand tools, or some of them, are in the cabinet above.

BELOW RIGHT He has made his own two stage dust collector using a generic lid and a metal garbage can. His fan does for many days, but when the desert heat gets rough, it's AC time.

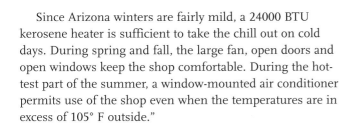

Since Arizona winters are fairly mild, a 24000 BTU kerosene heater is sufficient to take the chill out on cold days. During spring and fall, the large fan, open doors and open windows keep the shop comfortable. During the hottest part of the summer, a window-mounted air conditioner permits use of the shop even when the temperatures are in excess of 105° F outside."

Harry Wick's Turner's Shop

Harry Wicks and I have been bumping into each other since the middle or early 1970s, when Harry was Home & Shop Editor at *Popular Mechanics*. More recently (1990s, I guess), we'd bump into each other at press conferences, particularly the good ones Sears' Craftsman used to host.

A dozen or so years ago, Harry decided he'd had about all of the publishing game he cared for, so he retired to his Long Island (NY) area, and thought a bit about what he might do to stay busy, earn a few extra bucks and have some fun. He had started turning at PM, so it seemed a place to begin. At right, Harry's doorbell was given to him by his son Jim. The old hammer head is the clapper. Harry says it can be heard over the machines.

Harry got interested in turning and quickly became adept at various forms. Bowls are what have made his reputation

as an artist. He does almost all his turning in "rescued" wood, recovered from friendly landscapers and others.

As his skills increased, he needed a shop that was unaffected by home life, though near. The result is Harry's 30' × 30' copy of an historic barn in Essex, Connecticut. The plans came from a boatbuilder who works in the original barn. There's an 8' × 18' finishing section closed off from the main shop, reducing dust problems to nearly nothing. There's no basement, but there is a loft with drop-down stairs where lumber and other materials are stored. Heat comes from two, wall-mounted propane heaters — the external air combustion type with no flame exposed to the interior of the shop — making them safe in almost all conditions. The main room is air conditioned. The concrete floor has a broomed finished to make it anti-slip.

Harry milled his own wall covering of #1 pine, using shiplap joints. The wood walls are designed to allow him to "hang anything anywhere," he says. The ceiling is Sheetrocked™. About 30 duplex, 120 receptacles serve, while there are a dozen 4' light fixtures around the shop (and five more in the smaller room). The floor outlet for the table saw is 240 volts. There are several more 240 volt outlets around the shop, and two exterior duplex receptacles. The dust collector is held in a shed Harry built to reduce interior shop noise.

TOP Harry at the lathe turning a bowl.

ABOVE Harry says, "I mounted the vacuum chuck's pressure gauge on my lathe in a position that is out of the way while I turn yet is conveniently accessible when I want to turn vacuum pressure on or off."

TOP Harry uses the microwave to help keep wood dry, zapping the wood at 50% power in the morning and again in mid-afternoon.

LEFT This is a very simple tool holder made from a piece of plywood and a 1×4 piece of pine. 1" holes were bored down the center of the 1×4 pine and the board was then ripped down the middle, to make two facing pieces to hold the chisels. Hole sizes to bore are determined by the user's tools. Finally, a piece of ³/₄" pine is ripped to a width that is a snug fit in the space between lathe ways and screwed at center on the bottom side of the tool holder. It keeps chisels and scrapers safely at hand.

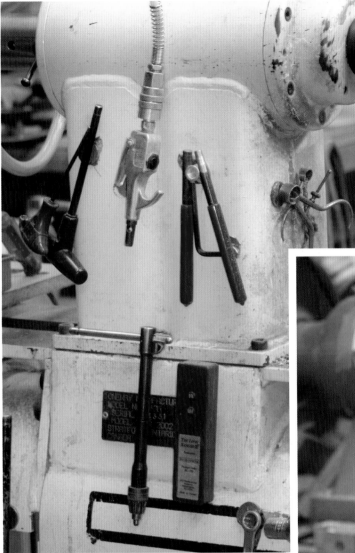

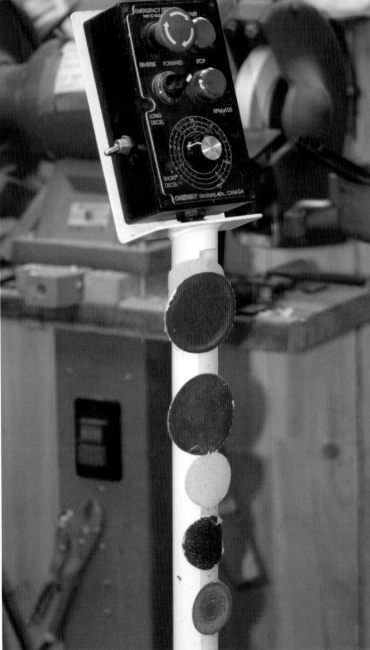

LEFT Super magnets are another of Harry Wick's enthusiasms, working well to hold small tools he doesn't want to chase around while turning.

BELOW He's also a big Velcro fan, as he says, "I have strategically placed strips of it around the studio to hold to assorted accessories. Here, a strip is attached to the post holding the lathe's speed pot. It is used to keep press-and-stick sanding discs corralled for re-use. These 1-, 2- and 3"-diameter discs are costly and this trick helps me get the most mileage from them."

He installed his Oneway 2436 and took off from there. Harry's "business" name is Harry Wicks, Woodturner, P. O. Box 1356, Cutchogue, N Y 11935, and he can be reached by phone at 1-631-734-5738.

And there you have ten shops from England to Arizona, with plenty of stops in between, that do a good job of running the gamut of today's woodworkers who put together shops in and around their homes. I regret not locating a real basement shop this time around, but their popularity seems to have slipped badly, for all the obvious reasons. Most people seem to be happier in a garage or freestanding woodshop whenever possible, even if the space must be shared with cars, lawnmowers, and, currently in my case, an old chest my wife recently inherited and wishes to refinish. She'll probably get that done about a dozen weeks after I finish building a kitchen cabinet for her.

ESTIMATING WORKSHEET: CONCRETE

CONCRETE WORK	LABOR	MATERIALS	CONTRACTOR	TOTAL
Staking				
Layout				
Excavate: hand				
Excavate: backhoe				
Form stems				
Form walls				
Form stairs				
Form walkways				
Form slabs				
Finish slab (if used as shop floor)				
Sand				
Gravel				
Concrete				
Membrane				
Rebar				
Wire				
Tie-ins				
Anchor bolts				
Vibrate				
Strip & clean				
Point & patch				
Hauling				
Backfill				
Unload & handle				
Other				

ESTIMATING WORKSHEET: WINDOWS & DOORS

WINDOW/DOOR	LABOR	MATERIALS	CONTRACTOR	TOTAL
Windows				
Skylights				
Extra Hardware				
Caulking				
Flashing				
Prime				
Doors				
Oversized Doors				
Jambs				
Hinges				
Prehung				
Locket Bore				
Hang				
Locksets				
Sills				
Thresholds				
Closers				
Weatherstrip				
Kick Plates				
Push Plates				
Overhead Doors				
Garage Door Closers				
Other				

Kick plates and push plates are not often used on swinging doors in woodshops. They do much to help keep the door in shape over a long period of time.

Garage doors (AKA overhead doors) are a great idea for woodshops. Otherwise, and even with, it's better to use no door under 36" wide, with preference given to 42" doors

ESTIMATING WORKSHEET: DRAINAGE

TYPE	LABOR	MATERIALS	CONTRACTOR	TOTAL
Excavate				
Gravel				
Filter Cloth				
Drain Fabric				
Solid Pipe				
Perforated Pipe				
Other				

ESTIMATING WORKSHEET: EXCAVATION

EXCAVATION TYPE	LABOR	MATERIALS	CONTRACTOR	TOTAL
Site				
Shoring				
Compaction				
Soil Treatment				
Finish Grade				
Hauling				
Rental Equipment				
Other				

For those without building experience, excavating and prepping a site is almost always better left to a contractor, working as your sub, unless you have a friend who has the time, equipment, knowledge and energy to give you a hand. In most areas these days, when soil is "opened" for construction purposes, it must be treated (by a pro) for termites.

ESTIMATING WORKSHEET: EXTERIOR FINISH

EXTERIOR WORK	LABOR	MATERIALS	CONTRACTOR	TOTAL
Felt/Tyvek				
Siding				
Siding Corner Boards				
Rafter Tails				
Rafter Molding				
Fascia				
Door Casing				
Window Casing				
Skirts				
Treads & Risers				
Stair Rails				
Other				

ESTIMATING WORKSHEET: FRAMING

FRAMING WORK	LABOR	MATERIALS	CONTRACTOR	TOTAL
Bolts				
Hold Downs				
Joist Hangers				
Tie downs				
Nails				
Post bases				
Post caps				
Other fasteners				
Foundation vents				
Rafter vents				
Layout				
Wall frame layout				
Wall frame mudsill				
Walls, cripple studs				
Walls, 2x4 studs				
Walls, 2x6 studs				
Walls, other				
Beams				
Posts				
Headers, door				
Headers, window				
Wall tie-ins				
Plumbing and line				
Ceiling frame layout				
Ceiling ledgers				
Ceiling joists				
Ceiling blocking				
Ceiling tie-ins				

ESTIMATING WORKSHEET: FRAMING P2

FRAMING WORK	LABOR	MATERIALS	CONTRACTOR	TOTAL
Floor frame layout				
Floor ledgers				
Floor girders				
Floor joists				
Floor rim joists				
Floor blocking				
Roof frame layout				
Roof ridge				
Roof ledgers				
Roof rafters				
Roof purlins				
Roof collar ties				
Skylights				
Fascia				
Soffit				
Blocking				
Plywood or board Subfloor				
Plywood or board sheathing				
Plywood roof sheathing				
Furring, drywall				
Blocking, drywall				
Blocking for accessories				
Blocking, misc.				
Other				

Notes: Just in case it isn't obvious, do not use any listing that isn't applicable to your workshop creation. If you're not using fascia or soffit, then don't include them in work time and cost estimates. Also, in areas where I've written "plywood" read as if I'd also added OSB or other acceptable sheathing or subflooring material.

Again, any time my recommendations bump into local or other codes, USE THE CODE.

ESTIMATING WORKSHEET: INTERIOR STAIRS

STAIR PARTS	LABOR	MATERIALS	CONTRACTOR	TOTAL
Stringers				
Skirts				
Risers				
Treads				
Newels				
Posts				
Rails				
Balusters				
Wall Rails				
Other				

Interior stairs are not common in woodshops, especially finished interior stairs, but there is always the off chance such work will need to be done, as you can see from some of our examples.

ESTIMATING WORKSHEET: INTERIOR TRIM

TRIM TYPE	LABOR	MATERIALS	CONTRACTOR	TOTAL
Hardware				
Nails				
Window Sills				
Extensions				
Window Apron				
Window Jambs				
Window Casing				
Finish/Floor				
Door Casing				
Base Pieces				
Base Inside joints				
Base Outside Joints				
Wall Caps				
Stair Skirts				
Shelves				
Other				

MACHINERY REQUIREMENTS: AMPS & CFM

MACHINE	AMPERAGE RATING	CFM NEEDED
10" Table Saw	8.3 @ 230v	300-500
10" Contractor's Table Saw	12.8	300-500
14" Band Saw (1/2 hp)	9	400-700
10" Radial Arm Saw	11.5.5 @ 120/240v	500
12" Miter Saw	13	500
6" Jointer	9.5	650-440
12" Planer	15	400-785
Drill Press	15	350-400
6" × 48" Sander	8.4 @240v	800?
2-hp Shaper	16/8 @ 110/220v	300-1,400
12" Lathe (3/4 hp)	11.4	350-500
Scroll Saw	1.3	200-350
Dust Collector (2 bag)	16/8 @ 115/230v	NA
Dust Collector (4 bag)	17 @ 230v	NA
20-gallon Shop Vacuum	10.5	NA
3 1/2-hp Air Compressor	15	NA
Router, 1 hp	6.8	200-350
Router, 3 hp	15	200-350
Belt Sander, 4" × 24"	10.5	300
Plate Jointer	6.5	200
Finish Sander	1.7	300
Spindle Sander	3.5	195
3/8" Hand Drill	4	NA
Bench Grinder	6	NA
Strip Sander, 1" × 30"	2.6	300
Jig Saw	4.8	200
Circular Saw	13	NA
Heat Gun	14	NA
Benchtop Mortiser	6	NA
HVLP Spray Gun Turbine	11.5	NA

BAND SAW BLADE SELECTION

HARDWOOD			SOFTWOOD		
RADIUS OF CUT	MATERIAL THICKNESS	BLADE WIDTH X TPI	RADIUS OF CUT	MATERIAL THICKNESS	BLADE WIDTH X TPI
$3/8$"	0 - $2^1/_2$"	$3/16$" × 10	$3/8$"	0 - $1^1/_2$"	$3/16$" × 10
$5/8$"	0 - $3/4$"	$1/4$" × 10	$5/8$"	0 - $1/2$"	$1/4$" × 10
	$3/4$" - $1^1/_2$"	$1/4$" × 8		$1/2$" - 1"	$1/4$" × 8
	$1^1/_2$" - $2^1/_2$"	$1/4$" × 6		1" - $1^1/_2$"	$1/4$" × 6
	$2^1/_2$" - 6"	$1/4$" × 4		$1^1/_2$" - 4"	$1/4$" × 4
$1^1/_4$"	0 - $3/4$"	$3/8$" × 10	$1^1/_4$"	0 - $1/2$"	$3/8$" × 10
	$3/4$" - $1^1/_2$"	$3/8$" × 8		$1/2$" - 1"	$3/8$" × 8
	$1^1/_2$" - $2^1/_2$"	$3/8$" × 6		1" - $1^1/_2$"	$3/8$" × 6
	$2^1/_2$" - 6"	$3/8$" × 4		$1^1/_2$" - 4"	$3/8$" × 4
$2^1/_2$"	0 - $3/4$"	$1/2$" × 10		0 - $1/2$"	$1/2$" × 10
	$3/4$" - $1^1/_2$"	$1/2$" × 8		$1/2$" - 1"	$1/2$" × 8
	$1^1/_2$" - $2^1/_2$"	$1/2$" × 6		1" - $1^1/_2$"	$1/2$" × 6
	$2^1/_2$" - 6"	$1/2$" × 4		$1^1/_2$" - 4"	$1/2$" × 4
$5^1/_2$"	0 - $3/4$"	$3/4$" × 10		0 - $1/2$"	$3/4$" × 10
	$3/4$" - $1^1/_2$"	$3/4$" × 8		$1/2$" - 1"	$3/4$" × 8
	$1^1/_2$" - $2^1/_2$"	$3/4$" × 6		1" - $1^1/_2$"	$3/4$" × 6
	$2^1/_2$" - 6"	$3/4$" × 4		$1^1/_2$" - 4"	$3/4$" × 4
7"	0 - $3/4$"	1" × 10		0 - $1/2$"	1" × 10
	$3/4$" - $1^1/_2$"	1" × 8		$1/2$" - 1"	1" × 8
	$1^1/_2$" - $2^1/_2$"	1" × 6		1" - $1^1/_2$"	1" × 6
	$2^1/_2$" - 6"	1" × 4		$1^1/_2$" - 4"	1" × 4

DRILL & ROUTER BIT SPEED CHARTS

BIT TYPE TWIST/BRAD	MATERIAL SOFTWOODS RPM	HARDWOODS RPM	ALUMINUM/BRASS RPM	MILD STEEL RPM
Point Bit				
1/16" - 3/16"	2500	2200	1250	1700
1/4" - 3/8"	1900	1700	1000	1250
7/16" - 3/4"	1000	1000	700	800
Spade/Forstner				
3/8" - 5/8"	2000	1600	NA	NA
11/16" - 1"	1200	1000	NA	NA
11/16" - 1 7/16"	800	600	NA	NA
2" - 3"	500	450	NA	NA
Hole Saw				
1/2" - 3/4"	500	500	650	500
1" - 1 3/4"	300	300	300	250
2" - 2 1/2"	200	200	200	170
3" - 4"	100	100	100	100
5"	75	75	75	75

ROUTER	BIT SIZE (DIAMETER)	MAX SPEED (RPM)
	0 - 1"	24,000
	Up to 2"	18,000
	Up to 2 1/2"	16,000
	Up to 3 1/2"	12,000

CFM DUCTING LOSSES

Correct duct sizing will make the difference between collecting 100% of the dust, and collecting poorly at the woodworking tool. You might be thinking, why not use an 8" duct? The bigger the better, right? Not really, we are conveying material, not just moving air. There has to be a minimum air speed in the duct (3500 FPM). Too large a diameter will decrease air speed and material will clog the duct.

The graphs at right show how pressure is lost in a 2HP system using a 6" and an 8" duct set up. Each component of the system adds resistance whether it's the corrugations of the flexible hose or the fabric of the filter media — it all creates friction losses for the moving air.

ONEIDA'S 2HP DUST GORILLA SYSTEM

Note that the fan adds pressure. Points on the suction side of the fan experience negative pressure (vacuum). Points past the fan in the system experience positive pressure since the air is being pushed from there forward.

The total loss from all the components in the system is calculated to be 8.4". This means that if we are to actually move 800CFM through this system we will have to have a fan that can move 800CFM @ 8.4" static pressure.

When looking for the same 800 CFM using smaller ducting, we have half as much cross sectional area in a 4" pipe as a 6" so the speed has to be twice as high. So just make the air go twice as fast right? You can't. Well, you could but not with the 2 hp fan we're using in this system. If you had a 10 hp, high pressure blower then maybe. The reason is that as airspeed in a duct increases, friction losses get exponentially higher. The chart bottom right shows pressure losses per 100' of 4"-diameter pipe at various CFM. Notice how the pressure loss increases sharply as CFM goes up.

Most dust collection fans only operate at a maximum of 8-12" total pressure. You can see that trying to move 800CFM very far through a 4" pipe will eat up all of your available pressure — and that's before you hook up any hose, elbows, filters, etc!

Notice how each section of the system uses up more pressure than before and that our total required pressure to move the 400 CFM is more than when we were working with 6". This system will need the fan to be able to move 400CFM @ 10.4" Static Pressure.

What really will happen with the 4" pipe setup is that the airspeed will try to increase in the pipe but very quickly friction losses will eat up all of the pressure the fan can supply and the air will only move a little faster if any than it did in the 6" pipe. Since the air is moving at roughly the same speed through a pipe that has half the cross section — you get half the total CFM.

Information and graphs compliments of Oneida Air Systems, www.oneida-air.com.

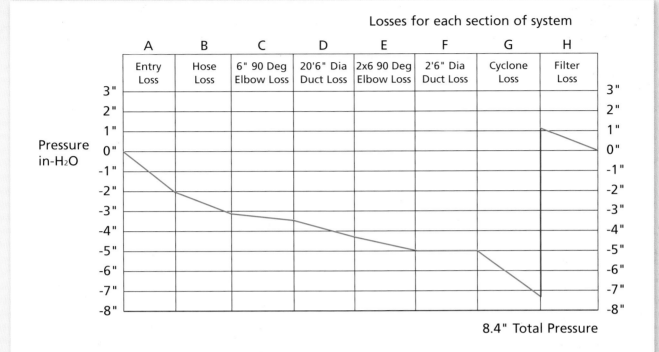

Losses for each section of system

8.4" Total Pressure

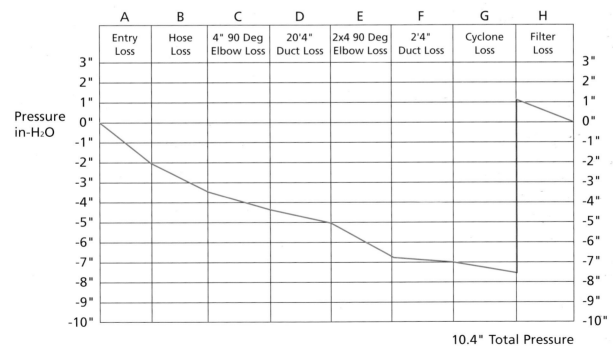

Losses for each section of system

10.4" Total Pressure

Source List

AJUST-A-BENCH
609-882-3300
http://adjustabench.com

AMERICAN WORKBENCH
843-367-6681
http://americanworkbench.com

APA
253-565-6600
http://apawood.org

BEISEMEYER
800-223-7278
http://deltaportercable.com

BENCHDOG
800-786-8902
http://benchdog.com

BOSCH
877-267-2499
http://boschtools.com

CRAFTSMAN
800-252-1698
http://craftsman.com

DAP
800-543-3840
http://dap.com

DELTA MACHINERY
800-223-7278
http://deltaportercable.com

DEWALT
800-433-9258
http://dewalt.com

DREMEL
800-437-3635
http://dremel.com

DRILL DOCTOR
800-597-6170
http://drilldoctor.com

FELDER
800-572-0061
http://felderusa.com

FUJI
800-650-0930
http://fujispray.com

FREUD
800-334-4107
http://freudtools.com

FESTOOL
888-337-8600
http://festoolusa.com

GARRETT WADE
800-221-2942
http://garrettwade.com

GEORGIA-PACIFIC
800-284-5347
http://gp.com

GRIZZLY INDUSTRIAL, INC.
800-523-4777
http://grizzly.com

HUSKY
http://huskytools.com

INFINITY
877-872-2487
http://infinitytools.com

JELD WEN
800-535-3936
http://jeld-wen.com

JET
800-274-6848
http://jettools.com

LEE VALLEY
800-267-8735
http://leevalley.com

ONEIDA
800-732-4065
http://oneida-air.com

PALMGREN
800-621-6145
http://palmgren.com

POWERMATIC
800-274-6848
http://powermatic.com

PORTER-CABLE
888-848-5175
http://deltaportercable.com

RIDGID
800-474-3443
http://ridgid.com/tools

ROUTER RAIZER
866-266-1293
http://routertechnologies.com

RYOBI
Sold, distributed and serviced
through third-party licensees of
the Ryobi® trademark.
http://ryobitools.com

SAWSTOP
503-570-3200
http://sawstop.com

SHOPSMITH
800-543-7586
http://shopsmith.com

SIMONTON WINDOWS
800-746-6686
http://simonton.com

STANLEY
800-262-2161
http://stanleytools.com

TORMEK
800-586-7635
http://tormek.com

TRITON
613-936-2955
http://tritonwoodworking.com

TYVEK
800-448-9835
http://dupont.com/tyvek

VELUX
800-888-3589
http://veluxusa.com

WOODWORKER'S SUPPLY
800-645-9292
http://woodworker.com

WORKSHARP/DRILL DOCTOR
800-597-6170
http://worksharptoolscom

Index

More great titles from Popular Woodworking!

WOOD FINISHING SIMPLIFIED WITH JOE L'ERARIO

The author guides you to a great finish. Learn how to:
- Select the proper stain
- Prepare the wood for finishing
- How to apply stains and colors (use the technique of building layer upon layer to the big finish)
- Apply final top coats the RIGHT WAY

No other finishing book is this easy to follow and understand — and not nearly as fun!

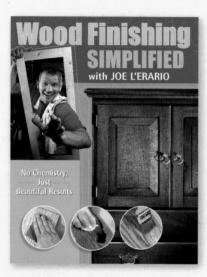

ISBN 13: 978-1-55870-807-5
ISBN 10: 1-55870-807-3
paperback, 128 p., #Z0639

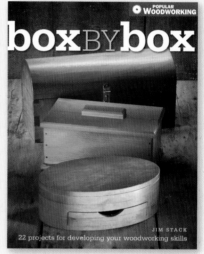

BOX BY BOX

By Jim Stack

Hone your woodworking skills one box at a time. In the pages of this book you'll find plans for 21 delightful boxes along with step-by-step instructions for making them. The projects include basic boxes that a novice can make with just a few hand tools to projects that will provide experienced woodworkers with an exciting challenge.

ISBN 13: 978-1-55870-774-0
ISBN 10: 1-55870-774-3
hardcpver with concealed wire-o
144 p., #70725

POPULAR WOODWORKING'S ARTS & CRAFTS FURNITURE PROJECTS

This book offers a collection of twenty-five Arts & Crafts furniture projects for every room in your home. Some projects are accurate reproductions while others are loving adaptations of the style.

A bonus CD-ROM contains ten projects and ten technique articles to provide even more information on construction and finishing.

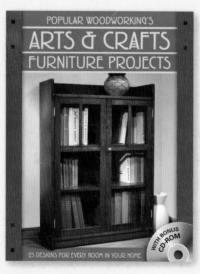

ISBN 13: 978-1-55870-846-4
ISBN 10: 1-55870-846-4
paperback, 128 p., #Z2115

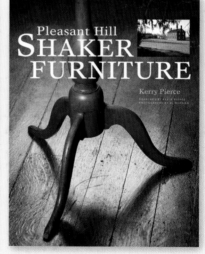

PLEASANT HILL SHAKER FURNITURE

By Kerry Pierce

Take a virtual tour through a restored Shaker community located in Pleasant Hill, KY. Study the history, the lifestyle and delve deeply into the furniture created by these gifted craftsmen. Includes painstakingly detailed measured drawings of the original furniture pieces and hundreds of beautiful photos. Learn the secrets of Shaker construction while learning about the Shaker's themselves.

ISBN 13: 978-1-55870-795-5
ISBN 10: 1-55870-795-6
hardcover, 176 p., #Z0564

These and other great woodworking books are available at your local bookstore, woodworking stores, or from online suppliers.
www.popularwoodworking.com